Trees and Woodland in the South Yorkshire Landscape

DEDICATION

This book is dedicated to the memory of
Bob Warburton (1943–2010)
naturalist, wildlife photographer and illustrator

TREES AND WOODLAND IN THE SOUTH YORKSHIRE LANDSCAPE

A Natural, Economic and Social History

Melvyn Jones

Wharncliffe Books

First published in Great Britain in 2012 by
Wharncliffe Books
an imprint of
Pen & Sword Books Ltd
47 Church Street
Barnsley
South Yorkshire
S70 2AS

ISBN 978-1-84563-150-5

A CIP catalogue record for this book is
available from the British Library.

Typeset in 10/12 Palatino by Concept, Huddersfield, West Yorkshire
Printed and bound in India by Replika Press Pvt. Ltd.

Pen & Sword Books Ltd incorporates the Imprints of Pen & Sword Aviation, Pen & Sword Family History, Pen & Sword
Maritime, Pen & Sword Military, Pen & Sword Discovery, Wharncliffe Local History, Wharncliffe True Crime,
Wharncliffe Transport, Pen & Sword Select, Pen & Sword Military Classics, Leo Cooper, The Praetorian Press,
Remember When, Seaforth Publishing and Frontline Publishing.

For a complete list of Pen & Sword titles please contact
PEN & SWORD BOOKS LIMITED
47 Church Street, Barnsley, South Yorkshire, S70 2AS England
E-mail: enquiries@pen-and-sword.co.uk
Website: www.pen-and-sword.co.uk

CONTENTS

AUTHOR'S FOREWORD AND ACKNOWLEDGEMENTS

WHEN I VISIT other parts of the country and give illustrated talks about the region's woodlands, including the fact that Sheffield is the best-wooded city in the country, I am met at first with disbelief, then surprise and finally envy. South Yorkshire is a region known in the rest of the country for its coal mining and steel industries and for its cities and towns rather than for its countryside, and yet the region is blessed with a large number of ancient woods (350 ancient woodland sites), thousands of miles of hedgerows, tens of thousands of street trees and some stunning veteran and ancient native and exotic trees in its country house parks and public green spaces. There are also some veteran and beautiful trees in our churchyards, along rivers and simply standing alone in the countryside. These all need to be celebrated and protected.

This book is designed to reveal the secrets of our wooded and treed landscape, to enable the reader to appreciate the beauty and the heritage of trees and woods and to become involved in their protection. The book is organised quite simply. The first three chapters describe and explain in chronological order the development of wooded landscapes and their management from prehistoric times until the end of the nineteenth century. There then follow four thematic chapters on woodland crafts, woodland archaeology, trees in parks and gardens and trees and shrubs in the wider landscape. The last chapter describes in detail some examples of woodland loss, rescue and restoration and records the outstanding work done in the last

twenty years by a variety of organisations. At the end of each chapter there is a short reading list and a selection of places to visit and things to do.

I owe a great debt of gratitude to many people. Over the years I obtained inspiration as well as information from Dan Lewis and Nick Sellwood when they were employed as woodland managers for Sheffield City Council and from Ted Talbot the current woodland's manager. I have also worked collaboratively – and gained many insights – on many woodland and related projects with Professor Ian Rotherham and Christine Handley. And this book, like many others, would be the poorer without the contribution of Bob Warburton's maps, line drawings and watercolours. To all the above many thanks. I would also like to acknowledge the assistance given over many years by the staff of Sheffield Archives and Rotherham Local Studies Library and Archives.

I have also received specific help for this book from a number of individuals: Bob Marsh and Jonathan Tesh of Doncaster MBC and particularly Colin Howes, formerly of Doncaster Museum, for information about woods and trees in Doncaster Metropolitan Borough; Ian Kennedy, Trees and Woodlands Team Leader at Rotherham MBC for information about Rotherham's street trees; John Gilpin of Parks & Countryside at Sheffield City Council for providing management plans for Bowden Housteads Wood; Nick Hetherington, Head of Streetscene, Streetforce, Sheffield for information on Sheffield's street trees; Anthea Greaves for a botanical illustration (Figure 1.12); Paul

Ardron for Figure 5.1; Avril Larent for Figure 5.9; Peter Wolstenholme for Figures 7.2, 7.15 and the photograph on page 168; and the Sandbeck Estate I also wish to thank His Grace, the Duke of Norfolk, the Milton Peterborough Estates Company, S.W. Fraser Esq. and the Head of Leisure Services, Sheffield City Council for permission to quote from the Arundel Castle Manuscripts, the Wentworth Woodhouse Muniments and the Spencer Stanhope Muniments in Sheffield Archives and for Figures 3.6, 3.8, 3.9 and 3.10 which are reproduced from the originals in Sheffield Archives.

Lastly I would like to thank my wife, Joan, for accompanying me on fieldwork, taking most of the photographs, proof-reading the entire book more than once and for her unstinting and uncritical support (except when we got lost in the car down some obscure country roads) during the nine month period when the book was being written.

Wood-sawyers at work in a woodyard.

IN THE BEGINNING …

A DIVERSE AND MANY-LAYERED LANDSCAPE

Five 'landscape character areas' have been identified in South Yorkshire: the Dark Peak, the Southern Pennine Fringe, the Yorkshire Coalfield, the Southern Magnesian Limestone and the Humberhead Levels (see Figure 1.1).[1] In the extreme west beyond Penistone and Bradfield are bleak uninhabited moorlands developed on the gritstones and shales of the Millstone Grit series. This is the Dark Peak landscape character zone. Here the skyline is periodically dominated by westward facing edges at their highest approaching 1,800 ft (*c*.550 m) above sea level and cut through by the headwaters of the Derwent and the Don and its tributaries. Large stretches are covered

Figure 1.1. South Yorkshire: landscape character zones

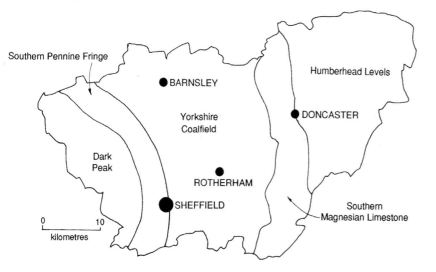

with heather moorland and blanket bog, without a sign of habitation. Deep narrow valleys fringe the area. Settlement is largely dispersed. To the east of this moorland country is the narrow Southern Pennine Fringe character area that embraces both the lower eastern fringes of the Millstone Grit country and the higher western parts of the Coal Measure country and includes the western half of the modern city of Sheffield. It is crossed by the steep-sided valleys of the Upper Don and by its tributaries the Little Don, Loxley and Rivelin. The altitude decreases eastwards when the exposed Coal Measures are reached (the Yorkshire Coalfield landscape character zone), and the country takes on a more rolling appearance and drops from about 800 ft (*c*.245 m) to less than 130 ft (*c*.40 m) in a dozen miles (19 km) between Grenoside and Thurnscoe. Another distinct but lower edge made of Magnesian Limestone is then met with rising to nearly 360 ft (*c*.110 m) at Hickleton, beyond which is a low plateau of fertile agricultural country. This gives way at Doncaster and beyond to a flat lowland, part of the Humberhead Levels, floored by Triassic rocks (Sherwood Sandstone and Mercia Mudstone) covered with glacial and post-glacial gravels, clays and silts, in places only a few metres above sea level.

This very varied physical environment has had an immense influence on the way in which human beings over thousands of years have created the complex human landscape of the region. And much of the complex modern landscape has resulted from the relentless clearing for six millennia of the primeval woodland that once covered the region. The rest of the chapter deals with the character and the clearance of the woodland cover across the region from the end of the last Ice Age until the end of the eleventh century; with the concept of an ancient wood; and with myth, legend and tradition of trees and woods.

THE 'WILDWOOD'

The woodland history of the British Isles in general and South Yorkshire in particular began about 12,000 years ago when the glaciers and ice sheets melted as the last Ice Age ended. Frozen ground thawed and climatic conditions improved to the point where trees could move in again from those parts of Europe that had lain beyond the grip of ice and freezing conditions. Seeds borne on the wind or spread in the droppings of birds and mammals enabled a wave of colonisation to make its way across the British Isles from the south-east. The progress of this arboreal colonisation has been reconstructed using the pollen grains produced by the trees and which are very resistant to decay, that accumulated in bogs, lakes and ponds. Using this evidence it has been possible to show that the first trees to colonise post-glacial Britain were Arctic trees such as aspen, birch and willow, the last two of which are usually still the first trees to colonise waste ground in the twenty-first century. Later came pine and hazel, then alder and oak. Later still came elm and lime and finally ash, beech, holly, hornbeam and maple. The later trees found it more difficult to spread because much of the bare ground had been occupied by the early colonisers. There then followed a long period of adjustment as particular species consolidated their dominance and others were pushed out by more invasive species. By about 4000 BC, unaltered by human interference, the so-called 'wildwood', a term invented by the woodland historian, Oliver Rackham, was fully developed.

In South Yorkshire we know something of the character of the wildwood from scientific research that has been undertaken over the last seventy years. Studies of the pollen record, the tree ring sequences of buried oaks and pines, and of fossil insects tell us much about the development and composition of the wildwood on Thorne and Hatfield Moors in the Humberhead Levels. Radiocarbon dating from the base of the peats has shown that peat began to develop about 2500 BC and this led to the drowning of the wildwood and the development of a raised mire. On Thorne Moors which was underlain by clay silts before peat development, a mosaic of mixed deciduous wildwood containing oak, wet 'carr' woodland and pine woodland had developed. In contrast, on Hatfield Moors, which was underlain by fluvio-glacial sands and gravels topped by wind-blown sand, almost the entire land surface was covered either by heath or a wildwood of native pines with occasional oaks. The fossils of at least sixteen extinct species of beetle, mostly associated with pine forest, have been preserved in the peats.[2] There are many records of bog oaks and pines surviving in the peat. The biggest one ever recorded in the Humberhead Levels was at the southern end of Thorne Moors. It was 120 ft long (36.5 m) and had a girth of 36 ft (11 m) at the bottom end, 30 ft (9 m) in the middle and 18 ft (5.5 m) at top where the trunk was broken off.[3] It is not certain whether the fallen trees were felled by humans or simply died. There is also evidence of woodland fires. Again it is not certain whether the fires were natural (by lightning strikes) or were set by humans. It is not clear whether the wildwood on Thorne and Hatfield Moors was 'managed' by early peoples, i.e., partially cleared by setting fires by Mesolithic groups to attract game to grassy clearings or by felling and burning by early Neolithic groups to create pasture land. Some writers certainly believe that fires were set deliberately by Mesolithic hunter-gatherers to change the vegetation to attract grazing game, for example, in a study of the North York Moors in the 1980s the authors concluded that Mesolithic hunter-gatherers had had a more influential impact on the wildwood than had previously been believed[4] and Oliver Rackham has written about the way that native Americans created 'prairies' in the forests of eastern North America in order to attract the wild animals which they hunted, although he does acknowledge that it was easier there than in Britain to create forest fires, because pine is our only combustible native tree.[5]

Studies of the pollen record on the gritstone moors in the west of the region have also revealed the composition of the wildwood there. A detailed study of three sites on Ringinglow Bog, a peat bog, near Sheffield, lying at an altitude of 1,300 ft (400 m), was carried out during the 1940s. The study showed that until the onset of peat development about 6000 BC the area was wooded with native pine dominant. As climate became wetter one part of the site became an alder-birch wood and other parts of the site became heather moorland.[6]

Until very recently the theory was that the wildwood stretched as a closed canopy forest without gaps virtually across the whole of Great Britain. This long-held theory has now been seriously challenged by the work of Dr Frans Vera (2000) who has put forward the theory that the wildwood consisted of a patchwork of woodland and large tracts of grassland with open-grown solitary trees, the natural or man-made large clearings being maintained by large herbivores such as deer and wild cattle. The Vera hypothesis is the subject of much debate.[7] What is clear is that the wildwood probably varied enormously in its composition, its density and its continuity. And that within the wildwood there must have

been some very old, very large trees and, where these had crashed down, grassy clearings or thickets of young growth. There must also have been many dead trees, standing, leaning against neighbours, and lying on the woodland floor in various stages of decomposition (Figure 1.2).

The first settlers of the wildwood were the Mesolithic (Middle Stone Age) peoples, nomadic hunter-gatherers who lived on animals that they hunted, fish that they caught and berries and other fruits, nuts and roots that they gathered. The bow and arrow had been invented by this time, perfectly fitted

Figure 1.2. No-one knows exactly what the wildwood would have looked like. There must have been very old, very large trees and where these had crashed down, thickets of young trees. There must also have been many dead trees. Scattered throughout the wildwood there would also have been permanent glades kept treeless by grazing animals

for silent and patient hunting in dense woodland. Mammals hunted included wild cattle, red deer, roe deer, horse, wild pig and beaver. And the rivers would have been teeming with fish including trout and salmon.

Their impact on the environment until lately was thought to have been negligible, but as noted above they may have had an influential effect on the wildwood through burning to attract game to newly regenerated grassland dotted with palatable trees and shrubs. Virtually all they have left behind are their tools and their weapons. The largest number of finds has occurred on the moorlands in the western part of the region where they have been preserved beneath peat deposits and then revealed as the peat has eroded. Further east on the Coal Measures important finds have been made at Wincobank, Hooton Roberts, Canklow and Hail Mary Hill. The latter site, for example, was on a hill rising to 275 ft above the River Rother near the village of Treeton, six kilometres south of Rotherham. 233 pieces of flint and chert (flint-like quartz) were found at the site, of which 188 pieces were classified as waste. Only thirty-two of the finds were recognisable tools or weapon heads.[8]

The most amazing local archaeological discovery of the Mesolithic hunter-gatherers was made at Deepcar in 1962. It was a camp site that dated from somewhere between 8,000 and 3000 BC and was the first of its kind discovered in England.[9] The site is located on a small hill overlooking the River Don, on the east side of the river opposite where Deepcar later grew up. It consisted of the stone footings of a tent or hut that would have been covered with tree branches and skins and beyond the hut there are what appear to be the footings of a windbreak (Figure 1.3). Such an elaborate arrangement suggests that the hut was occupied for some time, possibly months at a time and

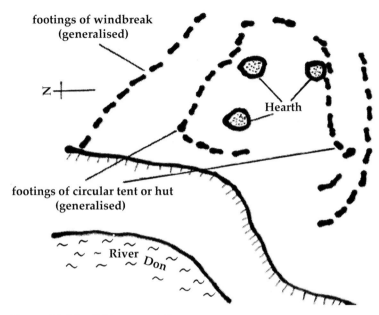

Figure 1.3. Mesolithic camp at Deepcar

on more than one occasion. This is emphasised by the remains of three separate hearths for fires. What is more remarkable is that the site yielded more than 23,000 artefacts including the debris from working flint into weapons and tools. The characteristic artefact of the Mesolithic period is the microlith, i.e., a very small worked stone, most commonly of flint or chert. A microlith is in the shape of a very small arrowhead or barb and a number of these would have been glued into a wooden shaft with birch resin to make a multi-faceted arrowhead, harpoon or spear suitable for hunting prey. Other flint artefacts were broader and rounder and these were scrapers for cleaning the flesh off skins. Small saws were also made as were awls for piercing holes in leather, wood or bone.

In the late Mesolithic period hunting became even more intensive and the wildwood environment appears to have been managed in places by felling and burning the wildwood to entice deer into areas of new, highly palatable growth on the woodland floor. This development foreshadowed the later domestication of pigs, sheep and cattle.

DESTRUCTION OF THE WILDWOOD
Deliberate large-scale clearance of the wildwood by humans has been taking place for the last 6,000 years, first by the Neolithic peoples, the first agriculturalists, who entered Britain about 3800 BC and then by the successive expansion of agricultural settlement and land use in the Bronze Age (2000–750 BC), the Iron Age (750 BC–40 AD), the Roman period (40–400 AD) and in the succeeding 600 years during which time Anglo-Saxon and Scandinavian colonists settled widely. By Domesday (1086) it has been estimated that only 15 per cent of England was still wooded. By the end of the medieval period only fragments of the original wildwood remained, but by then much changed by human interference, with each surviving wood known by a specific name and in many cases surrounded by a stock-proof fence to keep out foraging farmstock.

Woodland clearance continued throughout the Middle Ages and into the modern period, at first for agricultural land as before but later accompanied on a large scale by mining activity and industrial and urban expansion.

WOODLAND SETTLEMENT NAMES
It was the Anglo-Saxon (from the fifth century), Scandinavian (from the ninth century) and the later medieval occupants who left behind, in the names they gave to farms, hamlets and villages, widespread evidence of a countryside once covered by and gradually cleared of woodland. Some of these names tell us about the composition of the woods, names such as Lindrick (Old English for 'lime-tree ridge'), the name of a district that straddles the South Yorkshire-Nottinghamshire border and where there was a wood called *bosco de lyndric* first recorded in 1199. There is also Lindholme which means lime-tree island. In the west in Bradfield parish there are Ewden and Agden, both deep valleys first recorded as *Udene* (yew valley) in 1290 and *Aykeden* (oak valley) in 1329. Other tree species recorded in early South Yorkshire place-names include alder, elm, hazel, holly, maple, hawthorn and willow.

But it is the **woodland clearance names** that are most instructive. Many of these must indicate large clearings that had existed for many generations before the Anglo-Saxons and Scandinavians entered the region and they were merely re-naming them in their own languages. The Old English *leah* (woodland clearing) which gives us names such as Heeley, Tankersley and Cantley is the most widely distributed, with forty occurrences on the 1:50,000 OS sheets (110 and 111) covering South Yorkshire alone. Another widely distributed Old English element is *feld* (ten occurrences in South Yorkshire) which means a treeless area in an otherwise well-wooded landscape, as in Sheffield, Darfield and Hatfield. The Old Norse element for clearing is *thweit* (twelve occurrences across South Yorkshire) as in Ouslethwaite, Butterthwaite and Hangthwaite. Woodland clearance names are most densely located in the exposed coalfield and significantly the Magnesian Limestone belt, long thought to be the most attractive area in South Yorkshire for early settlement, has only three names indicative of a wooded countryside (Woolthwaite, Firbeck and Woodsetts) suggesting much woodland clearance had already taken place there before the appearance of the Anglo-Saxon and Danish Viking name-givers (Figure 1.4).

Old place-names in the modern English landscape are derived from four old languages, Celtic, Old English (Anglo-Saxon), Old Norse (Danish and Norwegian Viking) and Norman-French. It is wrong to try to come to conclusions based on the modern spelling of a place-name. It is necessary to study old maps and surveys and to consult place-name dictionaries in order to ascertain early spellings and meanings. It is also

Figure 1.4. Distribution of woodland and woodland clearance names in South Yorkshire

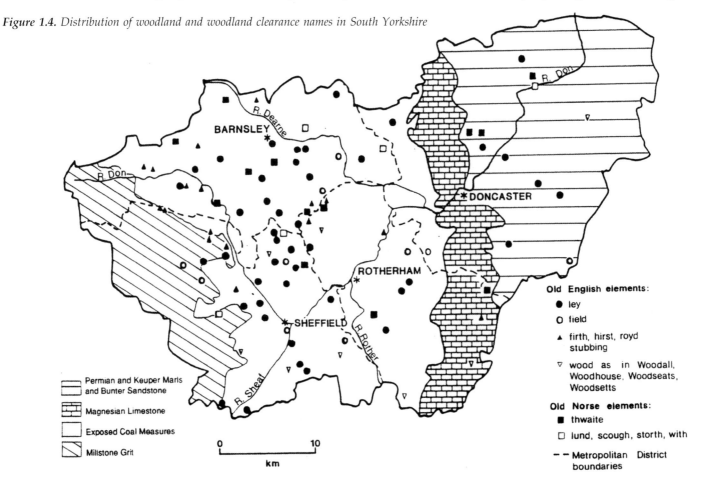

Old English elements:
● ley
○ field
▲ firth, hirst, royd stubbing
▽ wood as in Woodall, Woodhouse, Woodseats, Woodsetts

Old Norse elements:
■ thwaite
□ lund, scough, storth, with

– – Metropolitan District boundaries

Permian and Keuper Marls and Bunter Sandstone

Magnesian Limestone

Exposed Coal Measures

Millstone Grit

0   10
km

important to ensure that what appears to be an old name is not a modern invention.

The following is a list of place-name elements with a connection to woodland, woodland clearance and the names of specific trees that occur in place-names in South Yorkshire. The date after each example is the first date that the name was recorded in a document.

Celtic

ced or *coid* (modern Welsh *coed*) means 'wood' and occurs only rarely in England. Cat Wood in the Gleadless valley in Sheffield may be derived from this Celtic name for a wood.

Old English

ac (oak tree): as in Agden, 1290, Aughton, 1086, (oak tree farmstead) and Acomb (an earlier spelling is Akeholme = oak tree island).

alor (alder): as in Owlerton, 1310, (farmstead by the alders).

bearu (grove): as in Barrow, 1284, (near Wentworth) and Hazelbarrow (hazel wood).

denu (a long curving narrow valley): as in the South Yorkshire names of Dearden (deer valley) and Swinden, 1190–1208, (swine valley). *Denu* names are often associated with woodland as in Agden, 1329, (oak valley) and Ewden, 1290, (yew-tree valley).

feld (field): a treeless area in a well-wooded landscape as in Sheffield, 1086, (treeless area in an otherwise well-wooded landscape beside the River Sheaf), Ravenfield ,1086, (treeless area in an otherwise well-wooded landscape frequented by

ravens) and Austerfield, 715, (treeless area with a sheep fold in an otherwise well-wooded landscape). The name Ecclesfield, 1086, means a treeless area in an otherwide well-wooded landscape containing a Christian church. This would have been a name given by the early Anglo-Saxon settlers to a native British (Celtic) shrine. The *field* element occurs in every English county with the exception of Cornwall.

fyrth (firth): as in Firbeck, 1171–79, (woodland stream). 'Firth' is an old name for a wood and beck is from *bekkr* the Old Norse word for a stream.

graefe (grove or coppiced wood): as in Burngreave, 1440, (Byron's wood) and Leaveygreave, 1558, (leafy grove).

hesel (Old English and *hesli* Old Norse for hazel) as in Hazelhead, 1342.

holegn (holly): as in Hollings, 1385, and Hollin Hill, 1385.

hyrst (a wooded hill): as in Kilnhurst, 1331, (wooded hill with a kiln).

leah (ley): a woodland clearing as in Heeley, 1277, (high clearing), Barnsley, 1086, (Beorn's clearing), Woolley, 1259, (clearing frequented by wolves) and the less obvious Gleadless, 1512, (clearing frequented by kites) and Wheatley, 1086, (clearing used for growing wheat). This is the most widespread woodland settlement name. There are forty-three –*leah* place-names in South Yorkshire.

lind (Old English and Old Norse for a lime tree): as in Lindrick (lime-tree ridge), 1199, and Lindholme (lime-tree island), 1190–1202.

rod (a clearing): as in Armroyd and Gilroyd.

ryd and *rydding* (clearing): as in Herdings (high clearing). This is the word that has given us the modern word for a wide track through a wood – a ride.

sceaga (shaw): a wood, sometimes a narrow wood: as in Earnshaw, 1379, (eagle wood) and Crawshaw,1379, (crow wood).

stubbing (clearing where tree stumps have been cleared): as in Stubbin, 1344.

thorn (Old English and Old Norse for hawthorn): as in Thorne, 1086, Thorninghurst, 1483, and Cawthorne, 1086, (exposed thorn tree).

wilig (willow): as in Wilsick, 1086, (willow stream).

wudu (wood): as in Eastwood, 1379, Woodhall, 1253, (hall near the wood) and Woodsetts, 1324, (folds in the wood).

Old Norse
elmr (elm tree): as in Almholme (elm tree island).

elri (alder tree): as in High Ellers, 1210.

kjarr (carr, a wooded marsh): as in Elsecar, 1259–66, (Elsi's wooded marsh) and Deepcar, 1771.

lundr (wood): as in Lundwood, 1145–59, Lound Hill, 1379, and Lound Side, 1200–10.

skogr (a wood): as in Thurnscoe, 1086, (thorn wood).

storth (wood): as in Storrs, 1284, and the farm Rainstorth (boundary wood).

thveit (thwaite): a woodland clearing as in Butterthwaite, 1297, (clearing with rich pasture), Ouselthwaite, 1392, (blackbird clearing) and Hangthwaite, 1190, (Hagni's clearing).

WOODLAND AT THE TIME OF DOMESDAY
If we take the results of William the Conqueror's great national survey of 1086 at face value then woodland cover had been drastically reduced by the late eleventh century and the countryside was not covered by the boundless woodland of people's imagination. Rackham has calculated that the Domesday survey of 1086 covered 27 million acres of land of which 4.1 million were wooded, that is 15 per cent of the surveyed area. His figure for the West Riding of Yorkshire is 16 per cent.[10] My own calculation for South Yorkshire is just under 13 per cent. By way of comparison, woods today, including plantations, cover just over six per cent of the region. What this means is that in the eleventh century, South Yorkshire was relatively sparsely wooded even by today's standards.

The Domesday surveyors in South Yorkshire in 1086 gave woodland measurements for each manor in almost every case in leagues (12 furlongs or 1.5 miles) and furlongs (220 yards or one-eighth of a mile) and in most cases recorded how woods were utilised. When the data are mapped (Figure 1.5) noticeable variations in the distribution and types of woodland are clearly discernible. In the western half of the region, in the Dark Peak, Southern Pennine Fringe and in the Coalfield landscape character zones, woodland was relatively extensive with a substantial number of communities having more than 1,000 acres of woodland. In contrast, in the Magnesian Limestone belt and in the Humberhead Levels further east, the picture was different. In those areas woodland was more scattered, and amounts in individual communities were generally smaller than to the west. Additionally, the Magnesian Limestone belt, although only covering about one-eighth of the land area of the region, contained nearly a third (10 out of 33) of the places in which woodland was not recorded at all. This underlines the

Figure 1.5. *Domesday woodland in South Yorkshire*

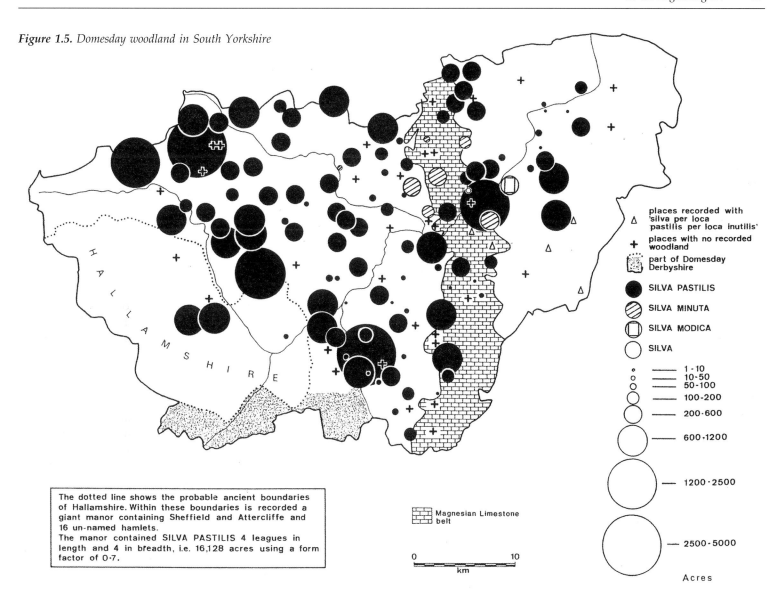

places recorded with 'silva per loca pastilis per loca inutilis'

places with no recorded woodland

part of Domesday Derbyshire

SILVA PASTILIS

SILVA MINUTA

SILVA MODICA

SILVA

1 - 10

10 - 50

50 - 100

100 - 200

200 - 600

600 - 1200

1200 - 2500

2500 - 5000

Acres

The dotted line shows the probable ancient boundaries of Hallamshire. Within these boundaries is recorded a giant manor containing Sheffield and Attercliffe and 16 un-named hamlets.
The manor contained SILVA PASTILIS 4 leagues in length and 4 in breadth, i.e. 16,128 acres using a form factor of 0·7.

Magnesian Limestone belt

0   10
km

HALLAMSHIRE

point made earlier about the lack of woodland clearance place-names suggesting very early clearance of woodland on the Magnesian Limestone.

The types of woodland recorded in South Yorkshire at Domesday also suggest a shortage of woodland in some places in the east of the region, particularly in the Magnesian Limestone belt, and a relative abundance further west. When woods were relatively abundant and populations relatively small, they would have been able to be exploited for timber and underwood <u>and</u> as pastures for cattle, sheep and pigs, i.e., as wood pastures (Figure 1.6). As populations grew and more woodland was cleared and the increased number of grazing

Figure 1.6. *Wood pasture*

animals prevented the regeneration of the remaining woodland, woods had to fenced to prevent animals entering them and a type of management which gave a continuous and self-renewing supply of timber and underwood had to be introduced, i.e., coppicing.

Domesday woodland in South Yorkshire was described in four main ways: as *silva*, *silva modica*, *silva minuta* and *silva pastilis*. *Silva* is simply woodland; the meaning of *silva modica* is not clear; *silva minuta* is coppice; and *silva pastilis* is wood pasture. Of the 111 manors in which woodland was recorded, 102 had wood pastures and seven had coppices. All seven occurrences of coppice woods were in the eastern half of the region, two in the eastern part of the Coal Measures (at Little Houghton and Barnburgh) and five on the Magnesian Limestone (at Adwick-le-Street, Hampole, Marr, High Melton, and a manor incorporating land at Sprotbrough, Cusworth and Balby). The coppices ranged in size from 12.5 acres (5 ha) in Little Houghton to 240 acres (98 ha) in Marr. On the other hand, although wood pastures were found throughout South Yorkshire they were very extensive and the only type of woodland found in the Millstone Grit country and throughout most of the Coal Measures.

THE CONCEPT OF AN ANCIENT WOOD
Throughout much of this book I shall refer to the old surviving woods as opposed to plantations and very recent second-ary woods as **ancient woods**. Most of South Yorkshire's ancient woods were once coppice woods. These are the woods that have the greatest heritage value. It is the inherited character-istics of ancient woods – their sites, their locations, their shapes, their variety of plant life and the animals that inhabit them, their archaeology and their often long documented history –

that make them so special. **They take us back to the roots of our history and are irreplaceable.**

An **ancient wood** is one that is known from documentary evidence or from a combination of archaeological, botanical and geographical clues to have already been in existence at some critical threshold date in the past, some writers such as George Peterken using AD 1600[11] and others such as Oliver Rackham, AD 1700.[12] The significance of these dates is that it was only after these dates that trees were planted on any scale in this country to form woods. What this means is that any wood already in existence by 1600 or 1700 would almost certainly have been the descendant of a medieval working wood, an area of woodland conserved, named and managed, not wildwood, not natural woodland but semi-natural woodland, influenced by human activity over hundreds and in some cases over thousands of years.

According to the Nature Conservancy Council's woodland inventory[13] there are 333 ancient woodland sites in South Yorkshire covering nearly 11,000 acres (4451 ha) or just 2.8 per cent of the land surface (Figure 1.7). Only one woodland exceeds 200 ha (494 acres), there are nine between 50–200 ha (123–494 acres) and 47 per cent are less than 5 ha (12.4 acres) in size. Ancient woodland is unevenly distributed across South Yorkshire, with less than 7 per cent of surviving sites on the Millstone Grit, only 7.5 per cent in the Humberhead Levels, and 12 per cent in the Magnesian Limestone belt. This means that nearly three-quarters of the surviving sites are on the extensive exposed Coal Measures. The topographic variety of this zone means that the observer is everywhere aware of woodlands in the landscape even though they cover only a small fraction of the land area. They clothe the scarps and back slopes of the highest edges, and on lower ground they cling to narrow scarps, and hang on steep valley sides right into the heart of the major urban areas.

An ancient wood is either **a primary wood or an ancient secondary wood.** A primary wood is a direct descendant, never cleared, of the wildwood that grew up after the last Ice Age. Much more common are likely to be ancient secondary woods that occupy sites that were cleared at some point before 1600 for settlement or farming, then abandoned, again before 1600, and reverted to woodland, and because of their age share the characteristics of primary woodland.

The surest way of determining whether a wood is an ancient wood is to find a documentary record of its existence before 1600.[14] These can be found in a variety of documents including manorial records, title deeds, accounts, leases, sales and rentals. A wide variety of documentary records are used throughout this book to cast light on the history of South Yorkshire's woods. In the minority of cases where there are no pre-1600 records a combination of pieces of physical evidence may also be used to identify a wood as an ancient wood. And even when documentary proof has been found the woodland historian would expect the wood to have most of the following characteristics.

Woodland names. A good clue as to whether a wood is an ancient wood is its name. But three words of warning are required. Just as in determining the meaning of settlement names it is wrong to try to come to conclusions based on the modern spelling of a woodland name. It is necessary to study old maps and surveys and to consult place-name dictionaries in order to ascertain early spellings and meanings. It is also important to ensure that what appears to be an old name is not a modern invention. Two South Yorkshire examples can illustrate the name substitution problem. The name Buck Wood for a wood in the Gleadless Valley in Sheffield is relatively new. In a survey of 1637 it was called Berrystorth, an ancient name of Old Norse origin and this continued to be used until the last quarter of the nineteenth century when the name Buck Wood was substituted. The name Treeton Wood (in Rotherham) is a late eighteenth century successor to the much older name 'Oaken Cliff', which tells us not only about the composition of the wood but also about its site. Lastly, some woodland names have been used indiscriminately. For example the name 'copse' originally signified a coppice wood, but more recently it is a

Figure 1.7. *Distribution of ancient woods in South Yorkshire*

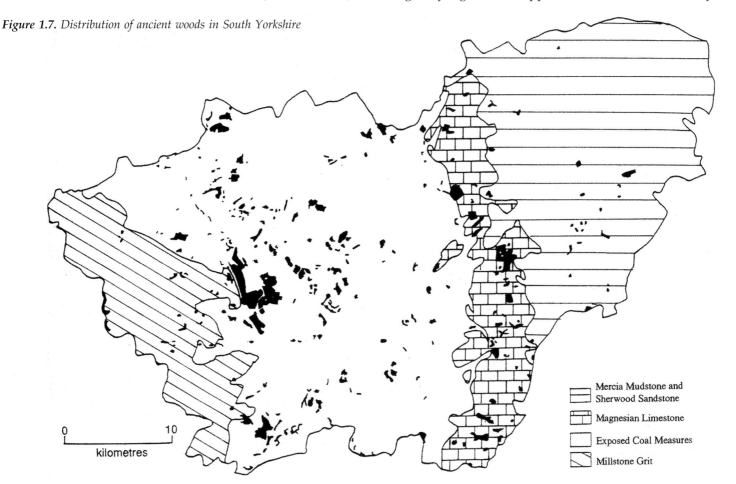

Mercia Mudstone and Sherwood Sandstone

Magnesian Limestone

Exposed Coal Measures

Millstone Grit

0   10
kilometres

name that has been given to new plantings, especially on country estates where field sports have been important. The Old English name *wudu* (wood) is also a name that has been used indiscriminately more recently to name plantations as in, for example, Sandall Beat Wood in Doncaster which is an early nineteenth-century plantation.

Below is a selection of the most common of these definitive old names that distinguish an ancient wood from a recent secondary wood.

Old English

clif (cliff or steep slope): as many ancient woods are on steep slopes this name occurs widely as in Hutcliff Wood, Thorncliffe Wood and Hooton Cliff.

cloh (a deep (wooded) ravine): as in Clough Wood and Raynor Clough Wood.

graefe (grove): as in Gibbing Greave and Haigh Greave Wood.

haeg or *haga* (enclosure or enclosed wood): as in West Haigh Wood, Hague Wood and Hag Wood.

hangr (a wood on a slope): as in Hang Bank Wood.

hyrst (wooded hill): as in Scraith Wood which was originally scraith-hurst which means a boulder –strewn wooded hill side.

rod (royd): which usually refers to a clearing whose name is transferred to an associated wood as in Birken Royd, Prior Royd and Broom Royd Wood.

sceaga (shaw): as in Shaw Wood, Hazelshaw and Oakenshaw Spring.

spring (a coppice wood): in South Yorkshire this word specifically meant a coppice-with-standards. The name survives widely as in Ladies' Spring, Snaithing Spring and Old Spring Wood.

Old Norse

storth (a wood): as in Storrs Wood, High Storrs and Duxter Wood (lost) which was originally Duckstorth, and Berrystorth (see above).

kjarr (carr, a wooded marsh): as in Carr Wood, Horse Carr Wood and Holmes Carr Wood.

Norman-French

coppeiz (coppice/copse): which is very widespread, but care needs to be taken to distinguish between ancient woods of that name and modern plantings.

Woodlands that have names containing reference to a neighbouring settlement are also reckoned to be of considerable antiquity, such names as Ecclesall Woods, Edlington Wood and Wadworth Wood.

Woodland locations. Ancient woods are often in the farthest corners of parishes and townships, often right on the boundary. Early settlement and clearance of woodland usually took place in the centre of territories that eventually became parishes or townships within large parishes. Clearance of woodland for agriculture would then expand outwards so that when woodland became scarce and was protected it often lay in remote parts of the territory and often right on the boundaries. A close look at the positions of ancient woodlands in Ecclesfield parish illustrates this point very clearly. Figure 1.8 shows the distribution of woodland in the parish in 1810 before they were

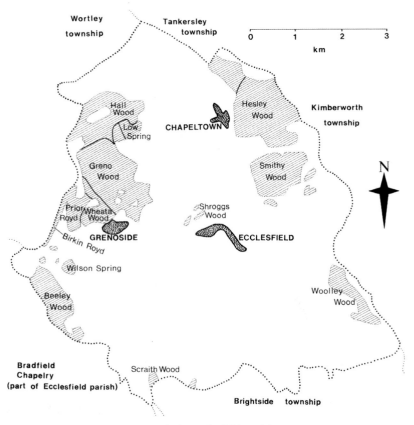

Figure 1.8. Ancient woods in Ecclesfield parish

affected by mining, by road development and settlement expansion. The large number of woods, twenty-five in all, is unusual as is the total woodland size of 1,500 acres (607 ha). What is also remarkable is that all the woods have survived to

the present day, if somewhat reduced in size. Looking at the parish as a whole only three small areas of woodland, known collectively as Lee Shroggs Wood, do not occupy parish edge locations. This locational pattern is repeated throughout South Yorkshire, for example, from Ecclesall Woods and Ladies Spring Wood in the south-west to King's Wood and Wadworth Wood in the east.

Woodland sites. Ancient woods often occupy sites that would have been the least attractive for clearance for settlement and farming. They are often on windswept hill tops, broad ridges, steep slopes and in narrow valleys. Parts of Greno Wood, for example, in Ecclesfield parish, rise to over 1,000 ft (305m). Pot Riding Wood at Sprotborough occupies the Don Gorge, Gallery Bottom Wood occupies a narrow valley that formerly marked the boundary between Rotherham parish and Ecclesfield parish. (Figure 1.9) In the western part of the Coalfield zone there are numerous woods on steep slopes often with the name cliff as in Thorncliffe Wood, Hutcliffe Wood and Top Cliffe Wood.

Woodland shapes. Ancient woods are 'left-overs' that have been attacked by axe over a very long period of time from different directions. Periods of rapid onslaught must have been followed with periods of inactivity. It is not surprising therefore that old woods commonly have irregular shapes, unlike plantations which often have straight sides (like Sandall Beat Wood) and regular or geometric shapes. Ancient woodland boundaries, therefore, tend to be sinuous or zig-zagged with well marked peninsulas and bays like a rocky coast. Ancient woods also tend to be surrounded by small irregular fields with medieval woodland clearance names like *intake* (land reclaimed from the waste), *ridding* and *royd* (land cleared of trees), *stubbing* (land from which the stubs and roots of trees

Figure 1.9. *The often steeply sloping, valley-side, site of Gallery Bottom Wood*

Figure 1.10. *Gillfield Wood, Totley showing the irregular shape of the wood and thick hedgrerows surrounding fields created by woodland clearance*

have been removed) and *ley* or *leys* (woodland clearing). Names meaning a wood such as *storth* and *spring* followed by the word *close* also point to the clearance of part of a wood or a whole wood in the past. Figure 1.10 is a vertical aerial photograph of Gillfield Wood in Totley showing its irregular shape and thick hedges showing former outlines of the wood. Surrounding field names include the elements *storth*, *ley* and *stubbing*. Gillfield Wood was first recorded in a document in 1561.

Botanical indicators. The distribution of trees and shrubs in ancient woods changes rapidly in response to soil and drainage conditions. An ancient wood is full of surprises as tree species suddenly disappear and others take their place within a short distance. Local ancient woods may also contain rare or uncommon species of tree or shrub. There are several rare or uncommon species of tree and one locally rare shrub found in South Yorkshire's ancient woodlands. Two of these trees, large leaved lime (*Tilia platyphyllus*) and wild service tree (*Sorbus torminalis*) (Figure 1.11) are restricted to the woods in the Magnesian Limestone belt. For example, wild service tree survives in Anston Stones Wood at South Anston, Kings Wood near Maltby, Old Spring

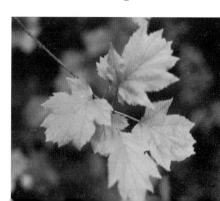

Figure 1.11. *The leaves of the wild service tree*

Wood at Thorpe Salvin and in Wadworth Wood and large leaved lime in Old Spring Wood, Hooton Cliff near Hooton Roberts and King's Wood at Sandbeck. The trunks of some of the large-leaved limes in King's Wood are more than 16 ft (5m) in circumference at breast height, a testimony to their great age, probably 500 years. In a recent article it has been suggested that the Anglo-Saxon name Lindrick, which means lime-tree ridge, and which occurs in the names Lindrick Common and Lindrick Dale in Laughton-en-le Morthen parish, in the town of Tickhill and in Carlton in Lindrick just across the county boundary in Nottinghamshire, refers specifically to the the Magnesian Limestone escarpment where large-leaved lime is so common in the surviving ancient woods.[15] Large-leaved lime is at the northern limit of its natural range in England and wild service is a tree largely restricted to south-east England and in South Yorkshire is at the northern extremity of its range. Small-leaved lime also occurs in woods on the Magnesian Limestone and it also occurs in the eastern part of the Coalfield zone in a wood in the Moss valley to the south-east of Sheffield. Although not as uncommon as large-leaved lime or wild service, the shrub, midland hawthorn (*Crataegus laevigata*) is very scarce in South Yorkshire. In Sheffield Metropolitan District, for example, it has only been recorded in the Ewden valley and in Lee Shroggs Wood in Ecclesfield, and in Rotherham it has been recorded in only seven locations, including Hooton Cliff Wood at Hooton Roberts. In Doncaster it occurs in a hedge adjacent to Wadworth Wood.[16] It is distinguished from the common hawthorn (*Crataegus monogyna*) by its much less deeply lobed leaves and berries that contain two stones rather than the one stone of the common hawthorn (Figure 1.12). Another uncommon native tree in South Yorkshire's ancient woodlands is the yew. In the Coalfield zone, where 75 per cent of the region's

Figure 1.12. *The leaves and berries of common hawthorn, left, and Midland hawthorn, right*

ancient woodlands lie, the only stand of yew occurs in Woolley Wood in Sheffield on what used to be the parish boundary between Ecclesfield and Rotherham. It is more widespread, yet still scarce further east, the largest stand being in Edlington Wood. Analysis of pollen from a pond in the wood suggests that it was growing there 1,500 years ago.[17] It also occurs in Pot Ridings Wood and Levitt Hagg Wood in the Don Gorge and in Howell Wood.

One of the greatest pleasures of visiting an ancient wood is to see the shafts of sunlight on the carpets of wild flowers in spring and early summer. Many of these are what are called **ancient woodland botanical indicators** and are typical of ancient woods but are uncharacteristic of other habitats.[18] The bluebell is the best known of these ancient woodland indicators in South Yorkshire. Other widely distributed and easily recognised wild flowers largely restricted to ancient woodland sites are wood anemone, wild garlic (ramsons), wood sorrel, yellow archangel, sweet woodruff (Figure 1.13) and the attractive grasses, wood melick and wood millet. The ancient woodland indicators are generally slow colonisers that often spread only vegetatively rather than by seed and find it difficult to colonise new plantations. Woods that have for centuries been managed as coppices tend to have a richer ground flora than woods that have long been managed as heavily shaded high forest.[19] It should also be noted that the behaviour of plants varies from region to region, and so many slightly varying lists have been compiled up and down the country. A provisional list of herbs, grasses, sedges, woodrushes, trees and shrubs strongly associated with ancient woodlands in South Yorkshire is given in Figure 1.14.

The use of ancient woodland indicators, and the caution that needs to be used if using these alone to identify ancient woods can be illustrated by looking at two ancient woods and six plantations created on former mined sites in the early and mid-nineteenth century at Tankersley (Figures 1.15 and 1.16).[20] It would be assumed that the ancient woods would have a rich ground flora and that the recent plantations would have none or very few indicators of ancient woodland. Bearing in mind that the soils are acid in this part of South Yorkshire and therefore not particularly species-rich, the results are very revealing. West Wood, an ancient wood, contained sixteen indicator species and the ancient part of Thorncliffe Wood had twelve indicator species, more than any of the other surrounding planted areas. Interestingly, though, the nine-teenth-century extension to Thorncliffe Wood contained eleven indicator species, only one less than the ancient part of the wood. The six plantations had between one and eight indicators. Even there, there were some striking differences. The four plantations outside the deer park that had been planted in areas that had been *assarted* (cleared of woodland for agriculture) in the medieval period contained between six to eight indicator species whereas of the two plantations in the

once heavily grazed deer park, one had four indicators and the other had one. Significantly, the site of the plantation with only one indicator, Bell Ground, was shown on an engraving of *c*.1730 as being in a particularly heavily grazed walled paddock within Tankersley deer park. The use of indicator species at Tankersley shows this to be a fairly reliable method of identifying ancient woods in South Yorkshire. The Tankersley surveys did, however, raise two other interesting issues. One is that care needs to be taken when surveying recent planted woods that are <u>attached</u> to ancient woods. Unless documentary research and ecological surveys are carried out simultaneously, 'recent' attached woods could be thought to be ancient. The one at Tankersley had many of the indicator species of the ancient wood to which it had been attached only 150 years previously. The other issue is that what indicators, if any, appear in a plantation may depend on what the vegetation was preceding the creation of the plantation. At Tankersley those plantations created on medieval assarts that may in part have been surrounded by long-established species-rich hedges contained substantially more indicator species than those created on sites in a heavily grazed deer park.

It should be pointed out that the ancient woods that have survived on the Magnesian Limestone are much richer habitats than the surviving ancient woods on the acid soils of the Southern Pennine Fringe and Coalfield zones. For example, as we have seen the two Coalfield woodlands, West Wood and Thorncliffe Wood contained sixteen and twelve botanical indicator species respectively from the provisional list of indicators shown in Figure 1.14, whereas in the Magnesian Limestone zone Old Spring Wood at Thorpe Salvin contains twenty-four, Pot Ridings Wood in the Don Gorge twenty-six, Edlington Wood twenty-nine and Anston Stones at South

Figure 1.13. *Ground flora botanical indicators of ancient woodlands: (a) bluebell; (b) ramsons; (c) wood sorrel; (d) wood anemone; (e) sweet woodruff; (f) yellow archangel*

Anston contains thirty-three. Wadworth Wood, although very heavily planted by the Forestry Commission, contains twenty-nine including (as also in Edlington Wood) the very rare lily of the valley.[21]

Ancient woods are also often full of **archaeological features**, in many cases never formally recorded or understood. These include boundary banks and ditches or stone walls that were essential to protect coppice woods from grazing animals in the early years of their re-growth. Almost all South Yorkshire woods except some in deer parks and on wooded commons were coppice woods. Archaeological features associated with coppice wood industries such as charcoal hearths (sometimes called pitsteads), white coal kilns, sawpits or the stone foundations of charcoal makers' or bark peelers' huts are often indicative of the long existence of a woodland. Ancient woods also contain prehistoric or medieval archaeological features that have nothing to do with the woodlands when they were working woodlands. These features have survived simply

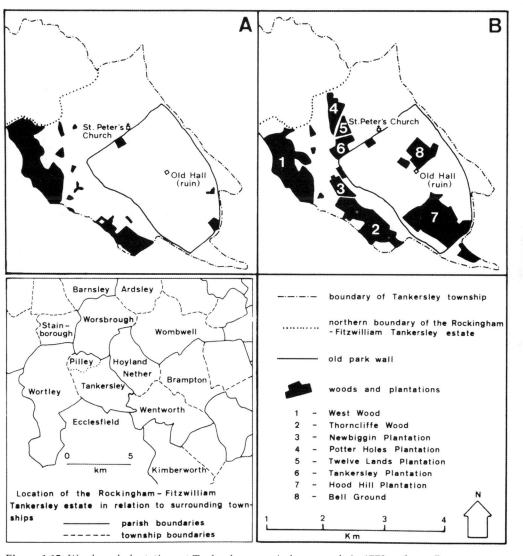

Figure 1.14. Provisional list of botanical indicators found in South Yorkshire's ancient woodlands

Figure 1.15. Woods and plantations at Tankersley: map A shows woods in 1772 and map B shows woods and plantations in 1906

Ajuga reptans (bugle)	
Allium ursinum (ramsons)	
Anemone nemorosa (wood anemone)	
Acer campestris (field maple)	
Adoxa moschatellina (townhall clock)	
Campanula trachelium (nettle-leaved bellflower) E	
Carex pendula (pendulous sedge) R	
Carex remota (remote sedge)	
Carex sylvatica (wood-sedge)	
Chrysosplenium oppositifolium (opposite-leaved golden-saxifrage)	
Conopodium majus (pignut)	
Corydalis claviculata (climbing corydalis)	
Crataegus laevigata (midland hawthorn) E R	
Epipactis helleborine (broad-leaved helleborine)	
Equisetum sylvaticum (wood horsetail)	
Fragaria vesca (wild strawberry)	
Frangula alnus (alder buckthorn) R	
Galium odoratum (sweet woodruff)	
Geum rivale (water avens)	
Helleborus viridis (green hellebore) E R	
Hyacinthoides non-scripta (bluebell)	
Hypericum hirsutum (hairy St John's-wort)	
Hypericum humifusum (trailing St John's-wort)	
Hypericum perforatum (perforate St John's-wort	
Hypericum pulchrum (slender St John's-wort)	
Ilex aquifolium (holly)	
Lamiastrum galeobdolon (yellow archangel)	
Lathraea squamaria (toothwort)	
Luzula pilosa (hairy wood-rush)	
Luzula sylvatica (great wood-rush)	
Lysimachia nemorum (yellow pimpernel)	
Malus sylvestris (crab apple)	
Melampyrum pratense (common cow-wheat)	
Melica uniflora (wood melick)	
Mercurialis perennis (dog's mercury)	
Milium effusum (wood millet)	
Myosotis sylvatica (wood forget-me-not)	
Orchis mascula (early-purple orchid)	
Oxalis acetosella (wood-sorrel)	
Populus tremula (aspen)	
Potentilla sterilis (barren strawberry)	
Primula vulgaris (primrose)	
Prunus avium (wild cherry)	
Quercus petraea (sessile oak)	
Sanicula europaea (sanicle)	
Scrophularia nodosa (common figwort)	
Sorbus torminalis (service tree) E R	
Stellaria holostea (greater stitchwort)	
Tilia cordata (small-leaved lime) E R	
Tilia platyphyllus (large-leaved lime) E R	
Vaccinium myrtillus (bilberry) W	
Veronica montanum (wood speedwell)	
Viburnum opulus (guelder rose)	
Vicia sepium (bush vetch)	
Viola reichbachiana (pale wood violet)	

Botanical indicators in South Yorkshire and adjoining parts of Derbyshire
W- west only; E - east only; R -rare.

List A Species from Peterken's 1981 list with a strong affinity for ancient woods in C. Lincs	West Wood 1	Old Thorn^cl Wood 2a	Ext to Thorn^cl Wood 2b	Newb Pl 3	Potter H Pl 4	Twelve L Pl 5	Tank^y Pl 6	Hood H Pl 7	Bell Gd. Wood 8
Anemone nemorosa (Wood Anemone)	*	**	*						
Galeobdolon luteum (Yellow Archangel)	**	**	*					*	
Galium odoratum (Sweet Woodruff)		*					*		
Luzula pilosa (Hairy Woodrush)	*								
Luzula sylvatica (Greater Woodrush)	*								
Melica uniflora (Wood Melick)	**	**	**	**			*	*	
Milium effusum (Wood Millet)	**	*	*	*			*	*	
Oxalis acetosella (Wood Sorrel)	**		*		*	*			
List B Species from Peterken's 1981 list with a mild affinity for ancient woods in C. Lincs.									
Allium ursinum (Ramsons)	**	**	*	*	*		*		
Comopodium majus (Pignut)	*								
Endymion non-scriptus (Bluebell)	**	**	**	*	*	*	*	*	
Fragaria vesca (Wild Strawberry)	*	*							
Mercurialis perennis (Dog's Mercury)	*	**	**	**	*	**	**	*	
Ranunculus auricomus (Goldilocks)	*								
Stellaria holostea (Stitchwort)	*	*	*				*		
Viola riviniana (Common Violet)	*	*	*			*			•
List C Species from Peterken's 1974 primary woodland species list for C. Lincs, omitted from his 1981 list.									
Quercus petraea (Sessile Oak)	**	**	*	*	*	*	*		
List D Species from Rackham's 1980 list of plants, additional to Peterken's 1974 list, with some association with ancient woodland in E. England.									
Epipactis helleborine (Broad-leaved Helleborine)					*				
Moehringia trinervia (Three-nerved Sandwort)							*		
	16	12	11	6	7	7	8	4	1

Figure 1.16. Botanical indicators in woods and plantations at Tankersley

because they have been preserved after their abandonment through the creation of a woodland that has not been cleared and converted to other uses. Such features in South Yorkshire include hillforts, linear earthworks, Romano-British settlement sites and abandoned coal and ironstone bell pits. Archaeological sites are dealt with in detail in Chapter 5.

The survival of ancient working trees in the form of large coppice stools within a wood and pollarded trees along the woodland boundaries, which some writers have labelled as living archaeology, may also indicate a woodland that has existed as a working wood for a long period of time. For example some coppice stools in Bradfield Wood in Suffolk are believed to have been in existence as early as the thirteenth century.

MYTH, LEGEND AND TRADITION

It is no surprise that if human beings have for millennia lived either in the woods or near woodlands, hedges and trees, that there are many associated myths, legends and folklore traditions. Perhaps the most intriguing of these are the medieval carvings that have survived throughout the country, and indeed throughout Western Europe, in stone and in wood in churches, cathedrals and abbeys that were originally called foliate heads but are now better known as green men. The carvings are usually in the form of a male face with leaves coming out of the mouth, and sometimes from the ears and/or eyes. The leaves have a resemblance to oak, hawthorn or maple (Figure 1.17). It is not absolutely clear what the meaning of the carvings is, but one interpretation is that they symbolise, rejuvenation or re-birth, i.e. the coming of Spring and the springing of vegetation into leaf once more. And with the majority of the population living in rural areas and dependent on the seasonal rhythm for the germination, growth and ripening of their crops, then the end of winter and the coming of Spring would always be greeted with joy and relief. Carvings of green men survive in at least fourteen of South Yorkshire's medieval churches. In St Mary's Church at Ecclesfield and at All Saints at Wath-upon-Dearne the carvings are in the form of roof bosses. In Rotherham parish church they are carved in stone on the columns of the nave.

Several trees and shrubs are surrounded by myth and legend. Rowan (Figure 1.18) has a special place in folk tradition, not only in this country but in Germany and Scandinavia. This is because of its long-thought-of magical properties, stemming from the long-held belief that Thor, the Norse god, was saved from an attempt by a sorceress to drown him in an overflowing river by holding onto the branch of a rowan tree. Hence it is said to offer protection against evil spirits, the devil and witches, giving rise to its local name *witchen* and variants on that name such as *wiggin*, which was its old South Yorkshire name. People would fasten sprigs of rowan to pieces of kitchen equipment or above cowshed and stable doors to keep their livestock safe. It was reported in 1888 that in Bradfield, the Pennine village to the west of Sheffield, people still nailed sprigs of rowan to their 'leaven-kits' (vessels for leavening oatcakes) 'to keep out the witch' and the same correspondent said that fifty years earlier the people of the same village would have no cups or bowls made from any other wood than rowan for the same reason.[22]

Holly has a very long history of being used in mid-winter celebrations. The Romans had a mid-winter celebration called Saturnalia that was introduced in 217 BC. At first it was celebrated on one day but soon became a week-long extravaganza. Presents included holly sprigs with best wishes for the recipient's health and well-being. The idea of holly bringing good luck or giving protection runs through the folklore of many regions and nations. It is the red berries that are at the heart of traditions. Red is the colour against evil. Holly was said to protect a house against lightning and its inhabitants against witchcraft. Another tradition is that a holly bush should never be dug up – it brings bad luck. Holly leaves were also used in divination practices. It was said that if you placed the leaves under your pillow you would dream about a future partner.

When Christmas beliefs and practices concerning holly began will never be known but it is easy to see why. Being evergreen it symbolised eternal life, the white flowers are a reminder of the immaculate conception, the berries allude to the blood of Christ and the prickly leaves represent the crown of thorns. When holly was brought into the house for the Christmas season it used to be said that if prickly-leaved holly was brought in first the man would rule the roost but if smooth-leaved holly was brought in first the wife would be dominant. And when made into a decoration with ivy, the entwining of the male-life symbol (holly) and the female symbol (ivy) would ensure fertility in the household.

Another Christmas decoration was the kissing bough or kissing bunch. This was constructed by making two hoops of willow (later replaced by wire) at right angles to each other and covering them with greenery usually holly and ivy to make a green globe. It was then hung from the ceiling. From it hung apples, oranges, sugar mice, streamers and most importantly

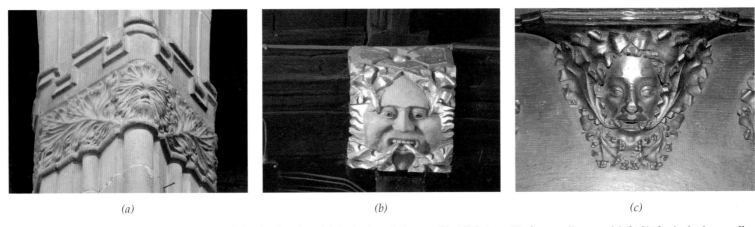

(a)   (b)   (c)

Figure 1.17. Green men in three of South Yorkshire's churches: (a) Rotherham Minster; (b) All Saints, Wath upon Dearne; (c) St Katherine's, Loversall

of all, a sprig of mistletoe. It was the centre of attraction at Christmas until it was replaced in the Victorian period by the Christmas tree. In a slightly different form it has re-appeared as the wreath fastened to doors at Christmas time. Holly was also part and parcel of the wassailing tradition, enshrined in the carol 'Here we come a-wassailing . . .' Wassail is from the Anglo-Saxon *waes-haeil* meaning 'good health'. It is a mid-winter custom that probably pre-dates Christianity but then became part of the Christmas and New Year festivities. Wassailing is a house visit-ing custom to wish health to neigh-

Figure 1.18. Rowan leaves and berries

bours. In its purest form it was a female custom with the girls and women garlanded and ribboned carrying a bowl of spiced ale and visiting local cottages and halls. Wassailing was also done around cowsheds and stables wishing health to the animals. The wassailers expected money or food in return for their visit. Holly was one of two woods (the other was maple) used in making the wassail bowl.

Hawthorn has an ambiguous folklore history. On the one hand under its alternative name of 'may' or 'may bush' it was used to adorn doors and windows on May Day, when young people went out into the woods in the early hours of the morning, 'gadding overnight' as one writer put it in 1583, to gather greenery to decorate houses to welcome the coming of Spring. This practice was first recorded as early as 1240. On the other hand it is widely believed to be unlucky and that to bring it into a house will cause illness or even death. This is related to the belief that the blossom smelled of death or the plague. The old saying 'ne'er cast a clout till may is out', meaning don't discard your winter clothing, is believed to refer not to the month of May but to the hawthorn blossom.

Some traditions related to trees are relatively modern, for example, oak apple day, 29 May, to celebrate the restoration of the monarchy in 1660, when King Charles II returned to England. Until well into the twentieth century it was the custom among children to wear either an oak leaf or an oak apple (i.e. a gall). And those not wearing an oak leaf or an oak apple on that day could be pinched, kicked or physically abused in other ways. Jean Huddlestone, who was born in 1923 and lived in Howbrook wrote that 'Our oak leaf protection we took care to pick on the way to school that morning and wore it carefully until noon lest we had our legs nettled, for that was the penalty'.[23]

Another tradition that was first recorded relatively recently is the game of conkers, using the fruits of the horse chestnut tree. In the season if you approach any horse chestnut tree there is likely to be evidence in the form of discarded sticks that children have been throwing up into the tree to dislodge the conkers. Yet the game of conkers was not recorded until 1856. The name conkers is thought to be derived from an earlier game called 'conquerors' or 'conquering' in which snail shells were squeezed together to see which one would shatter first. And in the seventeenth century there is a record of hazel nuts being strung and knocked together like conkers.

A tradition that may be ancient but continued into the 1940s and 1950s and possibly beyond was that chewing a sprig of hawthorn was good for you. In Barnsley and in Sheffield this was known as 'bread and cheese'.

Conkers

Conkers

What to read about the wildwood, ancient woods and tree and woodland folklore

ANDERSON, W. and HICKS, C. (1990) *Green Man*, Harper-Collins.

GELLING, M. and COLE, A. (2003), *The Landscape of Place-Names*, Shaun Tyas.

JONES, M. (1984) Woodland Origins in a South Yorkshire Parish, *The Local Historian*, **16**, 2, 73–82.

JONES, M. (1986) Ancient Woods in the Sheffield Area: The Documentary Evidence, *Sorby Record*, 24, 7–16.

JONES, M. (1995) *Rotherham's Woodland Heritage*, Rotherwood Press.

JONES, M. (2009) *Sheffield's Woodland Heritage,* 4th edition, Wildtrack Publishing.

ROTHERHAM, I.D., JONES, M., SMITH, L. and HANDLEY, C. (eds) (2008) *The Woodland Heritage Manual: A Guide to Investigating Woodland Landscapes*, Wildtrack Publishing.

SIMPSON, J. and ROUD, S. (2000) *A Dictionary of English Folklore*, Oxford University Press.

SMITH, A. H. (1961) *The Place-Names of the West Riding of Yorkshire, Part 1*, Cambridge University Press.

VERA, F. W. M. (2000) *Grazing Ecology and Forest History*, CAB Publishing.

Places to visit

Investigate your local wood to see which of the following attributes it possesses: a typical ancient woodland name; a parish edge location; a site typical of ancient wood (steep slope, deep valley, a broad ridge or a wetland site); ancient boundary and internal earthworks; ancient working trees (old coppice stools or boundary pollards).

Between late April and the end of June visit your local ancient wood and using the provisional list of ancient woodland indicators (Figure 1.14) identify and **record the number of botanical indicators** in the wood.

Go to the churches in South Yorkshire where there are carvings of **Green Men**: in Barnsley at Royston St John the Baptist and Silkstone All Saints (roof boss); in Doncaster at Hatfield St Lawrence, Loversall St Katherine (misericord) and Tickhill St Mary; in Rotherham at Harthill All Hallows, Laughton All Saints, Rotherham Minster (capitals), Treeton St Helen, Wales St John the Baptist and Wath All Saints; in Sheffield at Bradfield St Nicholas, Ecclesfield St Mary (roof boss) and Sheffield Cathedral.

DEER PARKS, CHASES AND WOODED COMMONS

WOOD PASTURES, in the medieval period and beyond, were wooded or partly wooded areas in which underwood and timber were harvested but in which animals were allowed to graze freely. As populations grew and settlements and therefore woodland clearance increased, sources of wood and timber became scarcer, wood pasture declined and was gradually replaced by a more intensive type of woodland management and production, coppicing. However, wood pasture survived alongside coppicing for many centuries. In the medieval period and beyond wood pastures were found in South Yorkshire, in deer parks and chases and on wooded commons.

MEDIEVAL DEER PARKS

Medieval deer parks were symbols of status and wealth. In South Yorkshire they were created by the nobility and they were also attached to monasteries. There were also two royal deer parks: Conisbrough Park, formerly the property of the de Warenne family that reverted to the Crown in the fourteenth century, and Kimberworth Park that became Crown property for a period in the late fifteenth century. As all deer were deemed to belong to the Crown, from the beginning of the thirteenth century landowners were supposed to obtain a licence from the king to create a park, although this appears not to have been necessary if the proposed park was not near a royal forest. The medieval parks at Conisbrough and Sheffield – now disappeared from the landscape except for place-names in the case of Conisbrough, and two important buildings – the

Manor Lodge and the Old Queen's Head public house, thought originally to have been a banqueting house in the deer park – in the case of Sheffield, predated the issuing of royal licences and so must have been of twelfth century or even earlier, possibly Saxon, origin. Thomas de Furnival, lord of the manor of Sheffield, when asked to explain before the *Quo Warranto* enquiry (an enquiry by the Crown into the privileges that lords claimed to hold) of 1281 by what right he held Sheffield deer park, said his family had held it (like the right to hold a market) since the Norman Conquest of 1066.

More commonly issued by the Crown was the right of free warren which gave a landowner the right to hunt certain animals – such as game birds, hare, fox, badger, wild cat, polecat and pine marten – within a prescribed area. This was often the forerunner to the fencing of demesne land to create a deer park. Searches of parish histories, principally Hunter's two-volume *South Yorkshire*[1] reveal that more than eighty grants of free warren were given in the medieval period in South Yorkshire and that in nearly a third of the cases, a deer park is known to have been subsequently created (Figure 2.1).

A number of the deer parks in South Yorkshire were created by the heads of the great Norman dynasties whose ancestors had accompanied the Conqueror to England in 1066 such as the de Warennes of Conisbrough Castle, who had parks at Conisbrough and Hatfield, the de Furnivals, who had a park at Sheffield and were also granted a licence to create a park at Whiston in 1316, and the de Buslis of Tickhill Castle who had a park at Tinsley. They were also created by other local lords of

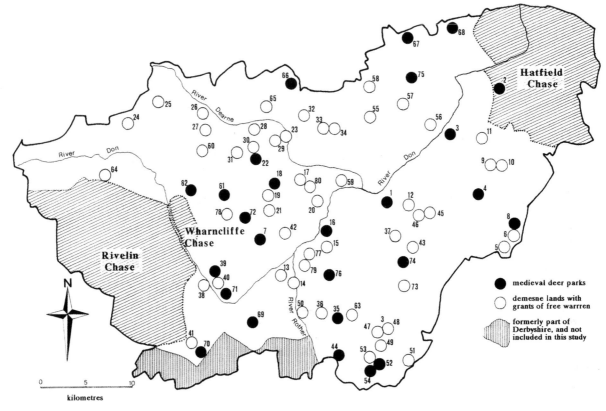

Figure 2.1. *Known medieval deer parks and grants of free warren in South Yorkshire. In some cases different landowners had parks/grants of free warren in the same parish or township. Deer parks are shown in bold.* 1 – **Conisbrough Park**; 2 – **Hatfield Park**; 3 – **Wheatley Park**; 4 – **Rossington Park**; 5 – *Bawtry*; 6 – *Austerfield*; 7 – **Kimberworth Park**; 8 – **Austerfield Park**; 9 – *Branton*; 10 – *Branton*; 11 – *Armthorpe*; 12 – *Edlington*; 13 – **Tinsley Park**; 14 – *Brinsworth*; 15 – *Dalton*; 16 – **Thrybergh Park**; 17 – *Newhall (Brampton Bierlow)*; 18 – **Rainborough Park**; 19 – *Linthwaite*; 20 – *Swinton*; 21 – *Wentworth Woodhouse*; 22 – **Woodhall Park**; 23 – *Newhall (Darfield)*; 24 – *Gunthwaite* 25 – *Cawthorne*; 26 – *Barnsley*; 27 – *Keresforth*; 28 – *Ardsley*; 29 – *Darfield*; 30 – *Wombwell*; 31 – *Worsbrough*; 32 – *Great Houghton*; 33 – *Thurnscoe*; 34 – *Thurnscoe*; 35 – **Aston Park**; 36 – *Aston & Aughton*; 37 – *Braithwell*; 38 – *Sheffield*; 39 – **Wadsley Park**; 40 – *Owlerton*; 41 – *Ecclesall*; 42 – *Greasbrough*; 43 – *Stainton*; 44 – **Northwood Park (Harthill)**; 45 – *Wadworth*; 46 – *Wadworth*; 47 – *North Anston*; 48 – *North Anston*; 49 – *North Anston*; 50 – **Treeton Park**; 51 – *Brancliffe Grange*; 52 – **Thorpe Salvin**; 53 – *Thorpe Salvin*; 54 – **Thorpe Salvin Park**; 55 – *Brodsworth*; 56 – *Bentley*; 57 – *Adwick*; 58 – *Hampole*; 59 – *Mexborough*; 60 – *Stainborough*; 61 – **Tankersley Park**; 62 – **Wortley Park**; 63 – *Hardwick*; 64 – *Langsett*; 65 – *Cudworth*; 66 – **Brierley Park**; 67 – **Norton Park**; 68 – **Fenwick Park**; 69 – **Sheffield Park**; 70 – **Ecclesall Park**; 71 – **Shirecliffe Park**; 72 – **Hesley Park/ Cowley Park**; 73 – *Roche*; 74 – **Maltby Park**; 75 – **Owston Park**; 76 – **Whiston Park**; 77 – *Rotherham*; 78 – *Ecclesfield*; 79 – *Rotherham*; 80 – *Wath*.

Norman origin such as the Fitzwilliams, Bosvilles, Chaworths and de Vavasors.

Religious houses were also granted permission to create parks in South Yorkshire. Some abbots and priors hunted in their parks – one of the secular practices of which they were accused by Henry VIII. A contemporary record states that Richard de Wombwell, prior of Nostell Priory from 1372–85, was fond of hunting. Significantly, the priory was granted free warren on its lands at Swinton, Thurnscoe, and Great Houghton (where there is still a wood called Little Park) during his term of office. Besides Nostell Priory other religious houses from outside the region were granted free warren on their South Yorkshire properties, for example Rufford Abbey and Worksop Priory, both in Nottinghamshire, and Bolton Abbey in Craven. One of the properties of Bolton Abbey on which they had a grant of free warren was at Wentworth Woodhouse, an antecedent of the surviving Wentworth Park (one of only two parks still containing deer in South Yorkshire). Monk Bretton Priory was granted free warren on its lands at Rainborough in Brampton Bierlow township and there is still a large wood there called Rainborough Park.

At least twenty-seven deer parks were created in medieval South Yorkshire. Nationally the great age of park creation was the century and a half between 1200 and 1350, a period of growing population and agricultural prosperity. Landowners had surplus wealth and there were still sufficient areas of waste on which to create parks. In South Yorkshire the majority of grants of free warren, which as already noted were often the forerunners of the creation of deer parks, were given in the period from 1250 to 1325 when forty-four grants were made. Significantly, no grants of free warren were given for thirty years following the Black Death (1349), but then there were twenty-one grants between 1379 and 1400. The last known medieval royal licence to create a deer park was given in 1491–92 when Brian Sandford was granted permission to create a park at Thorpe Salvin. This grant is also notable for the fact that it was accompanied by a gift of twelve does from the king's park at Conisbrough 'towards the storing of his parc at Thorp'.[2] The last-known local licence was granted to the 2nd Viscount Castleton in 1637 by King Charles I to create a deer park at Sandbeck (Figure 2.2). The licence states that Viscount Castleton was given permission to make separate with pales, walls or hedges 500 acres or thereabouts of land, meadow, pasture, gorse, heath, wood, underwood, woodland tenements and hereditaments to make a park where deer and other wild animals might be grazed and kept.[3]

Figure 2.2. The last known licence to create a deer park in South Yorkshire: Sandbeck Park, 1637. Source: the Lumley Archive, Courtesy of the Earl of Scarbrough

The creation of a park, emparkment, involved enclosing an area of land with a fence to keep the deer and other game inside and predators (in the early days wolves) and poachers outside. The fence – the park pale – consisted either of cleft oak vertical pales with horizontal railings, often set on a bank, or a stone wall (see Chapter 5). As parks could vary in size from under 100 acres to several thousand acres (Sheffield Park at its greatest extent covered nearly 2,500 acres and was 8 miles in circumference) fencing was a major initial and recurring expense. Because of this the most economical shape for a deer park was a circle or a rectangle with rounded corners, as was the case throughout South Yorkshire (Figure 2.3).

Figure 2.3. Characteristics of a typical deer park

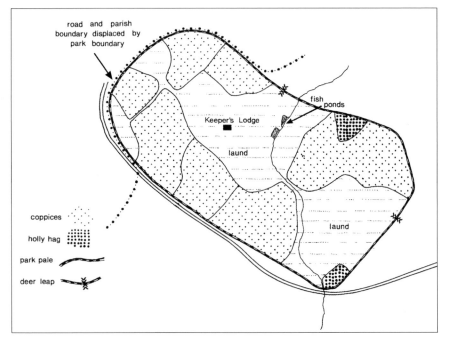

road and parish boundary displaced by park boundary

fish ponds

Keeper's Lodge

laund

laund

coppices

holly hag

park pale

deer leap

Deer parks were not created primarily for hunting although hunting did take place in the larger parks. The deer were carefully farmed.[4] Besides their status symbol role their main function was to provide for their owners a reliable source of food for the table, supplies of wood and timber, and in some cases quarried stone, coal and ironstone. They were, therefore, an integral part of the local economy. Besides deer, hares, rabbits (also introduced by the Normans and kept in burrows in artificially made mounds) and game birds were kept in the medieval parks of South Yorkshire. Herds of cattle, flocks of sheep and pigs were also grazed there. Another important feature of South Yorkshire's medieval deer parks were fish ponds to provide an alternative to meat in Lent and on fast days.

To use the modern term a deer park was also usually part of the manorial 'forestry' operation. Although there are records of parks without trees, deer parks usually consisted of woodland and areas largely cleared of trees. The park livestock could graze in the open areas and find cover in the wooded areas. The cleared areas, called launds or plains, consisted of grassland or heath with scattered trees (Figure 2.4). The Norman-French word laund is, of course, a predecessor of the modern word lawn. The king's park keeper at Conisbrough Park in the second half of the fifteenth century was referred to in a document written in French as *Laundier et Palisser de n're park de Connesburgh*, i.e. keeper of the un-wooded areas and the park boundaries at our park at Conisbrough.[5] Many of the trees in the launds would have been pollarded, ie, cut at least six feet from the ground leaving a massive lower trunk called a bolling above which a continuous crop of new growth sprouted out of reach of the grazing deer, sheep and cattle. In the launds regeneration of trees was restricted because of continual

Figure 2.4. A typical deer park scene: grazing deer in a laund with woodland in the background and an ancient oak tree in the foreground

grazing and new trees were only able to grow in the protection of thickets of hawthorn and holly. Some of the unpollarded trees might reach a great age and size and were much sought after for major building projects.

The woods within deer parks were managed in different ways. Some woods were 'holted', ie, they consisted of single-stemmed trees grown for their timber like a modern plantation. Most park woods were coppiced and were surrounded by a bank or wall to keep out the grazing animals during the early years of re-growth. Later in the coppice cycle the deer would have been allowed into the coppice woods. There were also in South Yorkshire's deer parks, separate woods or special compartments within coppice woods in which the dominant tree was holly and which were called holly hags. The holly was cut in winter for the deer and other park livestock.[6]

Sheffield Park is particularly well documented and a clear picture emerges of the woods and trees within it and the way they were used in the medieval period. This deer park, which at its greatest extent covered 2,462 acres (nearly 1,000 hectares) and was 8 miles (13 kilometres) in circumference, came right up to the eastern edge of the town of Sheffield (Figure 2.5). It

Figure 2.5. Sheffield deer park as described in John Harrrison's survey of the Manor of Sheffield, 1637

had a typical shape, a rounded rectangle. Harrison in his survey of the manor of Sheffield in 1637 named the various parts of the park including some with woodland names including Arbor Thorn Hirst and Stone Hirst (hyrst = a wooded hill) but they would only have been covered with scrub woods of hawthorn and holly. The cleared areas within the park are also precisely named in Harrison's survey: 'ye Lands', 'Cundit Plaine', 'Blacko Plaine' and 'Bellhouse Plaine'. Ye Lands is probably a corruption of laund.[7] These launds or plains contained large aged oak trees in the seventeenth century, that would have already been very large trees two or three hundred years earlier in the late medieval period. They were described in great detail by John Evelyn in his book *Silva*, first published in 1670. He appears to have obtained his information from Immanuel Halton, the Duke of Norfolk's auditor. Evelyn said that in 1646 there were 100 trees whose combined value was £1,000. He described one oak tree in the park whose trunk was 13 feet in diameter and another which was 10 yards in circumference. He also described another massive oak that when cut down yielded 1,400 'wairs' which were planks 2 yards long and 1 yard wide and 20 cords from its branches. A cord was a pile of wood 4 feet high, 4 feet wide and 8 feet long. He described another oak, that when felled and lying on its side was so massive that two men on horseback on either side of it could not see each other's hat crowns. On Conduit Plain (the Cundit Plaine of Harrison's 1637 survey), Evelyn reported that there was one oak tree whose boughs were so far spreading that he estimated (giving all his calculations) that 251 horses could stand in its shade.[8]

These mighty oaks, or veteran or ancient trees as they are now termed (see Chapter 6), had had a multiplicity of uses for centuries. As already noted when felled they provided not only timber for building projects, but also charcoal (from their branches), and wood for a multiplicity of crafts and industries. Standing, live, veteran oak trees also had an important function. These open-grown enormously-branched trees (the one on Conduit Plain described by Evelyn had branches extending for 15½ yards (14 m) in every direction) produced, unlike most woodland grown oaks, burgeoning crops of acorns. These not only provided the food for fattening pigs during the pannage season (Figure 2.6) but also for keeping the deer population in good heart in preparation for the long winter.

A 'Feet of Fines' document of 1268 and mid-fifteenth century manorial rolls give glimpses of the uses to which wood and

Figure 2.6. Pannage

timber in Sheffield Park were put in the late thirteenth and mid-fifteenth centuries respectively.[9] A Feet of Fines document was one relating to a judgement on a title to land. This one relates to the dowry of Berta, the widowed wife of Thomas de Furnival, lord of Hallamshire, and the father of the Thomas de Furnival who appeared before the *Quo Warranto* proceedings of 1281. The judgement stated that Berta de Furnival had rights to a third of the income from certain activities in the park. This income came from rents of the smithies in the park, from wood sold in the park, from pannage, herbage, eyries of sparrowhawks and 'forest pleas' from 'the said park'. The income from forest pleas, was presumably the income raised from fines imposed on trespassers, poachers and other persons found illegally entering the park and stealing from it. The income from the nests of sparrowhawks is less easy to explain unless the fledglings were sold to be hand-reared to keep small birds from cropped areas. What is clear, however, was that at this period, not all the park was reserved for deer or for producing material for the sole use of the lord: scarce resources were sold or rented out. Herbage (also known as agistment) was the renting of grazing space for cattle, sheep and horses and pannage (*pannagio porcorum*) was the autumnal grazing of pigs on fallen acorns (Figure 2.6).

The manorial rolls show that besides its role as a food larder for the lord, the park in the 1440s also supplied firewood for the castle, timber for building repairs at the castle stables and at the old tower next to the chapel in the castle. Pollarded oaks were felled (*pro prostatracione pollardruum quercuum*) to make scaffolding and hurdles for repairs at the castle. Brushwood and stakes were also taken from the park to repair the dam and weir of the fulling mill (inside the park) which had been damaged in a flood. Oaks in the park were felled to make posts, rails and palings for fencing the castle garden. Income was also derived from allowing holly trees to be cropped (for fodder), from the pannage of pigs, the sale of felled trees and a parcel of underwood, and from charcoal made from the branches of trees where they were being cleared to make a new pasture.

By the seventeenth century Sheffield Park was in decline but still contained a number of very important features, that reflected the continuance of medieval practices. By 1637, when John Harrison carried out his survey of the manor of Sheffield, more than 971 acres (more than a third of the park) had been let to tenants, including a coppice wood on Morton Bank.

Between the late fifteenth and eighteenth centuries many medieval deer parks either changed their function and hence their appearance, or, more commonly, disappeared altogether. When a landlord was absent (his main country seat may have been in another parish or county) or where his hall lay some distance away from his medieval park, there was increased possibility that the park may disappear altogether. John Speed's map of the West Riding of Yorkshire published in 1610 shows only ten surviving deer parks in South Yorkshire: at Wortley, Tankersley, Brierley, Sheffield, Kimberworth, Thrybergh, Conisbrough, Treeton, Aston and Austerfield. Only the outline of Tanksersley Park has survived to the present day in any recognisable form.

Well-wooded parks often simply became large coppice woods. Examples of the reversion to managed woodland in South Yorkshire are Cowley Park, Hesley Park, Shirecliffe Park and Tinsley Park. Cowley Park and Hesley Park, for example, became coppice woods of 163 and 135 acres respectively. A large part of the former Shirecliffe Park, survived into the twentieth century in the form of a large wood called Shirecliffe Old Park, which in Harrison's 1637 survey of the manor of

Sheffield was described as 'A Spring wood called Shirtcliffe parke' and covered 143 acres.[10] Tinsley Park by 1657 was a compartmented wood that was let by its owner, the 2nd Earl of Strafford, to the ironmaster, Lionel Copley, for felling for charcoal making. It covered 413 acres and comprised ten coppice woods and three holts.[11] Rainborough Park at Brampton became a coppice wood and the shape of the modern wood, a long rectangle with rounded corners, still suggests that it was once a fenced enclosure for deer.

Other medieval parks simply reverted wholly or largely to farmland. South Yorkshire examples include Aston Park, Brierley Old Park and Conisbrough Park. The outline of a small park at Aston still survives in the agricultural landscape as a rectangle with rounded corners. This small park appears to be the one shown on John Speed's map of 1610 and seems to be the one created by Osbert de Arches who had been granted a right of free warren in 1256–57. The park became part of a farm called Old Park Farm.

While hundreds of medieval deer parks were disappearing, many others took on a new lease of life and many new parks were created because the concept of the park was changing. Its primary function changed from being a game preserve and a valuable source of wood and timber to being the adornment of a country house. New residences were built within existing parks and the park boundaries extended. The parks surrounding the new country houses that were built in the sixteenth, seventeen and eighteenth centuries, were still essentially deer parks, although grazing cattle were a much more common sight than in the medieval period, with both the deer and the cattle being an aesthetic backdrop to the house as much as a source of food. Wentworth Woodhouse, the eighteenth-century residence of the Marquises of Rockingham and in the nine-

teenth and twentieth centuries of their successors, the Earls Fitzwilliam, provides the clearest South Yorkshire example of this change.[12] In 1732 Thomas Wentworth (later the first Marquis) embarked on the building of his magnificent Palladian mansion and the improvement of the surrounding park, or as he put it in a letter to his son, to 'beautifye the country and do the work ordered by God himself'. He extended the park until it was more than 9 miles in circumference, created 'a Serpentine river' and built a number of monuments, including a Doric temple and an Ionic temple. The sixth Earl Fitzwilliam in the second half of the nineteenth century also added a herd of bison to the red and fallow deer that grazed in the park.

Deer parks were still being created, remodelled or re-stocked in South Yorkshire in the eighteenth century. John Spencer, of Cannon Hall, for example, remodelled his parkland in the 1760s, building a new boundary wall and a ha-ha to separate the park from the gardens. Once these works were completed he set about re-stocking his park with fallow deer. He recorded in his diary on Wednesday 3 February 1762 that 'The Gamekeeper returned from Sprodborough with twenty bucks'. Two days later he noted that 'deer from Sir George Armytage's of Kirk Lees Hall' had been brought to his park and the next day he recorded that he had been to Gunthwaite and 'took the deer out of Gunthwaite Park & put them into my park'. By the end of the week he had a herd of eighty-nine deer in his park at Cannon Hall.[13]

The 750-acre (227ha) Tankersley Park, is a good example of a park that changed its function over time and then was destroyed. All that is known of its medieval history is that a right of free warren was granted to the lord of the manor, Hugh de Elland, in 1303–04 and that, presumably, subsequently the park was created. Only one reference to the park is known between the fourteenth and early seventeenth centuries when Henry Savile in a law suit of 1527 was said to have been 'hunting at dere wythe houndes in hys parke at Tankersley'.[14] The Saviles had inherited the estate from the Ellands in the late fourteenth century and in the sixteenth century they built a hall in the centre of the park.

The Tankersley estate with the park was then purchased by Thomas Wentworth, the 1st Earl of Strafford sometime between 1614–1635. The Wentworths and their successors, the Watson-Wentworths and the Wentworth-Fitzwilliams, as noted above, resided just a few miles to the east of Tankersley at Wentworth Woodhouse. In the eighteenth century from the time they built

their magnificent Palladian mansion and surrounded it with a large landscaped park, Tankersley Park went into decline, at first shrunken through enclosure for farming and then mined for ironstone from shallow bell pits and gin pits and also through deep shaft mining. An early eighteenth century engraving of the park made for the 1st Marquis of Rockingham has survived which shows many interesting features of its layout and management for deer. The engraving (Figure 2.7 (a)) dates from the late 1720s. It shows the park, in the form of a bird's-eye view looking from the east. Figure 2.7(b) shows the information in the engraving in map form, based on the first edition O.S. 6-inch sheet, with a number of key features identified.

Figure 2.7. *(a) engraving of Tankersley Park c. 1730 and (b) map based on the engraving*

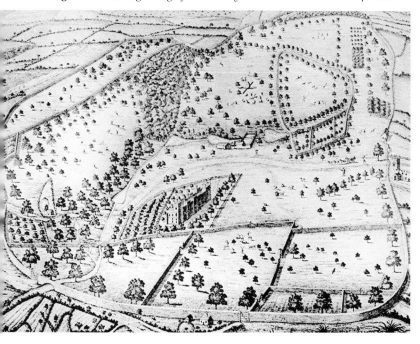
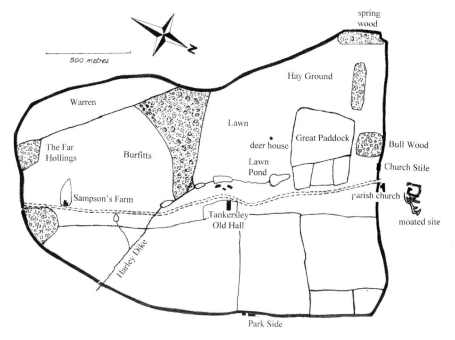

The park is a typical shape, rectangular with rounded corners in the south-west and south-east. Being in 'stone wall country' it is completely surrounded by a wall of locally-quarried coal measure sandstone rather than by a bank and cleft-oak pales and railings. In the centre of the park is the residence built by the once owner of the park, Thomas Savile, dating from the Elizabethan period, and known as Tankersley Old Hall from the eighteenth century and earlier as the Lodge. The hall seems to have been the successor to the moated manor house that lay outside the park to the north of the parish church, the moated site, by the early eighteenth century, being occupied by the rectory. The gardens and pleasure grounds of the hall are surrounded by a pale fence. Along Harley Dike, the stream running through the park and escaping through the park wall on the engraving, are four fish ponds, the largest one called the Lawn Pond on late eighteenth century maps.

The park is compartmented. The two largest compartments which both contain deer on the engraving, are separated by an area of dense woodland. One of these is the area in the south of the park shown on later maps as the Burfitts and the other area containing the deer shed named on some maps as 'the Lawn'. Two other distinct and walled areas were the Warren in the south-west and the Paddocks in the north. There was also a small wood shown on the engraving on the north-western margin of the park. On nineteenth-century maps this is called the Folly Spring, a spring wood in South Yorkshire being almost invariably a coppice-with-standards. The eastern part of the park was divided into a series walled enclosures, one of which is shown to hold deer, but others do not and may at that time have been tenanted. In a lease of the park and the Lodge to Sir Richard Fanshawe in 1653, three-quarters of a century before the engraving was completed, it was stated that certain parts of the park including the Paddocks and Swift Bank had been 'divided and severed from the deere' and were or had recently been in the occupation of tenants.[15.]

A feature of the park, strongly emphasised in the engraving, was that it was dotted with magnificent veteran trees, including oaks and yews. Hunter quotes one traveller who said that the 'Talbot yew' in the park was so large that 'a man on horseback might turn round in it'.[16] The first edition 6-inch Ordnance Survey map (Sheet 282, published in 1853) even points out the oak tree in the park 'in which it is said Lord Strafford was arrested'. The 1st Earl of Strafford was in fact arrested for treason in London and executed in 1641. Late nineteenth-century photographs have also survived showing magnificent pollarded horse chestnuts in the park (Figure 2.8).

The engraving also shows the careful way in which provision was made for the deer, which at Tankersley were mostly red deer. There were, besides the hundreds of acres of grass sward in which they could graze and the woodlands in which they could take cover, a number of special provisions made for the animals. There was the Warren, where hinds could be kept and looked after during the breeding season, and three specific ways in which extra feed in winter could be provided. First, between the Paddocks and Folly Spring, was an area called the Hay Ground where the grass was cut for hay for the deer. The 1653 lease specified that two loads of hay should be provided in winter for every hundred deer (the lease specifies that the number of deer should be increased to 280). The hay was stored in the deer house, deer shed or rotunda which is shown clearly on the engraving. Mangers would be erected at the deer house in which the hay was placed and replenished. In addition to hay, the 1653 lease specified that the deer had also to be fed in winter 'with holley to be cutt therein'. This was, as already

Figure 2.8. The deer shed and horse chestnut pollards in Tankersley Park c. 1900

noted, often grown in special woods or compartments in woods called in South Yorkshire 'holly hags'. The engraving shows a walled wooded enclosure in the south-eastern corner of the park. On late eighteenth-century maps this is called the Far Hollings. Bull Wood which is also shown on the engraving, survives to this day and is full of holly and may have been another holly hag in the park.

The engraving also shows the first stage in the disparkment of Tankersley Park in the form of buildings in their small enclosure not far inside the southern boundary of the park. This was Sampson's Farm which appears to have been carved out of the park in the late 1720s and early 1730s. A stone on

one of the surviving cottages bears the date 1729; in March 1732 'eleven thousand quicksetts' were planted as new field boundaries; and in the autumn of 1732 it is recorded that a barn was being built on the farm using stone from Tankersley Old Hall which was evidently being dismantled.[17] As the century proceeded more and more of the park was converted to tenanted farmland. By 1772 when a detailed survey of Tankersley was carried out more than two-thirds of the area of the park (nearly 500 acres) was in the hands of nine tenants and only 265 acres remained in the hands of the 2nd Marquis.[18] Despite the reduction in the size of the park the 2nd Marquis and Countess must have retained a great deal of affection for Tankersley Park, as in the 1760s the Marquis built a stone summer house/observatory called 'Lady's Folly' at the highest point in the park on the hay ground with extensive views in every direction.

But even more dramatic change was to follow, for the park is underlain by seams of coal measure ironstone – the Tankersley Ironstone, Swallow Wood Ironstone and Lidgett Ironstone – and these ironstones were systematically exploited between 1795 and 1879 to supply the Elescar and Milton ironworks in Hoyland township to the east.[19] The ironstone mining had the effect, slowly but surely, of leading to total disparkment. Earl Fitzwilliam's mineral agent, Benjamin Biram, noted in his diary on 15 January 1855 that there were 380 fallow deer and sixty-four red deer at Wentworth and Tankersley.[20] But within a year or two the remaining deer at Tankersley were removed to Wentworth. The deer house remained until after 1900, Lady's Folly was dismantled in 1960, the woods and ancient trees have disappeared and all that remains to remind the visitor that there was a deer park here are the silted up remains of the fish ponds and the ruins of Tankersley Old Hall.

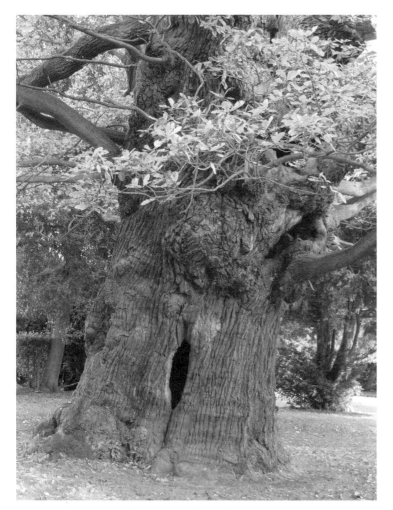

One final note on deer parks is called for. There is still standing in the gardens at Wortley Hall an ancient parkland oak that once stood in the medieval Wortley deer park (Figure 2.9). It is a sessile oak with its stalked leaves and un-stalked acorns. It has a massive girth of 23 feet (7 m) and is hollow. I estimate that it must be at least 600 years old so it must have been there in late medieval times. What a story it could tell if it could speak! And it must be remembered that ancient trees like the Wortley Hall oak harbour an unbelievably rich wildlife, particularly beetles. There are in Britain 650 different species that are rarely found very far from ancient woodlands and old trees and there are fourteen families of beetles that in their larval stage feed on living or dead wood including such spectacular beetles as the longhorn beetle, the rhinoceros beetle and the lesser stag beetle (Figure 2.10).

Figure 2.9. Ancient oak tree at Wortley Hall

Figure 2.10. Lesser stag beetle

FORESTS AND CHASES

Large tracts of the English countryside were turned into Royal Forests in the Norman period, for example, Sherwood Forest in Nottinghamshire, the Peak Forest in Derbyshire and the Forest of Pickering in Yorkshire. This is where hunting took place (Figure 2.11). The word forest does not imply woodland. Indeed the Peak Forest was mainly moorland. Forest here is a legal term meaning that Forest Law applied relating to the hunting of deer, the grazing of animals, the clearing of land and the felling of timber. Forests were not fenced and could include within their boundaries moorland, woodland, heath, fen, farmland and settlements. There were three chases in South Yorkshire which were the private equivalents of the Royal Forests. These were Hatfield Chase, Rivelin Chase and Wharncliffe Chase. In 1347 Hatfield Chase reverted to the Crown and became a Royal Forest until it was freed from Forest laws in the early seventeenth century.

The low-lying and often inundated 70,000 acres (28,000 ha) of Hatfield Chase became the private hunting ground shortly after the Norman Conquest of the de Warenne family of Conisbrough Castle. It became crown property in 1347 and became a Royal Forest until 1629, shortly after the Humberhead Levels began to be drained. The last royal hunt took place there in 1609 when it is said that the royal party in a flotilla of 100 boats pursued 500 deer across Thorne Mere. Abraham de la Pryme, writing in the 1690s, said that before the drainage deer were as common as 'Sheep upon ye hills' and had once been 'so unruly that they had almost ruined the country'.[21] Mature woodland would have been a rarity in Hatfield Chase and all there would have been were swampy scrub woods of willow, birch and alder (see wooded commons below).

On the western extremities of the region was Rivelin Chase, the generic name of adjacent private forests of the medieval lords of the manor of Sheffield. This chase included Rivelin Chase proper, the forest of Fulwood, Loxley Chase and a number of other areas under forest law called 'firths'. Rivelin Chase contained large areas of moorland over 1,000 feet (304 m) and extensive valley woodlands. As late as 1637 it still contained two large deer enclosures, one in the Rivelin valley and the other on the open moorland at Redmires 'reserved for ye Red Deere'.[22] The exact boundaries of Rivelin Chase are unknown but seem to have extended down the Porter, Rivelin and Loxley valleys to the Don valley and almost into Sheffield itself. The valleys were heavily wooded with some magnificent oak trees. John Evelyn in 1670 described a pollarded tree at the upper end of Rivelin called the 'Lord's Oak' which he said had a girth of 36 feet (10.9 m) and whose tops when pollarded about 1657 had yielded 21 cords of wood.[23] These would have weighed nearly forty tons when first cut. Just over twenty years earlier John Harrison in his survey of the manor of Sheffield in 1637 described an area of particularly stately trees in an area in the Rivelin valley that he called Hawe Park. Harrison's description is worth repeating in full:

> *Item Hawe Park lyeth open to Rivelin ffirth
> but it is at ye pleasure of ye Lord to inclose
> it ... This piece is full of excellent Timber of a
> very great length & very Streight & many of
> them of a great bigness before you come to a
> Knott in so much that it hath been said by
> Travellers that they have not seene such
> Timber in Christendome.*[24]

Figure 2.11. *A hunting scene showing the 'drive' or 'bow and stable' method where deer were driven into nets or towards a row of archers*

The illegal felling and carrying away of wood and timber must have been relatively common occurrences in royal forests and private chases and it was the foresters' duty to bring offenders before the manorial court. Cases from Rivelin Chase include, for example, Thomas Horsknave in 1385 who was fined three-pence for cutting wood in Grenofirth,[25] Thomas Beaumont in 1504 who was fined twelvepence for felling and taking away two loads of wood from 'le Firth de Revelinge',[26] and in 1595 in a letter to the 7th Earl of Shrewsbury it was reported that 'Edward Bromhall and his man have been taken for supposed hunting in Lockesley'.[27]

On a much smaller scale than Hatfield and Rivelin was Wharncliffe Chase, the private forest of the Wortley family which had been developed on the high plateau above the River Don and bounded by the dramatic Wharncliffe Crags (Figure 2.12). The chase was described in 1639 by the London poet John Taylor as a 'woody, rocky, stony vast wilderness'. It was probably originally created in the second half of the thirteenth century following the granting of a right of free warren in 1252. It was extended southwards in late Elizabethan times. In order to create the New Park, as the extension was called, tenants were evicted and two hamlets depopulated.

Figure 2.12. *Wharncliffe Chase today*

This ignominious episode is immortalised in the folk ballad *The Dragon of Wantley* published in 1685 which describes a dreadful combat between More of More Hall (which is in the Ewden valley opposite Wortley) and the Dragon of Wantley. The dragon is believed to be landowner Sir Richard Wortley who extended Wharncliffe Chase and More, his opponent, represented wronged yeomen and minor gentry.[28] There were still 1,200 head of deer on the chase in the 1820s,[29] by the 1890s there were fifty-seven red deer and fifty-one fallow deer and by 1945 there were just forty red deer. The severe winter of 1946–47 is said to have killed all but eight. Red deer, probably descendants of the Wharncliffe herd, still roam throughout the Wharncliffe area.[30]

WOODED COMMONS

Wooded commons were a widely distributed type of common in the Southern Pennine Fringe and Coalfield landscape character zones of South Yorkshire in great contrast to the moorland commons of the Dark Peak zone. Parts of the marshland commons of the Humberhead Levels also contained scrub wood in the form of willow carrs and alder carrs. Wooded commons were unfenced woods in which underwood and timber were harvested but in which the animals of commoners, i.e., those who had certain rights on the common land of a manor, were allowed to graze freely. Commoners usually also had the right of the underwood and dead wood but the timber trees usually belonged to the lord of the manor. In the manor of Sheffield as late as 1637 there were 21,000 acres of common land, much of it wooded.

In the Southern Pennine Fringe and Coalfield zones some commons disappeared quite early but others remained until enclosure in the eighteenth and early nineteenth centuries. The first record of a wooded common in South Yorkshire was in 1161 when the monks of the abbey of St Wandrille (who built Ecclesfield Priory) were given permission by the lord of Hallamshire, Richard de Louvetot, to pasture their flocks from January to Easter, their swine in the autumn, and to take dead wood in a large wood stretching from Birley Edge down to the Don all the way from Wardsend to Oughtibridge. In an undated charter of about 1297 Thomas de Furnival, the lord of the manor of Hallamshire, made a number of grants of common in the largely uninhabited uplands and river valleys in the western part of the manor. He gave to the men of Stannington, Morewood, Hallam and Fulwood the right of herbage and foliage (to gather green and dry wood) throughout his forest of Riveling (i.e. Rivelin Chase, his private hunting forest) all the way from Malin Bridge at the confluence of the rivers Rivelin and Loxley to Stanage Edge at a height of more than 1,421 feet (435 m) more than seven miles (11 km) to the south-west. In an inquisition *post mortem* of 1332 on the death of Thomas de Furnival it was recorded that his properties in the manor of Sheffield included pastures in among other places 'Greno, Billy Wood, Ryvelyngden and Baldwinhousteads'.[31] Ryvelyngden was the valley of the Rivelin occupied by his private hunting forest which continued in part to be wood pasture until the Parliamentary Enclosures but by 1600 the other three, Greno Wood, Beeley Wood and Bowden Housteads Wood, were all enclosed coppice woods. But some wood pastures continued in existence for more than two centuries longer.

Two interesting early deeds relating to the wooded commons at Rawmarsh are also full of interest. The first which dates from 1241 refers to the vicar's rights on the common of Rawmarsh for firewood, for housebote and for hedgebote.[32] The same wooded common was included in a marriage settlement in

1557 between Lancelot Mountforthe of Kilnhurst and Margaret Wentworth of Wentworth Woodhouse. The estate described in the settlement included access to the common and woods of Rawmarsh for pasturing animals and for 'wood for their fires, hedges and houses'.[33]

There are graphic descriptions of a number of wooded commons in the late seventeenth and early eighteenth centuries. In 1650 Loxley Chase was referred as 'one Great wood called Loxley the herbage common and consisteth of great Oake timber'. About ten years earlier, another wooded common, Walkley Bank, was said to have 'a great store of rough Oake trees & some Bircke (birch) woods'. In the same year Stannington Wood, formerly part of Rivelin Chase and which covered 217 acres (88 ha) in 1637, was said to consist of 'pt of rough Timber and part of Springe wood'.

The fen-edge settlements in the Humberhead Levels in the medieval and early modern periods were immediately surrounded by their townfields, closes and intakes, further away beside the slow-moving rivers and streams were meadows and beyond these were thousands of acres of fen made up of carr (scrub woodland) and peat bog utilised as commons. The uses that the commoners made of the fens were legion. First there was grazing. And turf from the peat moors was obviously a perquisite for all commoners, not only as a fuel but also as a building material. Reeds and sedges were cut to thatch cottages, outhouses and barns; rushes and other marsh plants were cut for hay; osiers in the willow carrs were made into wicker baskets and eel traps and bigger scantlings of wood would be used to make barges, turf barrows and sledges; and the wildlife was a food source: wildfowl and waders, birds' eggs and fish. There were also the remains of the prehistoric wildwood in the form of tree trunks and tree stumps buried in the peat deposits

on Thorne and Hatfield Moors. No doubt the bog oaks and bog pines unearthed during turf cutting were rescued by the commoners. There is evidence of these trees trapped in the peat for 4,500–5,500 years being sold for ships' masts.[34]

Like medieval deer parks, wooded commons have virtually all disappeared from the landscape. One of the lost commons, Brierley Common, once had a gigantic ancient oak, the lone survivor where there had previously been many (Figure 2.13). In 1831, Joseph Hunter, noting the survival of the venerable oak, known locally as Old Adam, wrote, 'May no unfeeling hand bring its venerable crown to the dust'.[35] Perhaps the best documented and interesting of the few surviving former South Yorkshire wooded commons is Loxley Common and the

Figure 2.13. Old Adam, Brierley Common. Source: Hunter (1831)

coterminous Wadsley Common. The area in question covers the valley side to the north of the River Loxley with Loxley Edge, a sandstone escarpment outcropping in the eastern half of the site and with a boulder-strewn slope below it (Figure 2.14). Loxley Common is variously referred to in historical documents as Loxley Common, Loxley Chase and Loxley Firth. Loxley Common was mentioned in a late thirteenth century document in which Thomas de Furnival, the lord of Hallamshire, granted common rights to the inhabitants of the area.[36] In an inquisition *post mortem* in 1332 on the death of Thomas de Furnival it was recorded that the pannage of the woods (*pannagium boscorum*), i.e. the pasturing of pigs on acorns, at 'Rivelyngden and Lokesley' was worth forty shillings.[37] Just over 300 years later in 1637 it was recorded in John Harrison's survey of the manor of Sheffield as 'A Common Called Loxley wood & ffirth' and covered 1,517 acres.[38] Incidentally in the same survey a croft on the north-western edge of Loxley Firth was said to contain the foundations of the cottage where Robin Hood was born! In 1650, as noted earlier, the common was referred to as 'one Great wood called Loxley the herbage common and consisteth of great Oake timber'. Two old oak pollards still survive on the site (Figure 2.15). At this time Lionell Copley, the successful South Yorkshire ironmaster was leasing Wadsley Forge and came to an agreement with the Howard family to fell woods on their estates for charcoal. The following verse is said to date from this time:

If Mr Copley had never been born,
Or in his cradle had died,
Loxley Chase had never been torn,
Nor many a brave wood besides.

In the early eighteenth century there are several references in the Duke of Norfolk's woodland accounts to the looking after of rabbits there. For example, in 1724 a payment was made to Edward Wilson 'for mending Rabbit Burs [=burrows] on Loxley & looking after the Rabbits there', suggesting that it was the site of a manorial rabbit warren.[39]

Figure 2.14. *Loxley Chase as portrayed on the 1893 6-Inch to One Mile Ordnance Survey map*

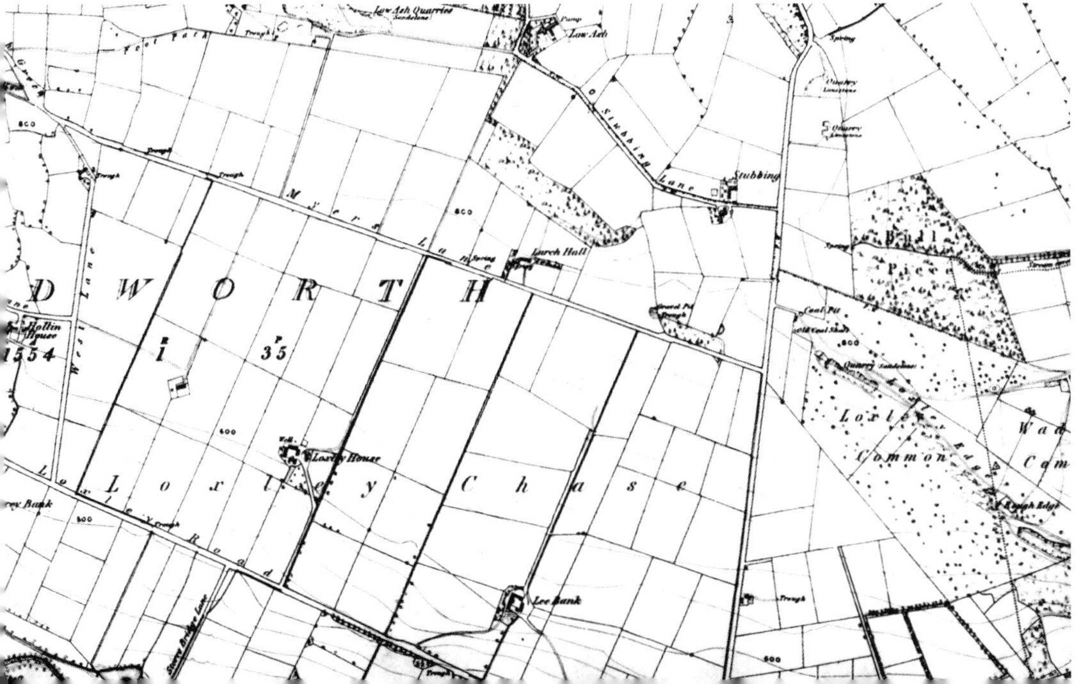

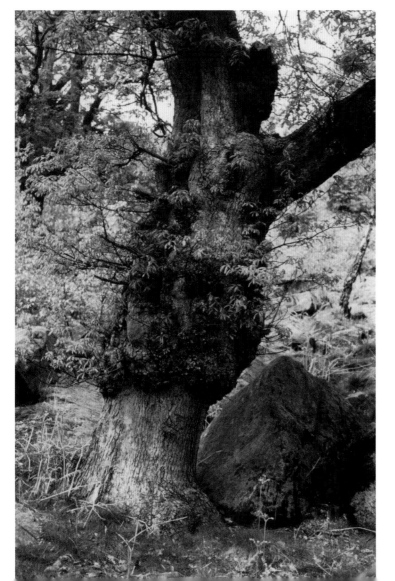

An enclosure bill for 'Loxley Chace' (partly in the manor of Loxley and partly in the manor of Wadsley) went through Parliament in 1784 and the final award was made in 1789. Most of the area was laid out as farmland, with the straight-sided rectangular fields bounded by dry-stone walls. Two absolutely straight enclosure roads, Myers Lane and Loxley Road, bound the northern and southern edges of the former Loxley Chase and another straight enclosure road, Long Lane, divides the former Loxley Chase from Loxley and Wadsley Commons. While the western half of the area to the west of Long Lane was used after enclosure as farmland, the eastern half of the area was the scene of quarrying until the 1920s for the Loxley Edge Sandstone, a much sought-after building stone; and of the mining, from drift pits, of coal and ganister (a fine-grained sandstone used to make refractory bricks for lining furnaces), which ceased about 1940.[40] These industrial activities inevitably scarred and reduced the quality of the lowland heath character of the site.

Most of Loxley Common had been in the ownership of the Payne family since 1800. In 1913, three surviving family sisters presented 75½ acres (30.5 ha) of the common to the City of Sheffield provided it retained its semi-rural character and was used as a public open space. In the 1970s it was designated a Site of Scientific Interest and it became a Local Nature Reserve in 1999, because of its status as lowland heath, an increasingly rare and threatened habitat. A ten-year management plan was drawn up in 1992 funded by the Countryside Commission's Countryside Stewardship scheme, followed by another of the same length ten years later. The major proposals centre around controlling the spread of birch and bracken, regenerating the

Figure 2.15. Oak pollard on Loxley Common

heather, and mowing meadowland. Not surprisingly the felling of trees has been greeted with consternation by many users of the common. A very active Friends group, the Wadsley and Loxley Commoners, was set up in 1993 and has more than 200 members.

What to read about deer parks, chases and wooded commons

HEY, D. (1975) The Parks at Tankersley and Wortley, *The Yorkshire Archaeological Journal*, **47**, 109–19.

HEY, D. (2002) *Historic Hallamshire*, Landmark Publishing, Chapter.6: Rivelin Chase and Hallam Moors and Chapter 9: The Dragon of Wantley.

JONES, M. (1995) *Rotherham's Woodland Heritage*, Rotherwood Press.

JONES, M. (2000) Sheffield's Medieval Park: a Re-examination of its Role, *Transactions of the Hunter Archaeological Society*, **24**, 4–15.

JONES, M. and JONES, J. (2005) *Historic Parks and Gardens in and around South Yorkshire*, Wharncliffe Publishing.

JONES, M. (2009) *Sheffield's Woodland Heritage*, 4th edition, Wildtrack Publishing.

LIDDIARD, R (2007) *The Medieval Park: New Perspectives*, Windgather Press.

MILESON, M.A. (2009) *Parks in Medieval England*, Oxford University Press.

MUIR, R. (2005) *Ancient Trees Living Landscapes*, Tempus.

RACKHAM, O. (1983) *Trees and Woodland in the British Landscape* (revised edition), Dent, chapters 7, 8 and 9.

RACKHAM, O. (1986) *The History of the Countryside*, Dent, Chapter 6.

Places to visit

It is still possible to walk most of the medieval boundaries of **Tankersley deer park.** Alternatively walk along Black Lane that takes you through the middle of the former park passing the ruins of the Tankersley Old Hall in the middle of the park. To the north of the railway bridge there is a footpath going off to the south that passes the sites of two of the old fish ponds.

You can also walk through **Wentworth Park** at Wentworth Woodhouse and see the herd of red deer grazing in a parkland landscape dotted with trees. At **Wentworth Castle** the park has recently been re-stocked with a herd of fallow deer and a herd of red deer. As at Wentworth Woodhouse they can be seen grazing in a park dotted with trees.

A visit to **Wortley Hall** is essential for anyone interested in ancient trees to see and (possibly) hug the ancient tree that once stood in Wortley deer park. It is 23 feet in circumference. It stands to the south of the hall in the gardens between the old pond and the ancient holly hedge avenue.

A walk through **Wharncliffe Chase** still manages to give the impression of an unfenced wilderness in which deer could roam freely in the past.

A visit to boulder-strewn **Loxley Common** will make it clear why it was not cleared of trees for use for agriculture. Visitors should also look out for the two old pollards that still survive there.

Extract from John Speed's map of 1610 of the West Riding of Yorkshire showing surviving medieval deer parks bounded by paling fences

COPPICE MANAGEMENT:
ITS RISE, DECLINE AND EXTINCTION

IN THE CENTURIES following the Domesday survey, although, as we have seen, the wood pasture tradition in South Yorkshire continued to be strong, in the form of wooded commons, chases and deer parks, coppice management gradually became dominant in order to conserve wood supplies which were in danger of becoming seriously depleted as the population grew and more woodland was permanently cleared for agriculture. Former deer parks and wooded commons became coppice woods.

THE RISE OF COPPICE MANAGEMENT

Throughout the region the form of coppice management called coppice-with-standards, which combined the production of underwood with that of single-stemmed timber trees, emerged as the most important form of woodland management, in economic terms, during the medieval period and continued to be so until at least the middle of the nineteenth century.[1] In this kind of woodland management in accordance with an overall plan, most of the trees were periodically (every fifteen to thirty years) cut down to the ground to what is called a stool (Figure 3.1(a)), and from the stool grew multiple stems, collectively called coppice or underwood (Figure 3.1(b)). Some of the trees were not coppiced but were allowed to grow on to become mature single-stemmed trees, and these were the standards (Figure 3.2). They would normally grow through a number of coppice cycles, as the coppice rotations were known, and therefore were of

various ages. Those that had grown through only one coppice cycle, i.e. less than thirty years old at most, were called wavers (usually written as weavers in South Yorkshire); those that had grown through two coppice cycles and were therefore between forty and sixty years old were called black barks; and those that had grown through three or more coppice cycles and were therefore at least sixty years old were called lordings.

The earliest-known surviving documentary record of coppice-with-standards management in South Yorkshire is a lease written in Latin at the relatively late date of 1421.[2] The lease refers to un-named woods on a farm at Norton (then part of Derbyshire) and contains a number of clauses concerning the right to cut underwood and timber, charcoal burning and keeping animals out of the woods for three or four years after cutting. The woods on the farm are referred to as le Spryng bosci, an interesting mixture of French, English and Latin, 'spring' being the usual name for a coppice-with-standards in South Yorkshire from the fifteenth to the nineteenth century. Timber in the document is called by the Latin word maerimium.

Two other late medieval records of coppice-with-standards have also survived, both in the same geographical area as the 1421 record. The first dated 1462, and written in English, refers to a number of woods in Norton parish including 'herdyng wood', the old name for the present Rollestone Wood.[3] The lease noted that the lessees, John Cotes and John Parker, had been granted permission by the lord of the manor, William

Chaworth, 'to fell downe cole (i.e., to make into charcoal) and carry the said Woddes', preserving for the owner 'sufficiaunt Wayvers after the custom of the contre'. Wavers, as already noted, were the young timber trees left to grow among the felled underwood, indicating that the woods concerned were coppices-with-standards. Wavers were also mentioned in the second document, which was written in 1496, also in English, and refers to two woods in the Sheaf valley in Sheffield, one of which was Hutcliff Wood, which still survives. The two woods were the property of Beauchief Abbey and the lease records that the 'abbot of Beacheff' had granted permission to the lessees 'to cooll (i.e., to make into charcoal) ii certen wodds', the woods to be left 'weyverd workmonlyke'. Significantly, the document also refers to a bloom hearth (a primitive furnace)

Figure 3.1. *(a) coppice stool (b) multiple stemmed coppice growth*

(a)

(b)

Figure 3.2. Coppice-with-standards

and a dam (the local name for a pond at a water-powered industrial site).[4] As we shall see, undoubtedly the increasing dominance of coppice management, at least in the western half of South Yorkshire, was closely related to the expansion of metal smelting and related trades such as nail-making and edge tool manufacture.

Nearly a century later, in 1574, William Dickenson, bailiff of Sheffield, recorded in his diary that he went to four spring woods in Totley called Fraunces Fields, the Carre, Husters and Long Spring, which were probably compartments of the present-day Gillfield Wood and marked 968 spyres or spyeres and '1 ashe'.[5] A 'spyre' was a spear or spire, terms which were generally used to refer to young oaks of about twenty years' growth which had been selected for growing on to become timber trees.

But coppice management was also a feature of the eastern part of the county by the sixteenth century at least. At the

dissolution of Roche Abbey in the Magnesian Limestone belt in 1546, a grant to Henry Tyrrell included 60 acres of coppice woods in four separate woods two of which (Norwood and Hell Wood) have survived to the present day. Two other woods belonging to the abbey, including a spring wood of 15 acres are also listed. There were also 800 oaks and ashes of sixty and eighty years' growth in the abbey's coppice woods and in other places in the abbey demesnes, 'parte tymbre and part usually cropped and shred'.[6] This reference to shredding – the cutting off of side branches to produce a crop of poles and leaf fodder for animals – is one of only two instances of this practice that I have found in documents relating to woodland management in South Yorkshire. Coppice woods on the Magnesian Limestone were also felled for charcoal making. In 1553 the 69 acre (28 ha) wood called Anston Stones, which still survives, was leased to two woodmen described respectively as a 'blacksmith' and a 'smetheman'. They were to 'wayve the said wood with all kind of oake', leave the wood 'wayved woodman lyke' and have 'sufficient turfe & hylling for the colyinge of the said wood'.[7]

From the outset owners and woodwards knew exactly what they were protecting in their coppice woods. The properties and uses of the various tree and shrub species, after thousands of years of use, were well known. The standards were mainly oak for building projects: for mansions and cottages, farm buildings and for early industrial sites such as water-powered forges. In the west, in the Southern Pennine Fringe zone and in the western half of the Coalfield zone, the native oak was the sessile oak (*Quercus petraea*) identified by its stalked leaf and unstalked acorns. Further east in the Magnesian Limestone zone pedunculate oak (*Quercus robur*) was also found, this time identified by its unstalked leaves and stalked acorns (Figure 3.3). The underwood that was coppiced on a regular

Figure 3.3. Sessile oak (Quercus petraea*), left and and pedunculate oak* (Quercus robur*), right*

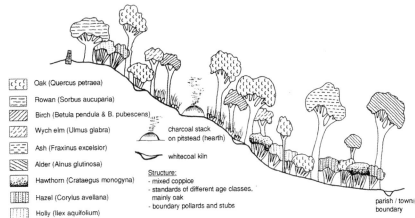

Figure 3.4. Cross-section through a typical Coalfield coppice-with-standards

basis was an intimate mixture of species: birch, hazel, holly, wych elm, ash, hawthorn, rowan, field maple, alder and willow, the last two in wet woodland (Figure 3.4). The Magnesian Limestone woodlands might contain additional species such as large-leaved lime, wild service, dogwood, spindle and native privet. All these trees and shrubs would have been coppiced for charcoal making, but some were also valued for their special properties, for example, willow for basket making, hazel for hurdle making, alder for clog soles and ash and rowan for tool handles. The rowan held a special place in the lives of people in early communities. The wood of the rowan is tough and besides tool handles it has been traditionally used for components of cart wheels and if the tree is large enough the timber was used for beams, planks and boards. If yew were not available it was used for making bows and, it was a favourite material for making walking sticks.

THE GOLDEN AGE OF COPPICE MANAGEMENT

By the early seventeenth century spring wood management appears to have been general. In an undated document written for the 7th Earl of Shrewsbury, the major landowner in south-west Yorkshire, who succeeded to the title in 1590 and died in 1616, forty-nine spring woods were listed. Significantly, they were listed as belonging to the Earl's forges and contained references to charcoal making such as 'Granowe Spring – 20 years ould redie to cole – 100 ac' and 'Thorncliff Spring one half about 9 years old tother halfe coalable – 30 ac' (Figure 3.5).[8] In 1637 John Harrison, in his survey of the manor of Sheffield listed thirty-six spring woods in which the underwood varied in age from four years to forty. Another aspect of coppice management becomes clear during the seventeenth century. This was the practice of subdividing large coppice woods into compartments and felling them at different times. In one

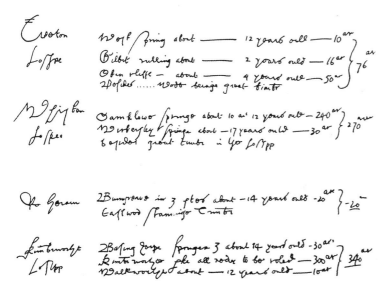

Figure 3.5. Extract from undated document, c. 1600 listing coppice woods on 7th Earl of Shrewsbury's estate. Source: Shr. P/LPL/Ms 698 folio 1 in Lambeth Palace Library.

of a pair of articles written in the 1950s on the vegetation of Sheffield in the seventeenth century, the authors, Scurfield and Medley, were puzzled by the fact that the wood growing in Greno Wood was described as being very young and of different ages, e.g., 'of 4, 5 and 6 yeares growth'.[9] The reason for this apparently youthful and uneven growth of the woodland in question was that, first of all it was described as a spring wood, i.e., a coppice-with-standards and the surveyor was referring to the age of the coppice poles and not the timber trees. And secondly, that it was so large that it was divided into different compartments which were treated as different woods,

often leased to different tenants, were felled at different times and had their own boundary fences. Ecclesall Woods, for example, were made up in the seventeenth century of more than twenty different woods varying in size from 8 acres (3.2 ha) to 45 acres (18.2 ha).[10] And a map drawn up in 1810 shows that the 243 acres (98.3 ha) of Canklow Wood had been divided since at least 1797 into eleven compartments, which had been coppiced between that year and 1807 (Figure 3.6).[11] The map also shows for most of the compartments the number of black barks and lordings (collectively called reserves) and wavers left standing in each coppiced compartment.

By the seventeenth century the iron industry in south-west Yorkshire had achieved a high degree of sophistication and was increasingly characterised by a large measure of vertical integration and horizontal combination.[12] By the 1650s, the most powerful ironmaster in the region was Lionel Copley[13] who entered into a succession of agreements with local landowners to fell and coal their spring woods. The surviving leases illustrate contemporary coppice practice. For example, in 1657 Copley entered into a ten-year agreement with the 2nd Earl of Strafford of Wentworth Woodhouse to fell the underwood and selected timber trees in thirteen of the Earl's woods. Under the contract Copley was to cut 1,000 cords of wood (in South Yorkshire, as already noted in Chapter 2 this was a pile of wood 4 feet wide, 8 feet long and 4 feet high) each year for charcoal making. He was allowed to cut 'young timber trees, Lordings, Black Barks, powles, coppices and Springwoode' together with 'the Bark thereof'. The lessee was also instructed to make sure that 'all the said Springwoode [is] well and sufficiently weavered' and that the coppice was 'workmanlike cutt downe ... and the stowens [stools] thereof neare to the roote so as best preserve for future growth and next springing thereof'. He was also

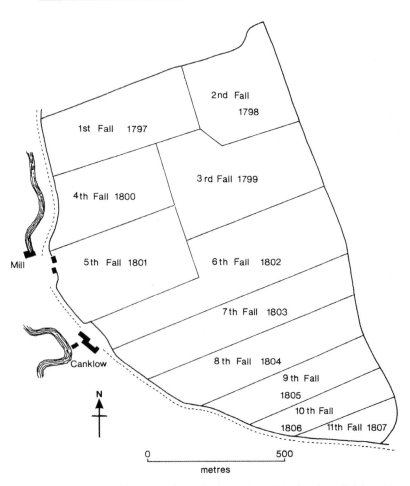

Figure 3.6. Canklow Wood, Rotherham, in 1810 showing division into compartments. Source: Arundel Castle Manuscripts, ACM She 169, in Sheffield Archives

asked to burn the 'Ramell' in places that would be 'least prejudiciall to the weavers and Springwood which shall be left to grow'[14]. 'Ramell' was the small brushwood.

To the east, coppice-with-standards management also continued to be important during the seventeenth and eighteenth centuries. On the Duke of Leeds' estate centred on Kiveton Park in the Magnesian Limestone belt, there were seventeen woods in the early 1700s, in Harthill, Thorpe Salvin and North and South Anston, five of them described in 1739 as 'timber woods', and another eight as spring woods including the surviving Anston Stones Wood, Hawks Wood, Lob Wells Wood and Old Spring Wood. Among the products made from the timber and wood cut in these woods during the period in question were hop poles, scaffold poles, cordwood, pit wood ('puncheons'), heft wood, hazel hoops, hedge bindings, and perhaps most interesting of all, 562 'straite oaken trees' which were taken by 'land and water to his majestys yard at Chatham' in 1701 and which yielded £473 in income.[15]

Various aspects of eighteenth century spring wood management in South Yorkshire are well illustrated in two schemes devised by Thomas Wentworth, Ist Marquis of Rockingham who inherited the Wentworth estates in 1723. In 1727 he devised what he called 'A Scheme for making a yearly considerable Profit of Spring Woods in Yorkshire' and in 1749 what he described as 'A Scheme for a Regular Fall of Wood for 21 years . . .' (Figure 3.7). In the 1749 scheme, a twenty-one-year rotation was used so that the woods coppiced in 1749 would be cut again in 1771, or as the Marquis put it '. . . & so begin the Circle again'. This meant that the Marquis' 876 acres (355 ha) of coppice-with-standards woodland in South Yorkshire would produce a regular crop of 40 acres of underwood a year. The Marquis stipulated that there were to be five black barks (mature

A Scheme for a Regular Fall of Wood for 21 Years to come from the Year 1749 of about 42 Acres a Year the Coppice Woods in Yorkshire amounting to about nine Hundred Acres, in which Calculation Scholes Wood, all timber Trees & Woods in the Park at Wentworth are not included, nor the Woods in Northamptonshire, particularly Withmail Park of 100 Acres nor a Wood of about 30 Acres at Yesthrop Park which was felled Anno 1726 – Reserves to be at least 5 Black Barks & 70 Wavers – Philip Wood 2 Acres 2 Roods being Holted is not included nor the Wood by the Pyramide.

		Acres
Tinsley Park at Nine Falls for the Years 1749, 1750, 1751, 1752 1753, 1754, 1755, 1756 & 1757		350
Anno 1758 Bassingthorp Spring		37
Anno 1759 Great Thorncliffe		37
Anno 1760 Harley Spring 18^A Luke Spring 8 – 2 Goss Wood 8 Acres Bank Spring 4 Acres	totall	38 – 2
Anno 1761 Giles Wood 24 Acres King's Wood 11 Normandale Springs 5 Bolderfall 2A 2R	totall	42 – 2
Anno 1762 Tindle Brig Spring 4A 2R Wadsworth Spring 1 – 2R Westfield Ing Spring 3 Acres Simon Wood 25 – 2 Birkfield Spring 7^A – 2^R Coney Garth Spring 2^A – 2^R	totall	43 – 2
1763 Law Wood – 40 Acres		40 – 0
1764 Street Wood – 13 Rowing Spring 4^A – 2^R Littlewood Ing Spg 5 Acres 2 Roods Thorncliff Bottoms 5^A Blackmoor Bottoms 1^A Longland Spring & Longley Bottoms 5^A Little Thorncliffe 3	totall	37 – 0
1765, 1766, 1767 upper Linthwait 5^A – 2^R Golden being three Years Fall Smithys 4 Rainbergh 115	totall	124 – 2
38 acres Per Annum		
Anno 1768, 1769 & 1770 Westwood exclusive of all Wasts being a Fall of 42 Acres Per Year. & so begin the Circle again		126 – 0
excluding all wast to fall		876

N.B. no Spinneys or Plantations in Wentworth Park & Demesnes are Included – There are also some little Reins & Spinneys up and down not taken notice of – also hedge Rows A Wood at Yesthorpe Park 30 Acres

1749

have now bought 400 Acres more called Edlington Wood 1750 bought Ld Gallway's Estate in Hoyland on which is 60 acres of wood so now the woodland is encreased near one half of that which may be brought into Regular Falls

Figure 3.7. The 1st Marquis of Rockingham's coppice wood management scheme, 1749. Source: Wentworth Woodhouse Muniments, WWM 1273, in Sheffield Archives

timber trees, forty to sixty years old) and seventy wavers (sapling timber trees) left in every acre of felled coppice.[16] The Marquis of Rockingham was fortunate that on his estate, besides hundreds of acres of coppice woods he also had deposits of ironstone, and he linked the charcoaling of the former with the mining of the latter. In 1749 he wrote that 'whereas it is the Iron Men that keep up the Price of the Wood, especiall care must be taken that the Iron Stone be never let for a longer time than the Woods are agreed for'.[17]

In the post-medieval period when a coppice wood or a compartment within a coppice wood was going to be felled and sold on the open market, the sale was preceded by a valuation of the wood which involved marking the timber trees that were to be left standing and marking and valuing the timber trees that were to be felled. The valuation of the compartment was called setting out and this involved marking (with paint and/or numbering with a scribe iron), valuing the timber trees to be felled and computing an overall value for the underwood. 'Top and lop' (branches of the timber trees) was often valued separately. If it were an oak wood the value of the oak bark would also be calculated. It was not unusual for the timber, the underwood together with the top and lop, and the bark to be sold separately.

The next stage was to advertise the sale and this was done in the nineteenth century through handbills (Figure 3.8). At the sale, normally held at a local inn, the woodward would write the valuation(s) on a ticket and put it folded on the table in front of him. Within a specified time all those bidding for the timber, underwood and other products included in the sale had to put their bids on separate tickets on the table. This was sometimes done three times, on each occasion the woodward announcing the highest bidder. The highest bidder became the purchaser

His Grace the Duke of Norfolk's
ANNUAL
Falls of Wood,
TO BE SOLD BY TICKET,

At the King's Head Inn, Sheffield, on Tuesday, January 24, 1815, betwixt the Hours of 2 and 4 o'Clock in the Afternoon, according to Conditions to be then and there produced:

LOT I.
GRENNO WOOD, 10th Fall.
85 Trees numbered
406 Oak Poles
104 Birch Poles
With the Bark, Shanks, Cordwood, and Underwood.

LOT II.
PRIOR WOOD, 1st Fall
571 Trees numbered
465 Oak Poles
309 Ash Poles
373 Owler and Birch Poles
With the Bark, Shanks, Cordwood, and Underwood.

LOT III.
LITTLE ROE WOOD.
238 Trees numbered
331 Oak Poles
14 Ash Poles
2 Owler Poles
With the Bark, Shanks, Cordwood, and Underwood.

LOT IV.
HEDGE ROWS in Edward Vickers's Farm.
130 Trees numbered, with the Bark and Tops.

THOMAS CROOKES, the Woodman, of *Pitsmoor*, will shew the Falls, and for further Particulars apply to Mr. *John Smelter*, at the King's Head Inn, *Sheffield*, on *Tuesdays* and *Saturdays*.

J. MONTGOMERY, PRINTER, SHEFFIELD.

Figure 3.8. Handbill announcing wood sale. Source: Arundel Castle Manuscripts, ACM S300, in Sheffield Archives

provided the bid equalled or exceeded the estate valuation. The successful ticket for a fall in Hall Wood in Ecclesfield parish in 1823 is shown in Figure 3.9.[18] The successful bidder, Joseph Tingle, was a steel-maker from Grenoside. The surviving contract for that fall drawn up and dated 14 January 1823, shows that the purchaser was given until the end of September 1824 to fell, saw and remove the timber, peel the bark and make charcoal. The contract specifically instructs the purchaser to cut down the trees in a 'workmanlike manner ... so as to encourage the future growth of the roots'. There were strict rules about making sawpits in the wood and gathering turf to cover charcoal stacks (called 'covering sods'). The brushwood (called 'ramel' in the contract) was 'reserved to the vendor'.[19]

Figure 3.9. Successful bid for a fall of wood in Hall Wood, 1823. Source: Arundel Castle Manuscripts, ACM S303, in Sheffield Archives

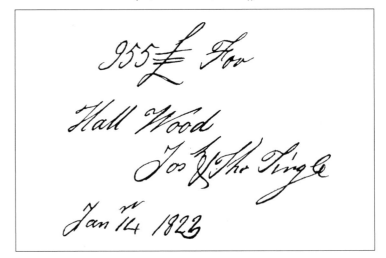

COPPICE WOOD SECURITY

Obviously the underwood and timber growing in coppice woods were valuable and had to be protected. This was done in a number of ways. Woods were looked after by woodwards who kept a vigilant lookout for trespassers and thieves. The proceedings of local manorial courts and woodwards' accounts are full of instances of waiting for and catching trespassers and thieves, of appearances in court, of fines and of payments to woodwards' helpers for tracking down wrongdoers and re-possessing stolen wood, bark and timber. For example, in 1564 William Dungworth was fined twelve pence for felling and carrying away wood from the Earl of Shrewsbury's Wincobank Wood[20] and at Oxspring in November 1645 Thomas Streete was fined twelve pence at the court of Godfrey Bosville for 'felling and carrying away a weaver from Storrs' and Thomas Ellis was fined five shillings for carrying away underwood and timber from the same wood. On the second day of that particular court hearing a general announcement was made that no person or persons should 'fell, cut or carry away timber and spring wood belonging to the lord of the manor without licence'.[21] In 1712 the Duke of Norfolk's woodward claimed a shilling for time spent in searching for stolen wood in Rotherham and Kimberworth. The next entry in the accounts reported that he was 'takeing Joseph Osborn's gun and searching for wood at Blackburn'.[22] In 1718, because of the 'great destruction' in the Duke of Norfolk's woods in Sheffield and Rotherham 'by being cut downe and Carried Away by Some Idle Disorderly persons', a warrant was issued by the justices of the peace to local constables who were, at the woodward's request 'All Excuses and Delays Sett apart' to 'make diligent search ... in the most suspitious houses ...' and to bring suspects before the magistrates.[23] That locating stolen wood and bringing thieves before the courts took up a good deal of the woodward's time can be judged by the fact that in 1719 William Ibbotson, the Duke of Norfolk's woodward, claimed three shillings for two days spent in searching in Ecclesfield parish 'for wood cut down in Roe wood'.[24] Nor were cases of theft necessarily only concerned with small quantities of wood and timber. In 1731 Mrs Letitia Pegge brought an action against Anthony Fox for carrying away twenty oaks and 104 cartloads of underwood from Park Bank Wood on the Beauchief estate.

Trespass, accomplished by making gaps in hedges or climbing the walls surrounding coppice woods was also a common offence. In 1441 Thomas de Housley was fined sixpence for trespassing in Greno Wood and breaking down the hedge.[25] On 20 May 1720 Joseph Shepherd and his wife were paid two shillings for 'watching to see who breaks ye Gapp open at ye upper end of Shertley Park'. The wood was Shirecliffe Park Wood. The woodward noted that on the same day 'M. Bamforth Pull'd it open'.[26] Six years later the woodward paid Richard Wainwright three shillings for waiting for, watching and catching Robert Rawson, a carrier, 'who was supposed to break ye old hedge' at the same wood. At certain times of the year, for example in September, October and November when foraging parties were out looking for winter firewood, game and autumn fruits, trespass must have been exceptionally common. The practice of collecting hazel nuts in local woods which had resulted in widespread damage prompted the Beauchief estate in 1809 and the Duke of Norfolk in 1812 to post notices to nutters warning of possible prosecution. The Beauchief poster refers to the damage suffered to the wood and the wood fences and the Duke of Norfolk's poster refers to the breaking down and destroying of the 'hazle wood' (Figure 3.10).

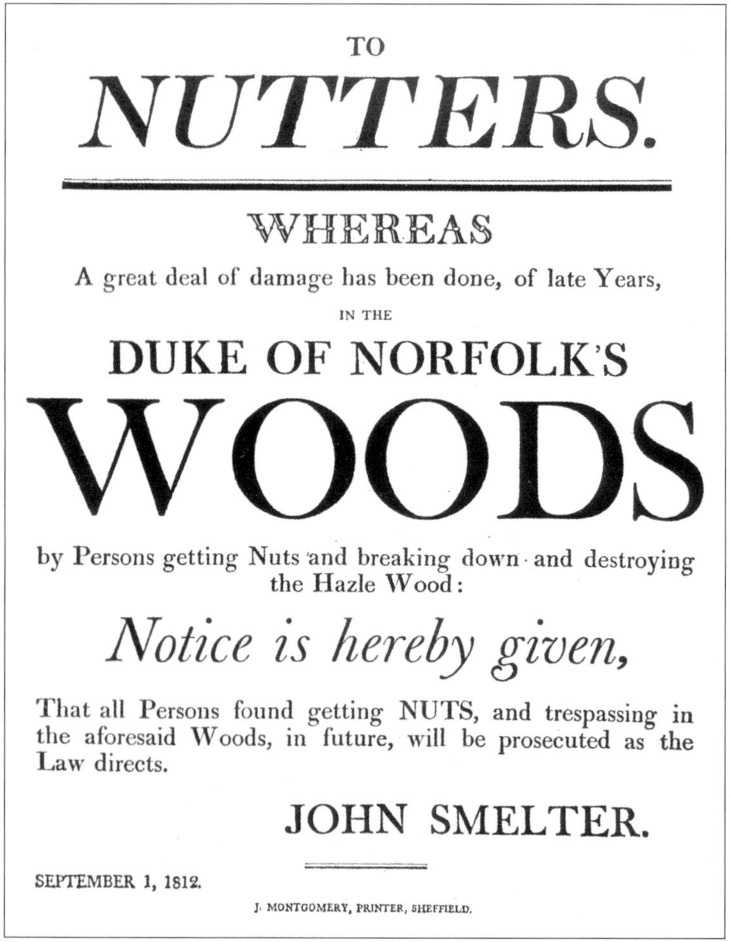

TO

NUTTERS.

WHEREAS

A great deal of damage has been done, of late Years,

IN THE

DUKE OF NORFOLK'S

WOODS

by Persons getting Nuts and breaking down and destroying
the Hazle Wood:

Notice is hereby given,

That all Persons found getting NUTS, and trespassing in
the aforesaid Woods, in future, will be prosecuted as the
Law directs.

JOHN SMELTER.

SEPTEMBER 1, 1812.

J. MONTGOMERY, PRINTER, SHEFFIELD.

Figure 3.10. 'Nutters' poster, 1812. Source: Arundel Castle Manuscripts, ACM S312 in Sheffield Archives

The problem of security was exacerbated by the fact that tenants' animals were allowed access to coppice woods for grazing on the woodland grasses and herbs once the coppice was well grown and beyond possible damage from browsing animals. There are records of horses and cattle being grazed in local coppice woods. The practice was known as agistment or herbage (Figure 3.11). Two records demonstrate the importance of only allowing grazing animals into coppice woods that were well grown. In 1710, for example, Joseph Ashmore, the Duke of Norfolk's woodward, charged himself two shillings for 'My Mare & fole in Woolley Woods this Spring a month' adding, just to make it absolutely clear that he was not contravening the normal custom, 'its old Cutt'.[27] Eight years later in 1718 the vicar of Ecclesfield, just after coppicing had taken place in

Figure 3.11. Typical scene of agistment in a well-grown coppice wood

Greno Wood, was paid twopence for giving notice to tenants at a Sunday service that they should 'take care that their cattle do no longer Continue to Graise in Greno Wood for Spoyling ye young sprouts'.[28]

Animals were likely to stray from pastures and commons into neighbouring coppice woods. When detected they were impounded and the owner fined. In 1718 Enoch Moor was fined one shilling when nine of his sheep were pounded out of Greno Wood[29] and in 1720 two men were paid three shillings and sixpence for their trouble in 'pounding 5 sheep belonging to Mr Watts that was trespassing in Little Hall Wood.[30] The village pinfold in which these animals would have been impounded still survives in Grenoside village.

The answer to preventing straying animals getting into coppice woods and to deter human trespassers and thieves was to build stout fences around the woods. These could be in the form of stone walls or banks with a wall or hedge on top and a ditch on the outside. The subject of identifying coppice wood boundaries is dealt with in Chapter 5.

THE ROLE OF THE WOODWARD

The surviving records of woodland management on a number of local estates provide us with a very detailed picture of the carefully implemented coppice management that took place between the late medieval period and the closing decades of the nineteenth century that guaranteed that the woods concerned became self-renewing and inexhaustible suppliers of wood and timber. And what has become clear in the surviving accounts is the vital role played by the woodland managers – the woodwards. They go by various names: woodward, head woodman, woodman, wood bailiff, wood steward and wood-reeve (Figure 3.12). There were woodwards who had

Figure 3.12. A nineteenth-century woodward

responsibility for all the woods on an estate and others just for a particular wood, especially if it was one of several hundred acres.

Such a woodward was David Glossop, woodward of Ecclesall Woods between 1756 and his death in 1793. He succeeded his father Abraham Glossop. He was in turn succeeded by his widow Sarah Glossop assisted by their son Benjamin Glossop. In the case of Ecclesall Woods the term 'woodward' was not used until the nineteenth century. David Glossop was simply described as 'looking after Ecclesall woods' or 'taking care of Ecclesall Woods' and on the monument of the wood collier, George Yardley (see Chapter 4) he is described as 'gamekeeper'. In 1793, the year in which he died, he was called 'bailiff'. He was paid an annual salary of £2.10.00 (£2.50).

Precise details of the duties he carried out have survived in the annual estate woodland accounts.[31] One of his major duties, which would have taken place on an annual basis in Ecclesall Woods, a compartmented coppice wood with coppice cycles coming to an end at different times in different parts of the woods, was marking the trees (the standards) that were **not** to be felled. These would have been the wavers, black barks and lordings, as noted above, known collectively as the 'reserves'. The accounts record David Glossop marking the reserves every year from 1761 to 1780. For example, in 1763 he was paid £3.7.2 for 'marking the reserves in Bright Spring, Snaithing Wood and the remainder of Upper Dale wood'. The trees were marked with a red paint called raddle (sometimes written as reddle or ruddle). In 1761, 1762 and 1763 the accounts show that he was paid for 'oil paint' or 'oil and paint' for accomplishing that particular task. In 1767 it is recorded that he supervised the peeling of bark from the oak trees in Andrew Wood and in other parts of Ecclesall Woods in 1777 and 1780. This would

have been on behalf of the buyer of the bark on trees that were being felled who would have been a leather tanner (see Chapter 4).

Another of his regular duties was to organise the re-building of the protective fences around the perimeter of the woods and between individual woods where they had fallen into disrepair, been deliberately broken by trespassers and thieves or where they had been removed temporarily during felling operations. This was an enormous task in a woodland covering nearly 300 acres (121 ha) and which was divided into more than twenty named woods. He is first mentioned 'fencing in Ecclesall Woods' in 1757 and was still engaged in repairing walls in 1792. It is also clear that he was not only involved in repairing walls but also in quarrying the stone and transporting it by horse and cart to the repair sites. In 1791, for example, it is recorded that in order to repair the wall around a wood that had been felled the previous year, he was paid for a 'hammer and a gavelock (a crowbar) for getting stone' and for the carriage of the stone. He was assisted by a specialist waller.

For most of the nineteenth century the woodwards for Ecclesall Woods were a father and son. James Smith was woodward from 1817 until 1836 when he was succeeded by his son Samuel Smith who held the position until 1881. The father, therefore, held the position for nineteen years and the son for forty-five years, a total between them of sixty-four years in service as woodwards. And they saw the woods change from coppice-with-standards supplying underwood and timber to a canopy wood providing timber only. Not only was Samuel Smith employed as woodward for forty-five years but by the time he died in 1881 he was eighty years old. James Smith's salary was £5 per year but in 1866 Samuel Smith's salary was increased to

£12 per year. Like David Glossop, James Smith, the father was described in the annual accounts as 'taking care of woods in Ecclesall' and this description of the woodward's role continued during the period when his son Samuel held the position. But interestingly, Samuel Smith's occupation in the 1851 census and in a directory entry in 1857 was described by the formal title of 'wood steward'.

Their roles as woodwards were basically no different from that of David Glossop, although during their tenure the accounts are silent about whether they had had the job of marking trees to be felled with oil-based paint. They were involved on a regular basis in the repair of the walls and hedges that surrounded the woods and supervised bark peeling from time to time. Between 1839 and 1843 Samuel Smith was also paid for catching moles, although in most years a specialist mole catcher was employed. They were also employed in cleaning out drainage ditches in the woods. Between 1840 and 1851 there was an outbreak of trespassing. In 1840 Samuel Smith was paid £1.5.6 in expenses for apprehending and committing George Gill for trespassing in Ecclesall Woods and other trespassers were prosecuted in 1841, 1844, 1849, 1850 and 1851.

DECLINE AND EXTINCTION OF COPPICING

From the late medieval period until the second half of the nineteenth century most woods were spring woods, i.e., coppices-with-standards, but not all woods. Some were treated simply as timber woods and were called 'holts'. For example, three of the thirteen woodland compartments in the former deer park at Tinsley in 1657 were called New Holt, High Holt and Old Holt. [32] A few woods also became ornamental woods in the new landscaped parks that sprang up in the eighteenth

century. This was what happened to Scholes Coppice in Kimberworth township. This had been a coppice wood in the former Kimberworth Park. It was bought by Thomas Watson-Wentworth of Wentworth Woodhouse in 1714 and coppiced for the last time in 1726. It was then 'cut into walks for beauty' and made part of Wentworth Park (Figure 3.13).[33]

By 1780 lead ore hearths had been replaced by coal-fired cupola furnaces and by the end of the eighteenth century iron furnaces were converted to or were rebuilt to use coke and new ironworks were, from the first, coke fired. The market for whitecoal (see Chapter 4), therefore, disappeared and that for charcoal was reduced, although it was still in demand locally for the production of blister steel in cementation furnaces. Nationally, coppicing did not decline in the immediate aftermath of the loss of the market for charcoal for iron smelting, and one author has suggested that the first half of the nineteenth century may be regarded as 'the golden age of traditional English woodmanship'.[34] This was not the case in South Yorkshire; its golden age was in the seventeenth and eighteenth centuries when production of charcoal and whitecoal were at their height. But coppicing continued to be very important during the first half of the nineteenth century and then gradually disappeared.

In the second half of the nineteenth century the surviving coppice-using industries could not sustain coppice-with-standards management in the region. As a result more and more coppice woods were gradually converted into high forests. In essence they were becoming plantations and forestry was replacing woodmanship. The changes in Ecclesall Woods, which had been acquired through marriage by the 2nd Marquis of Rockingham in 1750, mirror changes that were taking place, or would take place in the next half century, in other coppice

Figure 3.13. Scholes Coppice, shown 'cut into walks for beauty' at the southern edge of the park at Wentworth Woodhouse. Source: P. P. Burdett's Map of Derbyshire, 1791 edition

woods throughout the region.[35] In Ecclesall Woods sales from 1775 until 1847 were entered under some variation of the title of a 'fall of wood' or 'falls of wood' or 'fall of coppis'. But planting was also under way. In 1824 £68.7.6 was paid to a Mr Proctor for 27,500 larches and ashes for 'filling up the falls in Ecclesall Woods and Tinsley Park' and in 1826 a Mr Oldham was paid £99 for planting 'forest trees' in Ecclesall Woods, Tinsley Park and Edlington Wood, near Doncaster which the 1st Marquis of Rockingham had purchased in 1749. There was then a prolonged period of planting between 1830 and 1845 and planting took place either in Ecclesall Woods specifically or in woods in general on the estate of which Ecclesall Woods were part from the early 1860s until the end of the nineteenth century. A timber sale was recorded for the first time in 1848, again in 1851, and then continuously almost every year until the end of the century. No more sales of falls of wood are recorded after 1847.

Those purchasing wood and timber from Ecclesall Woods also changed dramatically between the 1750s and 1900: between 1750 and 1850 the main customers were ironmasters wanting coppice and branchwood for charcoal making or colliery owners purchasing pit wood; but from the 1850s industrial customers were replaced by timber merchants, William Toplis, a Chesterfield timber merchant, being the sole buyer at the Ecclesall Woods annual timber sales on twenty-seven out of the thirty annual sales that took place between 1869 and 1900–01.

Similar changes were also taking place in the many woods on the Duke of Norfolk's Sheffield and Rotherham woods. In 1898 the Duke's forester (a term that had supplanted the earlier 'woodward'), began to plant heavily in the declining coppice woods. In Hesley Wood and Smithy Wood he planned to plant

100 acres (40 ha) with ash, elm, sycamore, birch, lime, sweet chestnut and beech eight feet apart and 'filled up' at four feet intervals with larch. Another 120 acres (49 ha) were to be planted in the same way in Greno Wood, 75 acres (30 ha) in Canklow Wood, 60 acres (24 ha) in Beeley Wood, 40 acres (16 ha) in Bowden Housteads Wood, 35 acres (14 ha) in High-field Spring, 25 acres (10 ha) in Burnt Wood and Hall Wood and 20 acres (8 ha) in Woolley Wood, eight acres (3 ha) in Buck Wood and six acres (2.4 ha) in Treeton Wood. He calculated that he would need 109,000 seedlings for Greno Wood alone. He also planned to plant 60 acres (24 ha) in Scraith Wood and Old Park Wood, but noted that as they were both 'situated Nr Sheffield and therefore affected by smoke etc Larch & conifers would not grow well', he suggested broadleaves only planted six feet apart. On 16 November 1898 he placed his first order with Dicksons, 'Seed Merchants and Nurserymen' of Chester, for 20,000 larch, 10,000 sycamore, 5,000 beech, 2,000 birch and 2,000 sweet chestnut to be delivered at Wadsley Bridge Station.[36]

But it was not only planting and natural regeneration that re-structured the region's coppice woods from coppices-with-standards into high forest. A third way was by 'storing' the coppice. This means growing a multiple-stemmed tree past the normal coppice length. On each coppice stool only one or two, or exceptionally three, well-formed vigorous stems would be left to produce timber-sized material. Evidence of this process can still be seen in local woods in the form of large double or multi-stemmed trees, usually oak (Figure 3.14).

By the end of the nineteenth century coppicing, and its related trades and industries had all but disappeared.

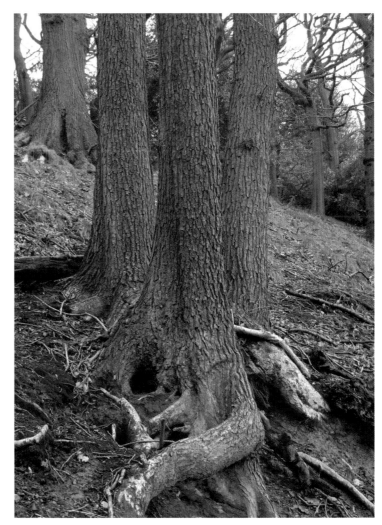

Figure 3.14. Stored coppice

What to read about coppice management

JONES, M. (1995) *Rotherham's Woodland Heritage*, Rotherwood Press.

JONES, M. (1997) Woodland Management on the Duke of Norfolk's Sheffield Estate in the Early Eighteenth Century in M. Jones (ed) *Aspects of Sheffield: Discovering Local History, Volume 1*, Wharncliffe Publishing Ltd, pp. 48–69

JONES, M. (1998) The Coal Measure Woodlands of South Yorkshire: Past, Present and Future in M.A. Atherden and R.A. Butlin (eds) *Woodland in the Landscape: Past and Future Perspectives*, PLACE Research Centre, pp. 79–102.

JONES, M. (1998) The rise, decline and extinction of spring wood management in south-west Yorkshire, in C. Watkins (ed) *European Woods and Forests: Studies in Cultural History*, CAB International, pp. 55–72.

JONES, M. (2009) *Sheffield's Woodland Heritage*, 4th edition, Wildtrack Publishing.

RACKHAM, O. (1983) *Trees and Woodland in the British Landscape* (revised edition), Dent, Chapter 4.

RACKHAM, O. (2006) *Woodlands*, Collins (New Naturalist Library), Volume 100, Chapter 3, 'Outline of Woodland History'.

Places to visit

Anston Stones, Rotherham (SK535830). A large wood in the Magnesian Limestone zone. Known to have been a coppice wood in Elizabethan times. Contains rare trees and rich ground flora.

Bagger Wood, Barnsley (SK304025). An ancient wood (first known record, fourteenth century) on a steep slope on an old township (Stainborough) boundary. Planted with trees not native to the site but a lovely bluebell wood. Now owned by the Woodland Trust.

Greno Wood/Wheata Wood/Prior Royd, Sheffield (SK330950). Extensive area of former coppice woods adjacent to a village that had a basket maker and a clog sole maker in the nineteenth century. Interesting woodland boundaries (walls, banks and ditches). Greno Wood is heavily coniferised. A leaflet on Wheata Wood and Prior Royd is available from Sheffield City Council's Parks and Countryside Unit.

Woolley Wood, Sheffield (SK385925). A former coppice wood on a steep slope on a parish boundary (between Ecclesfield and Rotherham). South Yorkshire's most beautiful bluebell wood that also contains woodland trees – yew, wild cherry and hornbeam – not found in other South Yorkshire Coalfield woods in such profusion. A leaflet on Woolley Wood is available from Sheffield City Council's Parks and Countryside Unit.

WOODLAND CRAFTS AND INDUSTRIES

THE WORK OF THE HOUSEWRIGHT

It was not until the seventeenth century that stone and brick supplanted timber as the main building material, timber holding prime place since the first permanent settlements were built in Neolithic times. As late as 1540, John Leyland, the antiquary, on his six-year tour of England, described the town of Doncaster as 'buildid of woode'. Even castles, like the ones at Sheffield, Conisbrough and Tickhill, and parish churches, were constructed of timber before they were rebuilt in stone. It is in the surviving timber-framed houses and barns that trees from the region's medieval woods can be seen. And it is trees that we see in timber-framed buildings, for the builder, called a house carpenter or housewright, did not obtain his timber in the form of ready-sawn or shaped planks and beams – he selected trees in woods and hedges that would roughly square up to the dimensions of the components required with the minimum of shaping, large trees for the beams and smaller trees for things like rafters. The timber used was mostly oak (although elm and sweet chestnut were also sometimes used) and it was sawn or shaped with an axe or adze while it was still 'green' for ease of working. It should also be noted that nails were not used to hold the timbers in place because the tannic acid in the unseasoned oak would corrode them. Instead, oak pegs sometimes called treenails were used, and were made in their thousands.

There are two traditions of timber-framed building that are likely to be met with in England: post-and-truss (or box frame) and cruck building. A **post-and-truss building** (Figure 4.1) consisted of a series of trusses or cross-frames formed by pairs

of vertical posts (principal posts) standing on large stones (stylobates) connected by tie beams. Longitudinally, the tops of the principal posts were connected by horizontal timbers called wall plates (at the top of the posts), girding beams (at mid-wall

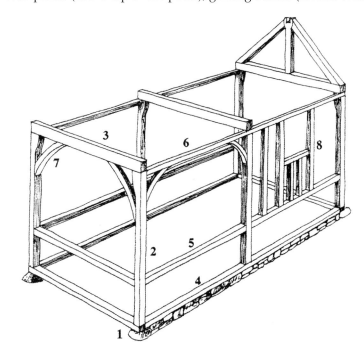

Figure 4.1. *Diagram of post and truss building: 1. stylobate or padstone; 2. principal post; 3. tie beam; 4. Sill beam; 5. Girding beam; 6. Wall plate; 7. Brace; 8. Stud*

level) and sill beams (at or near floor level). For extra stability, curved timber braces were added. The walls, where not of stone or brick, were formed by vertical timbers called studs with the spaces between filled with wattle and daub, stone slates or split oak laths, all covered with plaster, or with herringbone patterns of brick. The roofs of post-and-truss buildings were either of the common rafter or principal rafter type. There were many variations of principal rafter roofs. In the king post type, which was common in the north of England, a single vertical post rose from the tie beam; in East Anglia and the south-east the crown-post type, which had a vertical post rising from the tie beam to a collar purlin, was widely distributed. Only one crown post roof is known in South Yorkshire, in a house on Castlegate in Tickhill.

Most post-and-truss buildings have long since disappeared but there are a few outstanding examples still standing. Perhaps the earliest of these is Whiston manorial barn near Rotherham where a dendrochronological (tree-ring) analysis suggests that the original medieval timbers used in the building were felled between 1233 and 1252.[1] The barn has a simple principal rafter roof with two struts connecting the tie beam with the principal rafters. It is an aisled post-and-truss building in which extra building width was achieved by erecting the long walls beyond the principal posts to which they were connected by extensions to the roof trusses (aisle ties). The original building consisted of five bays (a bay is the space between two trusses) but in the sixteenth century the building was extended by two more bays and the original timber walls were replaced by stone. Figure 4.2 shows the interior of the barn looking west. On the left is a principal post with two braces to the wall plate and one to the tie beam. In the centre of the drawing is another principal

Figure 4.2. *Interior of Whiston manorial barn*

post with an aisle tie and a passing brace (a support between the aisle tie and the principal post).

A much later and much more sophisticated timber-framed structure is Bishops' House in Meersbrook, Sheffield, which is now a museum. This is an L-shaped yeoman's house built between 1500 and 1550. The original timber-framed house had two wings, the east wing containing the hall and the kitchen open to the roof and the west wing with a parlour and buttery on the ground floor and two chambers above on the first floor. It has a king post roof. The timber framing on the ground floor has largely been replaced by stone and a northern extension to the west wing was built in stone in the mid-seventeenth century.

A variety of patterns of timber-work was employed on the outside of the walls (Figure 4.3). Herringbone patterns were

Figure 4.3. *Exterior of Bishops' House*

used on both wings but that on the east wing points downwards and that on the west wing upwards. What is very noticeable is that timbers on the outside of the building (the studs) are closely spaced, with the spaces not much wider than the studs themselves. This close studding is a typical characteristic of timber-framed buildings in the north of England. The spaces between the studs at Bishops' House were filled with split oak laths and then covered with plaster. Inside the house there are several interesting features including carpenters' marks, adze marks on the shaped timber beside the stairhead and the thick oak planks to make the floor boards in the east wing of seventeenth century date.

Kirkstead Abbey Grange in Thorpe Hesley, Rotherham, is a stone building but with a very sophisticated timber roof structure. The first record of a house about to be built on the site was in 1161 when the monks of Kirkstead Abbey in Lincolnshire were leased land there to mine ironstone, smelt and forge iron and to build their headquarters.[2] The present building appears to be of late medieval date but incorporates stone and timber features from an earlier building, possibly the original one built by the monks in the twelfth century. Figure 4.4 shows the roof structure at the southern end of the building. It is a king post roof with the king posts (A in Figure 4.4) rising from massive tie beams (B) which rest on very thick (in places 36 inches (nearly 1 metre)) walls. The tie beam shown in Figure 4.4 is 14 inches by 9 inches (35 cm × 22 cm). Rising from the end of each of the tie beams are principal rafters (C) which are fitted into the tops of the king posts with mortise and tenon joints. Running from king post to king post and supported by braces (D) are ridge pieces (E). Halfway down the principal rafters are purlins (F). This superstructure supports a large number of common rafters, not shown in the diagram, running from the ridge to the top of the wall which in turn support the roof covering, in this case sandstone slates. In its original state the roof consisted of 212 timber components, all oak, including the shaped trunks of 183 individual trees. Treenails, long wooden pegs, are used throughout the roof structure to secure joints (Figure 4.5). A final noteworthy feature of the roof truss is the marking done by the carpenter in Roman numerals. Timber-framed buildings were often constructed in the house carpenter's yard, sometimes called a framing yard. For this reason, when originally assembled, each piece of timber had to be marked to ensure that every part was in its correct place when finally re-erected on the house or barn site.

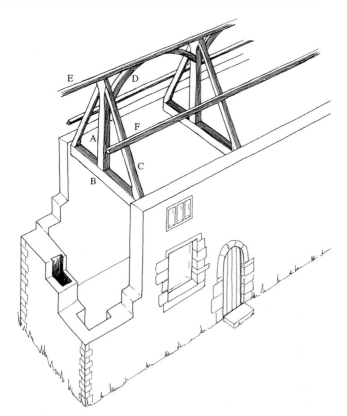

Figure 4.4. Diagram of roof structure at Kirkstead Abbey Grange: A. King post; B. Tie beam; C. Principal rafter; D. Brace; E. Ridge piece; F. Purlin

Cruck buildings were common in the upland areas of Britain and parts of the Midlands but are virtually unknown in eastern and south-eastern England. In South Yorkshire there are only three records of cruck buildings in the zone to the east of

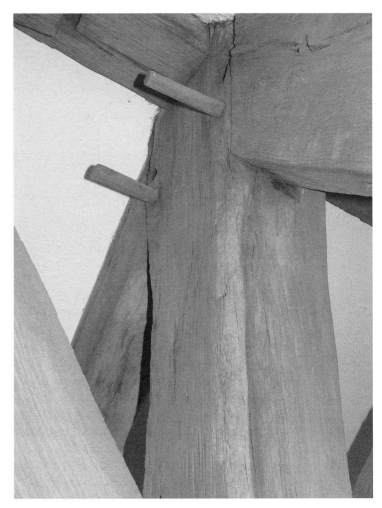

Figure 4.5. Tree nails in the roof structure at Kirkstead Abbey Grange

Rotherham, but to the west of the town there are records of nearly 150 cruck buildings either still standing or known to have been demolished since 1900.[3] In a cruck building the weight was carried on pairs of timbers called cruck blades which rise from or near the ground and meet at the apex of the roof (Figure 4.6). The blades are usually curved, having been selected from naturally bent trees. Often a bent tree was split or sawn lengthways to make two matching blades. The structure was strengthened by tie beams connecting each pair of cruck

Figure 4.6. Diagram of cruck building: 1. Cruck blade; 2. Stylobate or padstone; 3. Tie beam; 4. Wall plate; 5. Spur; 6. Sill beam; 7. Purlin; 8. Wind brace; 9. Stud; 10. Oak boarding

blades. The roof of the building was stabilised by struts called windbraces. As in post and truss buildings, the walls consisted of vertical studs rising from the sill beam to the wall plates with the gaps filled with a variety of materials as already noted or covered with horizontal oak boarding. One of the best surviving cruck buildings in South Yorkshire is Oaks Fold barn which stands near the entrance to Concord Park in Sheffield. It was described in John Harrison's survey of the manor of Sheffield in 1637 as 'a barne of 5 bayes'. The barn has long been encased in stone and when that was done the wall plates became redundant and were removed. Most of the windbraces have also disappeared. However, the cruck blades are on full view (Figure 4.7).

Figure 4.7. Interior of Oaks Fold barn

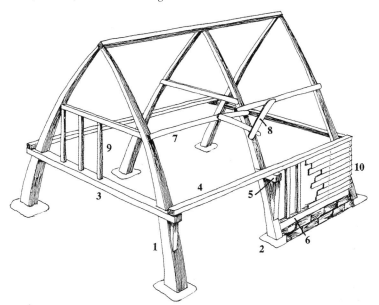

MEDIEVAL WOOD CARVERS

Another building with closely spaced studding is the Old Queen's Head public house in Pond Street in Sheffield. This is thought to have originally been a banqueting house in Sheffield deer park. A dendrochronological analysis of timbers shows that they were felled between 1506 and 1510. Interesting features on the outside of the building are the two carvings of heads (Figure 4.8). Other carvings, mostly in oak, will be found in the medieval churches throughout the region. Outstanding examples are the carvings on bench ends in the chancel at St Mary's, Ecclesfield and at Rotherham Minster, one of Mary holding the baby Jesus that may be the work of the same craftsman. Another remarkable carved wooden monument is to be seen at St Mary's

Figure 4.8. Carvings on the exterior of Old Queen's Head public house, Sheffield

Worsbrough. This is a double-decker effigy of Roger Rockley who died in 1534. On the top bunk the knight lies fully clothed but beneath is the cadaver with his skull and every bone in his body fully revealed (Figure 4.9). Another gem is the early

Figure 4.9. Double-decker monument at St Mary's church, Worsbrough

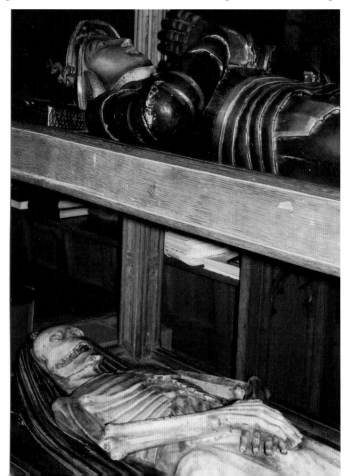

fourteenth-century knight in oak in St Peter's at Barnburgh. He lies cross-legged in his alcove with his heart in his hands.

BOAT BUILDERS

Within easy transport of the coasts, the woodlands provided the timber for shipbuilding and so the production of tie beams, principal posts and king and crown posts was joined in these locations by the manufacture of an array of ship timbers including keels, keelsons, bowsprits, gunwales and futtocks. The tree nails were sometimes known as 'shipp pins' when sold to shipbuilders. As already noted in the previous chapter, the only known record of South Yorkshire timber being used to build ships was in 1701 when oak timber from the Duke of Leeds' woods in North and South Anston, Thorpe Salvin and Harthill was transported to the royal shipyard at Chatham.

But if local timber was rarely used to make battleships it was used to construct smaller vessels that plied the canals, the lower reaches of the River Don and the Humber (Figure 4.10). These were keels, thought by many writers to be descendants of the Viking longships. They were of between 90–100 tons measuring in the case of the 'Sheffield size' 60 feet 3 inches long and 15 feet 3 inches wide. They had broad perpendicular bows and a large square sail. They were important in moving South Yorkshire coal and steel goods from Sheffield to the east coast. On the lower Don there were boatyards at Thorne, on the Don navigation at Sheffield and Masbrough, along the Worsbrough branch of the Dearne and Dove Canal at Worsbrough Dale and on the Dearne and Dove Canal at Old Mill, at Barugh and at was called Cawthorne Basin at Barnby.[4] There are a number of records of local boat builders buying timber from the Duke of Norfolk's woods in Sheffield and Rotherham. For example, in 1840 Joseph Scholey, boat builder of Worsbrough bought

Figure 4.10. Canal boats on the canal at Worsbrough Dale loading coal from Edmund Main Colliery. Source: The Illustrated London News, *July 16, 1859*

timber valued at £150 and James Thompson, also a boat builder of Worsbrough, bought timber valued at £245. In 1848 John Callis, boat builder of Masbrough bought timber valued at £82 and in the same year Joseph Scholey paid £250 for the fall of timber in Hesley Park.[5] John Callis was the manager of G.W. Chambers' boatyard at Masbrough where there had been a terrible accident in 1841. This was at the launch of a Billy Boy (a sea-going ketch), the *John and William*, when it was the tradition that children would be invited on board to enjoy the splash as the newly launched boat hit the water. On this occasion the boat capsized with the loss of fifty lives.[6]

CHARCOAL AND WHITECOAL MAKING

The preparation of charcoal for use as the fuel for iron smelting is the oldest recorded woodland industry in many parts of the country, not surprising as it would have been taking place since prehistoric times. Although the market for charcoal as the fuel for iron smelting gradually disappeared during the eighteenth century with the introduction and spread of the use of coke, some markets remained and others expanded. Most importantly, charcoal was used in making blister steel in so-called cementation furnaces where successive layers of bar iron inter-bedded with layers of charcoal were heated up to high temperatures for up to eight days. Over 250 such furnaces with their characteristic conical chimneys were built in the Sheffield area alone. Another industry based on charcoal was gunpowder manufacture that used charcoal from alder, willow and alder buckthorn trees. Charcoal was also used in large quantities as blacking by moulders in iron foundries.

During the 'coaling' season, that usually lasted from April to November, charcoal burners or 'wood colliers' as they were earlier known, lived a solitary life, often with their families about them, deep in the woodlands. Their work consisted of burning stacked lengths of coppice poles in the absence of enough air for complete combustion. The moisture was driven off during the early part of the process followed by volatile elements such as tar and creosote. The process left behind a residue of black carbon in solid form with a little ash.

Using the traditional method, a level spot, with many subtle variations in layout, was chosen and the turf removed, or, on a steep site, was dug out from the hillside. This was about 15 feet (*c.* 5 m) in diameter and was called the **pitstead**, **pit** or **hearth** (for more information about identifying charcoal hearths see Chapter 5). There are different traditions of building the stack.

One way, which may be a southern tradition, was to lay three short billets on the ground in the form of a triangle and then to build this up to form a central flue. A northern method was to drive in a long central stake which was removed when the stack was ready. Whichever method of flue construction was used, the remainder of the stack was constructed by stacking cordwood (four foot lengths of coppice poles and branch wood) facing inwards to form a stack looking like an upturned pudding basin, 15 feet in diameter and 5 feet high. The wood was then covered by straw, grass, bracken and turves, which were in their turn covered by dust and ashes. In this way virtually all air was excluded (Figure 4.11).

Red-hot charcoal and a few dry sticks were then dropped down the central flue. Once assured that the stack was alight, the wood collier sealed the flue and the fire spread throughout the stack. It was important that the stack burned steadily and that the fire did not burn through. For this reason the

Figure 4.11. Stages in the making of a charcoal stack

charcoal burner had to be in constant attendance, protecting his charge from sudden wind changes with hurdle fencing and sacking and closing any gaps in the stack with bracken, turf and soil. Burns lasted from two to ten days depending on size, weather conditions and the greenness of the wood. At first the stack emitted clouds of white smoke, that gradually turned to a blue haze and then died away altogether. When the burn was over, the stack was uncovered with a rake, allowed to cool and then packed in sacks or panniers.

The same charcoal hearths and the charcoal makers' hut sites were returned to repeatedly at the end of a coppice cycle. The huts were conical in shape built on a framework of poles like a wigwam sometimes around a low perimeter stone wall. The framework of poles was covered by sacking or skins and these were then covered with turves in the manner of tiles (Figure 4.12). Living in a hut made from wood, turf and tarpaulin was not without its life-threatening dangers. In Ecclesall Woods in south-west Sheffield there is a unique monument to a charcoal maker which demonstrates the dangers of his often solitary life in the woods. It consists of a monumental stone inside a small cast iron railing fence (Figure 4.13). The monument states that '**George Yardley, Woodcollier, he was Burnt to death in his Cabbin on this place Oct 11th 1786**' . Wood collier, as has already been pointed out, was the old name for a charcoal maker. There is then a list of the people who paid for the monument to be erected: William Brooke, salesman; David Glossop, gamekeeper; Thomas Smith, besom-maker; and Sampson Brookshaw, innkeeper. David Glossop was in fact the woodward of Ecclesall Woods and Sampson Brookshaw was the landlord between 1780 and 1806 of the Rising Sun public house on Abbey Lane just outside the woods. Searches have been made of the baptism and marriage registers for St Peter's parish church (now Sheffield Cathedral), the only church within Sheffield and Ecclesall where baptisms and marriages were recorded at this time. George Yeardley (the spellings Yeardley and Yardley were interchangeable in this period), wood collier, is recorded marrying Ann Turner, spinster, on 13 March 1755. This is almost certainly George Yardley, wood collier, who died in Ecclesall Woods on 11 October 1786. A search was then made for a George Yardley born in the parish between twenty-thirty years earlier, and the baptism of George, son of Samuel Yardley, filemaker, was found on 9 August 1734. If this is the George Yardley who died in Ecclesall Woods in 1786, he was twenty years and five months old when he married and fifty-two years old when he died.

It is possible to speculate about the circumstances of George Yardley's death. The fact that George Yardley was 'burnt to death in his cabbin' suggests that the fire that consumed him happened at night. A number of possible scenarios come to mind. The first is that it was a very windy night and that before retiring to the hut for the night he had cooked a meal and made a drink over the fire that was usually made within a few yards of the hut. He then went to sleep and while he slept either the gusty wind blew red hot embers from the cooking fire that had not been properly extinguished or that red hot embers had been blown on the gusty wind from a nearby burning charcoal stack. He may not have been aware of the advancing and consuming fire if he had been drinking heavily at the Rising Sun! The fact that Sampson Brookshaw, landlord of the Rising Sun, was one of those named on the monument suggests strongly that George Yardley was a regular customer at the public house. Alternatively it may not have been a windy night at all. But perhaps George Yardley had been drinking at the Rising Sun,

Figure 4.12. Charcoal maker's hut

Figure 4.13. Charcoal maker's monument in Ecclesall Woods

came back to his hut, lit a pipe and then fell asleep and dropped his burning pipe which started a fire in the hut.

There is one other tantalising fact about George Yardley's death. A thorough search has been made of the burial records of the churches in all the surrounding area (St Peter's, Sheffield; St Paul's, Sheffield, Beauchief; Norton; Rotherham and Ecclesfield). No burial for a George Yardley in October 1786 has been found. Does this mean that the fire was so fierce and that it burned for so long before it was discovered and extinguished that virtually nothing of George Yardley remained and that no burial took place in consecrated ground? Is the monument to George Yardley, wood collier, in Ecclesall Woods, also his last resting place? Significantly, the monument is very precise about where he died: in his cabbin on this place.

Between the last quarter of the sixteenth century and the middle of the eighteenth century in the woods along the south-western boundaries of South Yorkshire (and in neighbouring North Derbyshire) was another woodland industry making a fuel for smelting ore and sustaining the management of the region's woods as spring woods. The ore was lead and the fuel was **whitecoal**.[7] Local landowners are known to have been very active in the lead trade and they obtained their ore from the Peak District and smelted it at water-powered smelters called ore hearths using a mixture of whitecoal and charcoal as fuel. Whitecoal was small slivers of wood, dried in a kiln until all the moisture was driven out. According to William Linnard, charcoal and whitecoal were mixed together in lead smelting because 'charcoal made too violent a fire, and wood alone was too gentle'.[8] In 1657 Ecclesall Woods were leased to a 'lead merchant' who was permitted to make 'charcole or whitecole' and to 'make & cast pits & kilnes for the coaleing of the same'.[9] There are today in Ecclesall Woods some 300 surviving charcoal hearths and about 140 whitecoal kilns,[10] the latter in the form of deep round holes, usually on sloping ground, with a spout at the down-slope end. The spouts almost always face downhill. They are called whitecoal kilns and sometimes as **Q-pits** (Figure 4.14). The origin of the name Q-pit is surrounded with some confusion: some people say it is because the function of a Q-pit was not at first understood (Q = query or question mark), others are of the view that the letter Q mirrors the shape of the archaeological remains. Both explanations seem reasonable. Whitecoal kilns are described in more detail in Chapter 5.

Figure 4.14. Q-pit

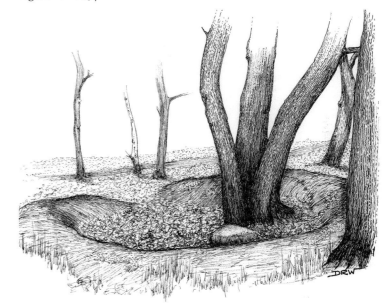

OAK-BARK LEATHER TANNING

During the 150-year period from 1680 to 1830, the production of leather and leather goods was, by value, the second most important industry in England after textiles, and one of the largest employers outside agriculture. Woodlands played a major role in supplying tree bark, which before the introduction of chemical substitutes, was the major agent, in the form of a liquor, used in the preparation or 'tanning' of the animal hides before their conversion into such everyday articles as boots, shoes, clogs, harnesses, saddles, breeches, aprons, gloves, bags, cases and bottles, and for use in industry for bellows and belting. Book binders were also important customers for fine leather. The tannic acid from ground bark seeps slowly through the pores of the hide, draws out the water and coats each fibre with a preservative. The tannin content of the bark of oak trees made oak bark the most efficient and therefore the most important tanning agent. Many of South Yorkshire's woods were predominantly oak woods and they became associated with the leather tanning industry at an early date. The best bark for tanning was obtained from coppice poles of about twenty years of age and so the bark obtained from the region's coppice woods was of the best quality.[11] Many of the surviving management records for local coppice woods include references to the peeling and selling of bark.

At a fall, the bark was peeled in large pieces from both the timber trees and the underwood poles. This was done by scoring a tree round its trunk at about two feet intervals and then making a longitudinal slit along the trunk. The bark could then be levered off in large plates with a bark peeler called a 'spud' (Figure 4.15). It was often the practice to remove as much of the bark as possible while the tree was standing, then felling it when other peelers, often women and children, would peel it from the branches, even down to branches one inch in diameter, and their product was sometimes called 'pikt bark' or 'sticking bark'. In 1722, for example, £1-14-04 was paid to 'seven Pillars [peelers] of bark' in Hesley Park at Thorpe

Figure 4.15. Peeling bark

Hesley 'for such Bark as stuck to ye wood after ye first pilling thereof'[12]. The peeled bark was stacked to dry and then, as tannin is soluble in water, it was protected from rain in thatched stacks until it was sold to tanners.

For Treeton Wood near Rotherham in 1710 the whole process from the letting of the peeling contract to the selling of the bark to tanners is preserved in the account book of the Duke of Norfolk's woodward:

> ... *Pd for Ale when we let the Pillings 00-01-00*
> *Paid Thomas Lee and partners for pilling 1420 fathoms of bark 18-14-05*
> *And for stacking the same 2-07-04*
> *Spent at Treeton when I met the Wath Tanners 00-01-00*
> *Pd Mt Turner 104 Thack Sheaves for thatching Bark Stacks 00-04-04*
> *Pd Jno Clayton for covering 5 Bark Stacks with Sods and 11 Stacks covered with straw 00-14-00*
> *Jno Oldham 100 quarts of Bark from Treeton Wood 16-13-08*
> *Lyonel Keyworth bt 62q & 2 from Treeton Wood of Bark 10-09-09*[13]

'Jno Oldam' was John Aldham, a member of a well-known tanning family from Upperthorpe in Sheffield. The inventory of William Aldham in 1696 records that he had £400 of leather in stock and 'in ye pitts'.[14] Lyonel Keyworth was a tanner in Woodhouse on the eastern fringes of Sheffield and just over three kilometres from Treeton Wood. The 'Wath Tanners' would have included Richard Jackson who had 340 hides in stock when he died in 1728.

At the tanyard the hides were first washed and cleaned up, usually in a water pit. This was followed by immersion in pits in slaked lime to open the pores on the hides and facilitate the removal of hair. The hair and any remaining flesh were then removed with 'de-hairing' and 'fleshing' knives while the hide was hanging over what was called a fleshing beam. After rinsing the hides were cut into sections known as heads, necks, shoulders, bends and butts. They were then ready for the tanpits.

In the meantime the bark had been ground in a bark mill worked either by horse- or water-power. The ground bark was added to cold water to make a tanning liquor and hides were passed through a succession of tanpits with increasingly strong tanning solutions. The hides were suspended in the pits from sticks or a wooden framework and care was taken that they did not touch each other so that they did not display touch marks or be uneven in colour. After months or in some cases years in the tanpits, the hides were dried, rolled and oiled before being sold to 'curriers' for final preparation and colouring.

Despite the fact that tanning was a complicated and protracted business in which capital investment was high in order to maintain a smooth-running operation and where large numbers of hides and large amounts of bark were involved, South Yorkshire was dotted with tanyards throughout the medieval and post-medieval period. For example, a tanyard was recorded at Thorne in 1483 and in medieval Doncaster there were tanneries in Fishergate. Tanners are mentioned in Sheffield in the lay subsidy rolls of 1297 and the poll-tax returns of 1378–79. William Rawson of the parish of Sheffield was described as a tanner when he died in 1550 and his descendants were still in the same business in the eighteenth century. They then occupied a tanyard on the tributary of the Don at Owlerton, in the past called Toad Hole Dike, the dam (pond) of which survives to this day as the fishing pond called Rawson Dam to the north of Herries Road. The site would have had a good water supply for the tanpits and a water-wheel for grinding bark. The mill was called Rawson Mill or Bark Mill. Thomas Rawson, tanner, occupied the mill in 1783 and took out a ninety-nine-year lease in 1789.[15] Sheffield continued to be an important centre for tanning in the nineteenth century and in a directory for 1833 six tanners are listed including John Aldham of Upperthorpe.

It should be noted that as leather tanning was a smelly business, tanneries were often located in the countryside or on the edges of towns, as in the case of the Rawson tannery at Owlerton and the Aldham tannery at Upperthorpe, both just outside the early town of Sheffield. Tanneries were also often infested with rats. This is probably the reason why the 25 Inch Ordnance Survey map published in 1904 shows a short street opposite the Tanyard at Dodworth Green named Ratten Row. There was also a Ratten Row near to the site of the Russell family's tannery at Upper Hoyland.

In the seventeenth and eighteenth centuries there was at least one tanner in Cawthorne and two in Dodworth. When William Smith, tanner of Cawthorne died in 1722 his goods and chattels were valued at the very high figure of £1,000 of which his hides, tanned and partly tanned and his bark were valued at £660. When John Brooke of Dodworth died in 1694 he had nearly 300 hides in his tanpits. John Hobson of Dodworth, who kept a diary, recorded in the 1730s buying hides from a butcher as far away as South Shields and collecting debts from customers as far away as Durham and Darlington.[16]

Woodhouse to the east of Sheffield has already been mentioned as the location of a tanyard in the early eighteenth century. By 1800 there were three tanyards in the village. In 1851 a Peter Birks, was a tanner living in Tannery House on Tannery Street. His business must have been prospering because the census records that he employed eight men. By 1881 William Birks

employed twenty-two men and eight boys. The tanyard closed in the early 1900s.

One of the most successful late Victorian tanning businesses was run by Henry Clegg of Barnsley. In the 1881 census Clegg was described as a 'Tanner, Currier, Leather Merchant, Mill Strap and Boot Upper Manufacturer. He had thirty-two employees and owned tanneries at Cawthorne and Denby Dale. In 1882 he purchased more than 62 tons of bark from Hall Wood, Parkin Wood and Woolley Wood in Ecclesfield parish and from Canklow Wood in Rotherham.

Before leaving the subject of oak-bark one very peculiar use for it must be mentioned: the growing of pineapples. It is believed that the first pineapple was grown in England in the late 1670s when gardener John Rose presented one to King Charles II. But pineapple growing on any scale did not begin until the 1720s and by the 1730s large landowners were said to be in the grip of 'Pineapple Fever'. For example, Thomas Watson-Wentworth of Wentworth Woodhouse, the future Marquis of Rockingham, stated that he started growing pine-apples in 1737 noting that they were 'very scarce in England'. By 1740 he recorded that he had got their cultivation 'to great perfection'. In 1745 he said some were ripe as early as 24 March and by the second week in June of that year he had cut more than 200.[17]

The pineapples were first grown in so-called 'tan-pits'. Tan pits were brick-lined pits sometimes with a back wall to which sloping glass frames were fixed. The brick pits were then filled with a layer of rubble on which used tan bark was laid that would remain in place for between three and six months. Tan bark was used oak bark from tanneries. While used oak bark was fermenting it produced a constant temperature to the roots of between 75–85 degrees Fahrenheit. The pineapples were grown in pots sunk into the tan bark from March to October. In October they were moved into heated glasshouses or 'stoves' and then moved back into the tan pits in spring. Eventually all-year-round pineries were built incorporating bark pits and heating from warm-air flues and later hot water boilers. The first reference to buying used bark in the Wentworth Woodhouse garden accounts (which began in 1750) was in 1766 when 'old bark' was obtained from a John Payne and such purchases went on until the 1830s when boilers and under-soil hot water pipes were installed in the stoves. William Smith from the nearby Chapeltown tannery was an important supplier.

THE SMALL CRAFTS

Less well-known than building in timber, charcoal and white-coal production and peeling bark and tanning leather, but once widespread, were a number of specialist, often outdoor woodland crafts that have all but disappeared because the product is no longer required, other materials are used or they are made in factories. Such crafts include turnery, coopering, chair bodging, wheel making, clog sole making, basket making, hurdle making, thatch spar making, rake making and besom making, hazel hoop making (to put round barrels) and birch wine making. For example in the 1851 census in Rotherham there were two wood turners, two master coopers, a wheelwright and a basket maker and in neighbouring Masbrough there was a timber merchant, a cooper, a house carpenter and a boat builder.

Turners made not only wooden dishes and plates but also a wide range of kitchen and dairy implements (Figure 4.16). With the advent of cheap china, plastics and stainless steel and the almost complete disappearance of domestic butter and

Figure 4.16. Pieces of turnery including spoons, ladles, butter pats, a cabbage squeezer and a potato masher

cheese making, the turner is now more likely to be making decorative objects and toys, often in imported woods. Medieval court rolls, records of marriages in local churches from the late sixteenth century to the nineteenth century and early census returns all mention turners, dishturners and dishmakers. Until forty years ago turners also made dolly pegs and wringer rollers but these objects are no longer required in an age of automatic washing machines. The turner worked on a simple lathe called a pole lathe and worked with woods such as rowan, ash, birch, beech and sycamore. By the nineteenth century sycamore was the wood most commonly used because it does not taint food-stuffs and it can be repeatedly immersed in water without warping or cracking. It has a pale colour without any marked figuring and it can be worked and turned while green.

Like turners, **coopers** also made vessels for food and drink. There were three branches of coopering: dry coopers made casks to hold non-liquid goods such as flour, tobacco, fruit or even gunpowder: white coopers made articles for domestic and dairy use: and wet coopers, the most specialised branch, produced casks for storing liquids. The dry cooper used a whole range of timbers, the white cooper worked in oak, sycamore and ash, and the wet cooper only in oak. Much oak timber from South Yorkshire's woods in the past was turned into staves for coopering work. No homestead before the nineteenth century would have been without a number of specialised vessels made by a local cooper: pails and piggins for carrying water and milk, churns for making butter, tubs called keelers for cooling liquids, tubs called kimnels for general use, lidded kits for holding milk, butter and other foods and hogsheads for storing ale (Figure 4.17).

The following three examples show the ubiquitous usage of the vessels made by the local cooper. The inventory of William

Figure 4.17. Pieces of coopery: a flour bin, butter churn and an apple press

Blythe of Bishops' House at Meersbrook in Sheffield, compiled on his death in 1665, included two barrels, nine half hogsheads 'with some beare in' one flour kit, three flesh kits 'with some meate in them', two churns, two kimnels and a cheese tub.[18] Some thirty years later the inventory of Thomas Yeardley, farmer, of Kimberworth Park Gate (now Kirkstead Abbey Grange) in Thorpe Hesley, Rotherham, in 1694 included in the kitchen a water kitt, a milking kitt, a leaven kitt (in which bread would be kneaded and left to rise), a water tub, a butter churn, and a flasket (an oblong or oval tub for washing clothes). In the buttery next door was a kimnel, a flesh kitt, two wooden bottles, six milk pails, a tub and a barrel.[19] And lastly the inventory of William Walker in 1718, draper and alderman of Doncaster where he was mayor in 1689 and 1692, included a salting kitt, a 'kimling', a hogshead, six half-hogsheads and four tubs.[20]

Wooden soled footwear was common in the past, not just for wearing in factories and coal mines, but for everyday wear and for when working on the farm. There were two distinct crafts: clog making and **clog sole cutting**. The clog sole cutters used alder, willow, birch, sycamore and beech trees, though alder was preferred because it was waterproof and easy to work. Trunks were cut into short logs that were about the same lengths as the four standard sizes: men's, women's, children's and middles. These short logs were then riven (split) into sole blocks using a mallet called a beetle and a metal wedge, and finally shaped with a special tool called a stock knife which was attached by a hook at one end to a ring on a low bench. The Dronfield family at Grenoside were well-known clog sole cutters in the nineteenth century. William Dronfield Senior, born in North Derbyshire, embarked on his apprenticeship as a woodman in Dore in 1809 at the age of fifteen before coming to Grenoside. He and his son, also called William who died in 1916, operated from the woodyard at the entrance to Wheata Wood at the top of Bower Lane. They were regular buyers of alder, sycamore and birch trees from the Duke of Norfolk's woods in Ecclesfield parish. They also made brush heads, tool handles and beetles for the Duke of Norfolk's woodmen.

Another woodland craft associated with Grenoside is **basket making**. Members of the Sharp(e) family were basket makers there in the nineteenth century and there are references in the Duke of Norfolk's wood accounts of the Sharpes being given permission (i.e. wood leave) to cut hazel and willow rods in local woods. They also bought oak coppice poles probably for swill making as described below. Their small pond ('Sharpe's wood 'oil') from which they obtained water and where they

soaked willow rods prior to weaving them into baskets is still in existence in Greno Wood (see Chapter 5). A locally-made type of basket used by, among others, charcoal burners and potato pickers, was the spelk or swill (Figure 4.18). This was made by weaving thin strips of oak (spelks) around a hoop of ash or hazel. The spelks were obtained by boiling oak coppice poles and thinly splitting (riving) them while still hot. An undated letter from George Sharp of Grenoside to Newton Chambers' Thorncliffe Ironworks has survived in which he explains that he has set himself up as a basket maker after having served a ten-year apprenticeship. He goes on to say that he can supply large coke baskets for 18 shillings per dozen, brays for 12 shillings per dozen, box baskets for 8 shillings per dozen and half-box baskets for 6 shillings per dozen. The letter ends with a request for a pan (presumably in which to boil his oak poles for swill making) 4 feet 5 inches long, 12 inches deep and 10 inches wide in exchange for a selection of his baskets.

Besom making was also a widespread local craft until the beginning of the last century. A besom is a tied bundle of twigs with a handle (in South Yorkshire called a *steyl*) inserted into it and used for sweeping flagged cottage floors, factory floors and dirt roads and paths. Besoms without handles, known as swales, were used in vast quantities in the steelworks of Sheffield and Rotherham until very recently. These swales removed the 'scale' from red-hot rolled steel as it emerged from the rollers. The besom handles were made from young ash, birch or hazel poles and the brooms were made from bundles of birch or hazel twigs (*rammel* in local dialect) or from heather, tied together originally with strips of willow, riven oak or even bramble. Later wire was used. The brooms made use of the lightest brushwood referred to as *ramayllis* or *ramelia* (ramell) or *tynsellum* (tinsel) in medieval documents in South Yorkshire. The manufacture of a

Figure 4.18. A swill basket maker

besom is a simple and short task – something like ten minutes – when performed by a skilled 'broom squire' as besom makers were called. A production rate of four dozen a day was not unusual (Figure 4.19).

Nothing was wasted. The smallest branches and twigs were bound together and called faggots or bavins or kids. They were made in large quantities and in 1720 1,000 kids were made from the tops of trees felled in Scraith Wood for the use of the Duke of Norfolk's tenants. Faggots had two main uses in South Yorkshire. They were used as the fuel in fires needing

Figure 4.19. Besom makers

very high temperatures in a short period, for example, in bakers' ovens, which were then scraped clean and the dough put in. And in 1719 there is a record of kids being used to burn bad meat in Sheffield market.[21] Faggots were also used to protect riverbanks and the sides of goits and dams at water-powered sites. There are many records of 'long kids', faggots up to ten feet long, held in place by stakes or hurdles, being regularly installed along waterbanks. Raddlings were also used for this purpose. These were thin rods interwoven between vertical stakes. In 1717, for example, 300 'radlins' were supplied from Sheffield's woods to repair the 'water banks above Neepsend' and another 100 to repair the waterbanks at the Old Park Corn Mill. In 1717 a payment of £2-15-00 was made for 'staking and radling 55 yards and filling up with Brush Wood' the water-bank near Rhodes Mill.[22]

Even the sap of birch trees was used to provide an income for the poorest members of rural communities. In 1717 Sarah Lockwood of Stannington leased the right, for ten shillings a year, to collect the sap from the birch trees in Stannington Wood.[23] The sap, which would have been collected in Spring by cutting a slit in the trunk, was made into sugar or mixed with honey, cloves, lemon peel and ale to make a mead-like drink.

It was during the Industrial Revolution that local woodland crafts were progressively 'industrialised' and taken out of the small woodland communities in which they had been created and perfected. This is clearly shown by the advertisement below (Figure 4.20) for Garsides' saw mill and factory at Worksop in 1853. The firm was a regular customer for timber at wood sales in the Sheffield area. Another sign of the industrialisation of local woodland crafts and industries and the change from coppice management to canopy woods and the planting of many timber trees was that not only timber merchants became

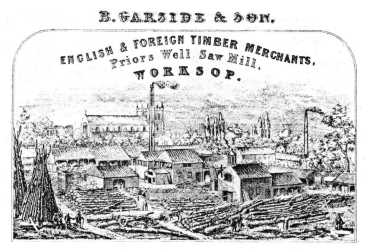

Figure 4.20. Advertisement for Garside's saw mill and factory at Worksop. Source: Worksop Public Library

important purchasers from local woods and plantations but that two rapidly expanding industries devoured large quantities of timber. These industries were coal mining and railway building. Coal mines had been a market for local timber from a very early period for as early as 1637 John Harrison in his survey of the manor of Sheffield recorded that in Cook Wood at Shirecliffe 'they get Punch wood (a puncheon was a pit prop) for the use of the coale pits'.[24] But in the nineteenth century the market increased enormously. For example, between 1840 and 1900, more than a dozen colliery companies bought timber from the Duke of Norfolk's estate in Sheffield and Rotherham, some repeatedly.[25] The timber would presumably have been for use as pit props, for lining shafts and for coal wagons. The significance of the coming of the railways can be seen from the fact that in 1853 the Sheffield, Rotherham, Barnsley and Wakefield Company paid £1,160 for timber from woods on the Duke of Norfolk's estate in Ecclesfield, which was one-third of the total estate income from wood and timber sales in that year.[26]

Despite the fact that most wooden objects are now factory-made and what used to be made from wood may now be made from metal or plastic, craftsmen in wood still survive. There are still local turners, basket-makers, rocking chair makers, hurdle-makers and even one small firm specialising in the construction of timber-framed buildings and other structures.

What to read about woodland crafts and industries

ARDRON, P. A. and ROTHERHAM, I. D. (1999) 'Types of charcoal hearth and the impact of charcoal and whitecoal production on woodland vegetation', *Peak District Journal of Natural History and Archaeology*, **1**, 35–47.

EDLIN, H.L. (1949) *Woodland Crafts in Britain*, Batsford

BROWN, R. J. (1986) *Timber Framed Buildings of England*, Robert Hale.

HARRIS, R. (1978) *Discovering Timber-Framed Buildings*, Shire Publications Ltd.

KELLEY, D. W. (1986) *Charcoal and Charcoal Burning*, Shire Publications Ltd.

RYDER, P. F. (n.d.) *Timber Framed Buildings in South Yorkshire*, South Yorkshire County Council, County Archaeological Monograph No 1.

TABOR, R. (1994) *Traditional Woodland Crafts*, Batsford.

Places to visit

Visit those buildings mentioned in the text that are **open to the public** to inspect the carpentry and/or carving. These are Bishops' House Museum, The Old Queen's Head public house, St Mary's church, Ecclesfield, St Peter's, Barnburgh and Rotherham Minster. Whiston manorial barn is only open to the public when public events are taking place. Permission to inspect the interior of Oaks Fold barn should be sought from the rangers who work there.

A visit to **Ecclesall Woods** is a must for three reasons. First to inspect George Yardley's monument; secondly to search for charcoal pitsteads and whitecoal kilns (see Chapter 5); and thirdly to visit the Working Woodlands Gallery ('Hector's House') to inspect the building materials and techniques employed in this modern timber-framed building and to see the products on sale from a variety of local craftsmen and artists. Woodland craft courses can also be attended.

Lastly, a visit to **Penistone Open Market Hall** enables the visitor to view an excellent example of a large modern timber-framed building completed in 2010. It is the largest oak structure in the country open to the public. Market day is on a Thursday.

THE ARCHAEOLOGY OF
SOUTH YORKSHIRE'S WOODLANDS

ARCHAEOLOGICAL FEATURES in South Yorkshire's woodlands are of two distinct types. First, there are those features which have nothing whatever to do with woodland management or with woodland crafts and industries. They have survived for hundreds or thousands of years because the area has become wooded or remained wooded and they have not been disturbed. Such features include caves and rock shelters used from as early as the Upper Palaeolithic (*c.* 10,000 BC) and as late as the earlier Neolithic (4000–3000 BC), cup and ring marked stones, Bronze Age settlements, Iron Age forts, linear earthworks, Romano-British settlement sites and field systems, old quarries and bell pits resulting from the mining of ironstone and coal, and even a bomb crater from World War Two. Secondly, there are those features which are directly the result of woodland management and the carrying on of woodland crafts and industries. These include boundary banks and walls, charcoal making sites, whitecoal making sites and a pond used by basket makers.

PREHISTORIC AND ROMANO-BRITISH ARCHAEOLOGICAL FEATURES

Among the oldest archaeological sites in a South Yorkshire wood is a **rock shelter** in Anston Stones Wood, an ancient wood in the Magnesian Limestone zone between South Anston and Woodsetts. The wood occupies a valley whose northern edge is in the form of a limestone cliff which contains a cave called

Dead Man's Cave. The cave consists of a fissure just over 8 feet (2.5 m) wide and 5 feet (1.5 m) high which leads to a narrow passage which in turn widens out into a chamber 14 and a half feet (4.5 m) long and nearly 10 feet (3 m wide). The remains of flint knives and blades have been discovered together with the bones of wild animals including wild horse and reindeer. These indicate that people of the Old Stone Age (Upper Palaeolithic) must have used the cave as a shelter just after the end of the last Ice Age before the wildwood developed. Similar sites have been discovered in Edlington Wood and Pot Ridings Wood in Doncaster.

One of the most interesting archaeological sites in South Yorkshire's ancient woods, the Mesolithic camp site near Deepcar, has already been described in Chapter 1. The next oldest archaeological features to survive are probably **cup and ring** marked boulders. Three rocks with cup and ring marks have been found in Ecclesall Woods in Sheffield (Figure 5.1). Cup and ring marks are a form of prehistoric art. A cup consists of a circular concave depression a few centimetres across sometimes surrounded by a concentric circular channel (the ring). Sometimes there were multiple rings and complex patterns of cups, rings and grooved channels linking or enclosing the whole design. They occur on natural rock outcrops, boulders and on standing stones. They have been pecked into the rock surface by either a deer antler or a flint or metal tool. They are thought to date from the late Neolithic or Bronze ages. Their

Figure 5.1. Cup and ring marked stone, Ecclesall Woods

exact meaning may never be known, although various theories have been put forward, including that some may be route markers, and that others had religious or ritual purposes.[1]

Another set of finds relating to the earlier Neolithic (4000–3000 BC) was in a rock shelter in Scabba Wood above the Don valley between High Melton and Sprotbrough. This time it was not, like the cave in Anston Stones Wood, a shelter from the elements, but a burial place. The site has been excavated on two occasions, in 1992 and 1998, by South Yorkshire Archaeological Service, following the discovery by the owner of human bones and who had then contacted the police. The police soon decided that the bones were not recent. The first excavation revealed that a human burial had taken place below the overhanging limestone and had been sealed by a cairn made of limestone rubble. Subsequently the overhanging limestone had broken

off and slid down the slope and the cairn had been disturbed revealing the human remains. When the bones were examined at least two bodies were identified, one male aged between twenty-thirty and another, possibly female, aged twelve-fifteen years. The more extensive 1998 excavation revealed more bones of Neolithic age, possibly those of two more individuals, an adult and a child of eight-nine years. Neolithic arrowheads, flints and part of a quern were also discovered. Objects dating to the Bronze Age (pottery fragments), Iron Age (pottery fragments), the Roman period (pottery sherds and five coins) and a pendant whetstone of the Anglo-Scandinavian period (*c*. 900–1100 AD) were also revealed. The writers of the report on the 1998 excavation wondered whether the site had acquired a 'supernatural significance' in the later prehistoric period.[2]

Another set of earthworks thought to date back as far as the Bronze Age occupies the summit areas on the eastern fringes of Canklow Wood in Rotherham. The most recent survey by the South Yorkshire Archaeological Service (1992) revealed a far more complex system of domestic enclosures, field systems and boundaries and droveways than previous work had shown. It is suggested that the archaeological features reflect occupation from as early as the Bronze Age (*c*. 1000 BC) and extending through the Romano-British period (*c*. 50–400 AD).[3]

Prehistoric forts have also survived in the region's ancient woods. For example in Ecclesall Woods in the western corner of the bird sanctuary is what is believed to be a promontory fort of late prehistoric or Romano-British date. It covers an area of about an acre (0.4 ha). On the north-west and south-west there is a naturally steep slope into the valley of the Limb Brook but on the south-east and north-east sides there are traces of a bank and ditch.[4] In Scholes Coppice in Rotherham there is another well preserved fort once known as Castle Holmes and Caesar's

Camp (Figure 5.2). This earthwork consists of a single rampart and ditch enclosing a flat area of about one acre (0.4 ha) in extent. The rampart, 50 feet (15 m) wide in places, still stands several feet above the interior and rises more than 15 feet (*c.* 5 m) above the bottom of the ditch which is also about 50 feet (15 m) wide. The counterscarp beyond the ditch rises in places to 7 feet (*c.* 2 m). The bank and ditch are both continuous except in the north-east and in the south-west where they are cut through by a wide ride, possibly one of the walks cut 'for Beauty' in the wood in the eighteenth century. There is no obvious entrance to the interior and originally the entrance may have been via a timber bridge. Excavations carried out by South Yorkshire Archaeology Service in 1992 showed what are believed to be

Figure 5.2. Caesar's Camp, Scholes Coppice

post holes of a timber palisade on top of the bank.[5] It is presumed it was a defensive site and if so its location is curious. It is located not at a high point but on a back slope at about 300 feet (91 m) in a slight depression and is overlooked on all sides except the north.

Another well preserved hill fort commands extensive views over the lower Don valley in Wincobank Wood. It consists of an oval, defensive enclosure of just over 2.5 acres (one ha) surrounded by a single rampart with an external ditch. The material from the excavated ditch has been thrown up into an outer bank. Today the grass covered rampart, which at one point rises about 9 feet (2.8 m) above the bottom of the ditch, is more or less complete except for three breaks, through two of which – in the south-west and north-east – passes a long-established track, called Wincobank Wood Lane. The ditch and outer bank are absent along most of the western side of the fort and along the northern half of the eastern side. Excavations by Sheffield City Museums in 1899 and 1979 have shown that the rampart was originally built as a very substantial stone wall. The interior of the wall was composed of earth and sandstone rubble bonded together by timbers. The inner side of the wall was faced by small un-mortared dressed stones, and the outer side by large, un-mortared dressed stones. It is not clear how high the original rampart was, but it would almost certainly have been topped by a timber palisade. No excavations have been made inside the fort and so whether there are any signs of occupation in the form of post holes for buildings or storage or other pits is unknown. When the excavations were made in the rampart, charred timbers were recovered, and in the rubble core there were signs of vitrification, i.e., the filling had been fused into a glass-like substance by intense heat. The charring suggests that the rampart was destroyed by fire. Using radiocarbon dating

(C14) it is possible to put an approximate date on some archaeological objects. Charcoal from burnt timber taken from the rampart in 1979 gave an approximate date of 500 BC. This suggests that the main rampart was built in the middle of the Iron Age. It was probably built as a result of conflict between neighbouring tribes wishing to control the Don valley. It has long been believed that the Wincobank hill fort was occupied during the early Roman period to check the northern advance of the Roman armies. The Romans built their own fort in AD 54 only two miles away on the opposite side of the Don valley at what became known as Templeborough.

All the three forts described above in Ecclesall Woods, in Wincobank Wood and in Scholes Coppice, would have required sites with good visibility in all directions. They would not therefore have been constructed deep in woodland. What this means is that the three woods cannot be examples of primary woodland, i.e. woodland that is a direct descendant of the wildwood and never cleared. They must be examples of ancient secondary woodland that has grown up once the forts were abandoned.

Other features that suggest that woodland has grown up since features were constructed include a number of **Romano-British field systems** in addition to the one in Canklow Wood that is now believed to have been occupied since the Bronze Age. Romano-British field systems have been identified in Wheata Wood and Greno Wood at Grenoside, in Edlington Wood, Pot Ridings Wood and Wadworth Wood. The one identified in Wheata Wood, which is typical of such sites, consists of four widely spaced lynchets (raised strips of land), rubble banks, an orthostat (boulder) wall, a rectilinear enclosure and a number of stone and rubble clearance mounds.[6] The features are subdued, eroded and covered by vegetation and only discernible to a professional archaeologist. In Wombwell Wood in Barnsley there is a set of features thought to be of Iron Age/Romano-British date not found elsewhere in South Yorkshire. The site consists of two enclosures joined by a 'drove-way' between two parallel banks. Field boundaries radiate from the enclosures.

Also surviving in dense woodland at the foot of the Wharncliffe Crags in Wharncliffe Woods is a **quern-making 'factory'**. Querns were hand-operated grindstones for converting cereal grains into flour. The site at Wharncliffe used the outcropping Wharncliffe Sandstone and covers 178 acres (72 ha). On-site evidence of querns of different types and sizes suggests that the 'factory' may have had its origins in the Bronze Age and that it was still active in the medieval period with its main phases of production in the Iron Age and Romano-British period. More than a thousand 'flat-disc' and 'beehive' querns in various stages of production survive on the site.[7] The name Wharncliffe is simply a corruption of 'Quern-cliff'.

Part of the **linear earthwork**, the Roman Ridge, that once stretched for almost 11 miles (17.6 km) along the northern side of the Don valley from Sheffield to Mexborough is well preserved in Wath Wood (Figure 5.3). The earthwork splits into two at Kimberworth, with the northern arm continuing to Mexborough and the roughly parallel southern arm ending at Kilnhurst. In Wath Wood the northern arm, as a broad bank with a ditch (to the south), runs through the southern part of the wood. The line of the bank here formed part of the boundary between the ancient parishes of Wath and Swinton. Speculation still surrounds its date and its function. It may be purely a defensive feature or it may have been created to delineate a demilitarised zone. Suggestions as to its date range between the period of Roman advance into the southern

FEATURES RELATED TO THE QUARRYING OF STONE AND THE MINING OF COAL AND IRONSTONE

Quarries occur in a number of ancient woods and in a few cases abandoned quarries have become woods. For example there are abandoned sandstone quarries in Wickersley Wood, Walkworth Wood and Canklow Wood in Rotherham, in the latter case this was where Mexborough Rock (Rotherham Red) was quarried. There are also three old sandstone quarries in Barber Wood in Grange Park at Kimberworth, the largest of which is reputed to have supplied dressed stone for the neighbouring Thundercliffe Grange. Abandoned limestone quarries are also found in the Don Gorge woodlands at Sprotbrough. At least three abandoned quarries for the extraction of ganister occur in Ecclesall Woods. These date from the late nineteenth and early twentieth centuries. Ganister is a fine-grained sandstone that occurs beneath the thin coal seams of the Lower Coal Measures. It was ground into a powder which was mixed to form a clay for making refractory bricks to line the interior of steel furnaces. The 25-inch Ordnance Survey map for 1920 shows tramroads linking ganister quarries in Ecclesall Woods with Abbey Lane where the ganister must have then been transported to the brickworks by road.

Bell pits, for mining coal and ironstone, were sunk in the western parts of the Coalfield zone where seams outcropped at the surface or were near the surface before they dipped away eastwards. Some surviving spoil heaps from bell pits could well be medieval but this method of mining continued until the mid-nineteenth century. In a bell pit a short vertical shaft was sunk to the coal or ironstone seam and the coal or ironstone was 'got' in all directions from the bottom of the shaft. Because of fear of roof collapse, after the mineral had been removed a short distance from the shaft, it was abandoned and another pit

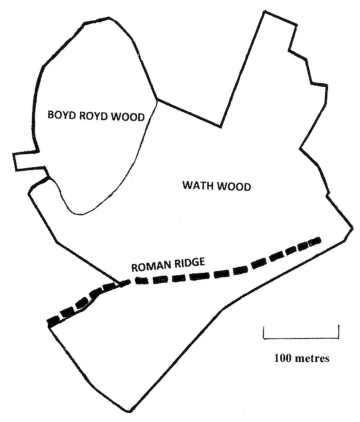

Figure 5.3. Roman Ridge in Wath Wood

frontier of the Brigantian peoples, and the Dark Ages, sometime between 450–600 AD, after the collapse of the Roman empire to defend the Celtic kingdom of Elmet from the advancing Anglo-Saxons.[8]

was sunk. Miners went down and were brought up the shaft, as was the coal or ironstone, by windlass, but in larger bell pits, called gin pits, a horse was used to operate a pulley system (the gin). It appears that as one pit was abandoned and another one was sunk at least some of the spoil from shaft sinking and making headway into the coal or ironstone seam in the new pit was dumped over the shaft of the old pit. Thus, today all that is normally left of an old bell pit is a mound of shale, that can be as high as 17 feet (5.17 m) and 80 feet (24.3 m) in diameter, with a central hollow where subsidence has occurred over the shaft (Figure 5.4). In one pit in Gallery Bottom Wood in Grange Park

Figure 5.4. Bell pit in Bray Plantation, Kimberworth

at Rotherham subsidence is so severe that it is possible to see the top of a round brick-built shaft. Bell pit spoil heaps tend to be simply sprinkled throughout a wood or plantation in a random pattern but they also appear in neat rows. The remains of many bell pits can be found in a number of ancient woods including Thorncliffe Wood and Smithy Wood near Chapeltown and in Gallery Bottom Wood in Grange Park, Rotherham. In an area in Cawthorne Park Woods ironstone bell pits occur near much slag and cinder debris and it has been suggested that this marks a medieval iron smelting site.[9] In the lease drawn up between the owner of Thorncliffe Wood (Earl Fitzwilliam) and iron manufacturers, Newton Chambers & Longden, it was stipulated that before any pits were sunk in the wood the Earl's steward had to be informed so that he could fell any timber trees on the site of the pit and if the company injured, damaged or destroyed any tree during mining operations then they had to pay in compensation double the value of that tree. When a particular pit was abandoned the pit hills were supposed to be levelled ready for planting with young trees.[10] And as is detailed in Chapter 7, a number of plantations were created in the nineteenth century on land previously mined using bell pits.

FEATURES DATING FROM THE SECOND WORLD WAR

It may be surprising to learn that a small number of features relating to the Second World War survive in South Yorkshire's woods. One of these is a 'ghost feature', i.e. the location is known but no artefacts remain, just a series of irregular breaks in the slope in the Iron Age fort rampart in Wincobank Wood, Sheffield, overlooking the Lower Don Valley, which in the Second World War was full of steel works manufacturing a wide range of armaments for the army, the Royal Navy and

Air Force. This was the site of an anti-aircraft gun site and searchlight emplacement. More obvious are the markers on the boundary of an ammunition depot with the ammunition hidden underground in grass-covered bunkers. The depot was on land now largely occupied by Grenoside crematorium. Here were stored bombs used in raids on Hitler's Germany and taken on a regular basis by convoys of lorries to the airfields in Lincolnshire. Now all that remain are boundary stones on the edge of what was one of the earliest recorded wood pastures, now the scrub-wood at Birley Edge. The stones have the initials W D (War Department) etched into them. One stands immediately behind the Birley Stone, a medieval boundary marker.

In the Sheffield 'blitz' in December 1940 hundreds of heavy bombs, six parachute mines and thousands of incendiary bombs were dropped on the city and at least some of these must have landed in woodland. On guided walks round Ecclesall Woods in the 1970s numerous bomb craters were pointed out by the guides, members of the city's Estates Department. These 'bomb craters' were in fact whitecoal pits (see below). One bomb crater that has been more or less identified as such lies in Wheata Wood at Grenoside (at grid reference SK 324 943). It consists of a large circular hollow about 26 feet (8 m) in diameter and more than 7 feet (2.25 m) deep. Around its edges there is a low and intermittent rim of debris.[11]

ARCHAEOLOGICAL FEATURES RELATED TO THE MANAGEMENT OF WOODS AND DEER PARKS
Boundary banks and walls are some of the longest surviving archaeological features of former deer parks and coppice woods. But they are often missed. The first thing that anyone interested in the history and archaeology of a woodland ought to do on visiting it for the first time is to carefully walk its boundaries.

And if there is no bank or wall on the modern boundary look inside and outside the wood for surviving boundary features – in case the wood has been enlarged or reduced in size.

These boundaries were created, as already discussed in chapters 2 and 3, in the case of deer parks, to keep the deer and other livestock inside and poachers and predators outside; and in the case of coppice woods to keep trespassers (who may be poachers, thieves, berry-gatherers or nutters) and grazing animals out. Deer park boundaries are important to woodland historians for two reasons. First, inside a deer park there was a wood pasture regime where growing wood and timber was coupled with grazing, and secondly because many deer parks were later converted into compartmented coppice woods.

The creation of a park – called emparkment – involved enclosing an area of land with a fence. The fence was called the **park pale** and consisted of either cleft oak stakes attached to a rail, often set on a bank, or a stone wall. If there was a bank, there would be a ditch on the inside to make it more difficult for the parkland deer to escape, as already pointed out in Chapter 2. As parks could vary in size from under 100 acres to several thousand acres fencing was a major initial and recurring expense. Because of the expense of fencing the most economical shape for a deer park was a circle or a rectangle with rounded corners. It is also interesting to note that parish and township boundaries were often displaced by the creation of a deer park. One additional characteristic of park pales is worthy of note. Park pales contained **deer leaps.** These were devices which allowed wild deer to enter the park but prevented them and the herd of deer already in the park from escaping.

In South Yorkshire surviving recognisable deer park boundaries are in the form of banks, which would originally have had either a wall or cleft oak stakes attached to a rail on top, or simply in the form of high stone walls. For example, the part of the boundary of Tinsley Park, which was also a township boundary was in the form of a broad bank, whereas the boundary of Tankersley Park, as we have seen in Chapter 2, was in a the form of a stone wall.

Ancient woodland shapes, unlike deer park outlines, as pointed out in Chapter 1, tend to be zig-zagged with well marked peninsulas and bays like a rocky coast as if giant bites had been taken from them. This unevenness is the result of the unplanned, piecemeal clearing process, which in the medieval period was known as *assarting* and resulted in the creation of small irregular fields outside the woods.

Despite their irregular shapes good fences were absolutely essential around coppice woods. Indeed the verb 'to encoppice' means to protect the underwood prior to rotational felling in a <u>fenced</u> wood. Like deer parks the boundaries were either in the form of banks or walls. Wood banks have ditches on the <u>outside</u>. The higher and broader the bank and the deeper the ditch, the older the bank is likely to be. Thick hedges or wooden post and rail fences surmounted these banks and where trees grew on them they were often pollarded so that animals grazing along the woodland edge could not feed on the new shoots. These woodbank pollards, if they still survive, are usually by far the oldest trees still growing in a former ancient coppice wood. Walls took the place of banks and ditches where good wall stone outcropped. The walls protecting woods in South Yorkshire come in a variety of forms: a wall on its own, a wall on a bank, a wall revetted into a bank and even a wall on the outside of a wood-bank and external ditch. Walls are not uniform features. The oldest walls were made from orthostats, boulders removed from the land as clearances were made. The lower parts of walls made with orthostats can

still be found surrounding woodlands and these are likely to be of medieval date at the very latest. After the Middle Ages double-skinned dry-stone walls with rows of topping stones became general. During the Parliamentary Enclosure period (1750–1830), very professional dry-stone walling techniques were employed, walls of this period being typified by double-skins filled with small waste stone fragments, the generous use of strengthening through stones, tapering cross-sections and mortared-in rows of top stones. It can be very difficult to try to date stone walls around old coppice woods because through human and animal interference and through demolition to remove wood and timber, an enormous amount of patching (called 'gapping' in some areas) has taken place over the centuries, and so many walls are made of a combination of the work of the original waller and patches made at various times since its erection.

Figure 5.5 shows five different types of boundary around former coppice woods in the Coalfield zone. The Rollestone Wood boundary is in the form of a weak bank with an external ditch. It is not clear whether this once had a hedge or a wall on top of the bank. The boundary around Low Spring is also in the form of a bank, stronger than the one around Rollestone Wood and this time with the remains of a stone wall surmounting the bank. The Tinsley Park boundary is very broad and this is reckoned to indicate an ancient origin. The first of the two boundaries around Smithy Wood is simply in the form of a thick stone wall. The second Smithy Wood boundary is a broad bank with a stone wall revetted into it.

Because many ancient woodlands are on township and parish boundaries, a woodland boundary in the form of a bank or wall may have a double function: to mark a territorial as well as a working woodland boundary. On rare occasions a parish or

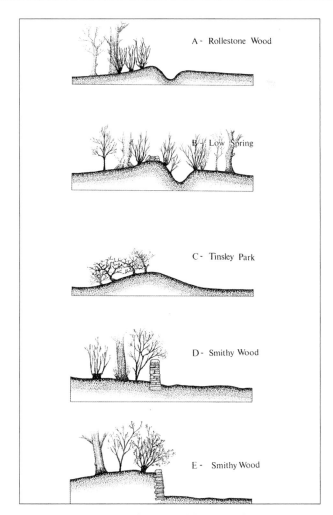

A - Rollestone Wood

B - Low Spring

C - Tinsley Park

D - Smithy Wood

E - Smithy Wood

Figure 5.5. Five types of woodland boundary feature

township boundary may be found within an ancient wood. This is the case, for example, at King's Wood which sits astride the boundaries between Brampton, Hoyland and Wentworth townships in the ancient parish of Wath. Within the wood following a tortuous route, running south-west then turning abruptly north-west and then again north-east is the boundary bank between Brampton and Wentworth townships (Figure 5.6).[12]

One curious ecological note can be added to the discussion of woodbanks. The grass, wood melick (*Melica uniflora*) has a 'circumboscal' distribution, i.e. it tends to occur along woodland boundaries, often occurring on medieval woodbanks, indeed Oliver Rackham refers to it as the 'woodbank grass'. The woodbank around Rollestone Wood in the Gleadless Valley in Sheffield shown in Figure 5.5 is covered in wood melick.

Another characteristic feature of deer parks that has survived in a few cases is the **fish pond**, in one case, at Beauchief Abbey, still in full view but in another lost among trees and in a third case deep in woodland. There are still two recognisable fish pond sites, now dry except in the very wettest weather, in Tankersley Park along a footpath among the trees on the left just beyond the railway bridge up Black Lane. That they are the original deer park fish ponds can be confirmed by comparing their position with the engraving of the park of *c*. 1730 (Figure 2.7(a) and 2.7(b) in Chapter 2). The best preserved deer park fish pond sites occur in Gallery Bottom Wood in what was once part of Kimberworth Park. In a narrow valley on the southern edge of the wood are the silted remains of three ponds (Figure 5.7). Stone-built sluices are still in place in the dam walls (earthern banks). The bottom pond is 98 feet (*c*. 30 m) long, the middle pond is 125 feet (38 m) long and the top pond, which is more difficult to define is more than 197 feet (60 m) long.[13]

Figure 5.6. Township boundary bank in King's Wood, Elsecar

Figure 5.7. Fish pond remains in Gallery Bottom Wood

Of the archaeological features related to woodland crafts and industries, those related to charcoal making are the most common. Careful searches of former coppice woods in winter when the vegetation does not conceal subdued features will reveal charcoal making sites, variously called **charcoal hearths** and **pitsteads**. These are most difficult to identify when they are on naturally level ground, although when the circular or oval sites have been re-used over many coppice cycles they are usually dish-shaped. Careful inspection to find blackened soil and small pieces of charcoal may confirm the feature's identity as a charcoal hearth. Charcoal hearths are much easier to identify in woods on sloping sites. Here the charcoal maker

had to prepare a level stable site. The characteristic features of these 'platform' sites are a low bank on the upper side where the charcoal maker has cut into the slope to create a circular, oval or sub-rectangular level surface. In some cases the lower edge of the hearth may have stones revetted into it to give extra stability. Figure 5.8 shows a measured hearth on a sloping site in Parkbank Wood in the Sheaf valley in Sheffield. To give some idea of the density of charcoal hearths in local coppice woods, about 300 have been identified in the 290-acre (117.5 ha) Ecclesall Woods and more than 20 in the 27-acre (11 ha) Parkbank Wood.[14]

Another feature that is much rarer than a charcoal hearth is the foundation of a **charcoal maker's hut**. These huts in which the charcoal maker lived in order to keep a 24-hour a day vigil

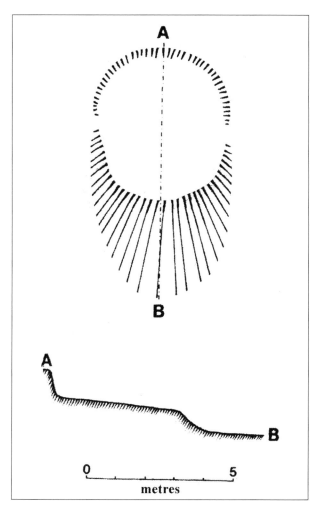

Figure 5.8. Measured plan and elevation of charcoal pitstead

beside the slowly burning stack were in the form of a wigwam made of long narrow poles sometimes set into a low perimeter stone wall, as already described in Chapter 4. They were typically 10–12 feet in diameter and 12–14 feet high. A lintel was lashed in place over a gap that was left as a doorway. Over the framework of poles sacking or skins were laid and these were then covered with turves in the manner of tiles. A stake was often driven into the ground a few feet from the entrance. The door often consisted of wood battened together which could be pulled in front of the doorway at night and merely pushed outwards to rest on the stake when the charcoal maker emerged in the morning. A particularly evocative but faded photograph of a charcoal maker's hut has recently been unearthed in a Sheffield attic (Figure 5.9). The hut is typical of its type with a turf covering over tarpaulin covered poles (one pole in the doorway is clearly birch). Note also the tiny cabin built for the dog. The underwood and timber trees would have been felled in the wood in the previous winter and, as can be clearly seen, the 'reserved' trees left to grow to maturity have been marked with white paint. Leaning against the hut is a woodman's two-handled cross-cut saw used to cut the cordwood to length together with a series of long pointed poles that were probably rake handles. In the foreground is a sieve used for riddling the dust that was used to form the outer cover of the stack and two swill or spelk baskets for carrying work on the site.

The remains of these huts in the form of a circle of stones (the remains of the low perimeter wall, with a gap for the doorway) can sometimes still be found if a thorough search is made in winter when the ground vegetation has died down. The author has photographed several examples of these stone foundations in various parts of the country but only one example has been

Figure 5.9. Charcoal makers and their hut in a Sheffield wood

found in South Yorkshire, in Walkworth Wood in Kimberworth. No doubt others remain to be identified. Perhaps some of the sites identified as charcoal making sites may in fact be the sites of charcoal makers' huts that did not have a low perimeter wall.

In woods in southern Sheffield on the border with Derbyshire charcoal hearths are accompanied by **whitecoal kilns** in which slivers of wood from which the moisture had been dried out, whitecoal, was produced. Whitecoal was the fuel for lead smelting. The basic characteristics of whitecoal kilns have already been described in Chapter 4 , although there are a number of variations on the basic type. Besides the circular and ovoid-shaped kilns there are square shaped kilns, others that

appear to have a channel or leat running from the spout and even paired kilns with a long leat running away from their spouts. More than 140 whitecoal kilns have been identified in Ecclesall Woods, ten in neighbouring Ladies Spring Wood and at least fifteen in Parkbank Wood. Figure 5.10 shows a measured whitecoal kiln in Parkbank Wood clearly displaying the spout at the downslope end.

A unique feature related to the carrying on of an ancient craft in or the near a wood is the **small pond** that has survived in Greno Wood at Grenoside. This is 'Sharp's wood oil', a small stone-lined pond where members of the Sharp family, basket makers, obtained their supply of water. Water from the pond would have been used in two ways. First it would have been used for soaking willow rods prior to their being woven into baskets and secondly it would have been used for boiling their rived (split) oak poles to make them supple enough for making swill or spelk baskets (see Chapter 4).

As the coppice woods in South Yorkshire, as elsewhere, were felled in rotation, usually between twenty-thirty years, with standard trees also being felled and removed on a regular basis, it would have been important to maintain **a system of tracks** through the largest woods to enable easy entry and exit of horse drawn vehicles to remove the wood, timber and bark. The oldest tracks tend to be sinuous 'hollow-ways' between high or low banks, some natural others artificial. Hollow-ways, some well-defined others much less so, occur in, for example, Ecclesall Woods and Wheata Wood in Sheffield and Hawks Wood at Thorpe Salvin in Rotherham. The best defined hollow-way is the one in Wheata Wood at Grenoside. This hollow-way runs roughly parallel to the Woodhead Road in the northern narrow extension of the wood. It runs sinuously in a north-north-westerly to south-south-easterly direction. In parts it

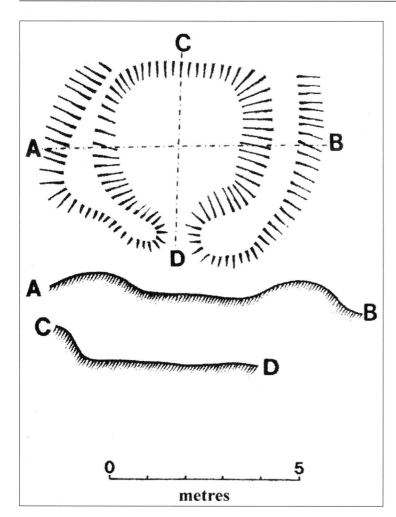

Figure 5.10. *Measured plan and elevation of whitecoal kiln*

forms a flat floored gully 6.5 feet (2 m) wide and in places has steep sloping sides.[15]

Later post-medieval tracks are often in the form of straight 'rides'. They may be metalled in part in boggy areas and small stone bridges may have been built to carry the ride over small woodland valleys containing streams. There are well preserved rides in Bowden Housteads Wood in Sheffield and Rainborough Park between Wentworth and Brampton. In Bowden Housteads Wood a wide ride follows a former compartment boundary in the northern half of the wood, crossing via a small bridge a small tributary of the Car Brook and emerges from the eastern edge of the wood next to the site of a woodman's cottage, now demolished. In Rainborough Park a virtually straight ride bisects the wood from north to south. From this central ride two subsidiary rides extend to the eastern and western edges of the wood. The main north-south ride is 800 metres long, is wide and forms an important species-rich habitat. It is dry in some places, wet in others, and there are ride-side ditches. It contains a rich variety of herbs, grasses and sedges including pignut, lady's mantle and ragged robin.[16] Although there can be no doubt that the north-south ride was closely related to the management of the wood, it seems to have had another function as part of the planned wider estate landscape. To the south of the wood it links directly to the Needle's Eye monument built by 1732 which leads directly to the North Lodge at the entrance to Wentworth Park and to the north of the wood it leads to a pair of ornamental gates called the Lion Gates.

The most elaborate layouts of rides are found in the largest woods, for example, in Maltby Wood and Edlington Wood. Maltby Wood, for example, now mostly obliterated by the opening of Maltby Colliery in 1911 and the spread southwards and westwards of its large spoil heap, had the most elaborate system of straight rides forming a starburst pattern. The rides are clearly shown on Thomas Jefferys' map of Yorkshire published in 1771 (except he shows an extra ride in the north-east part of the wood (Figure 5.11). In all there are five rides,

or 'ridings' as they are called, shown on successive editions of Ordnance Survey maps. Each riding was named: Laughton Riding, Grange Riding, Stainton Riding, Tickhill Riding and Upper and Lower New Riding. The names of the first four ridings relate to four villages and one grange (Lambcote Grange) to which the ridings would lead if they continued into the neighbouring countryside. The rides separated the wood into seven compartments called 'quarters': Grange Quarter, Stainton Quarter, Lower and Upper Castle Lidget quarters, Stone Park Quarter and most interestingly, High and Low Shoulder of Mutton quarters. Only Upper and Lower Castle Lidget quarters survive, still separated by the Lower New Riding.

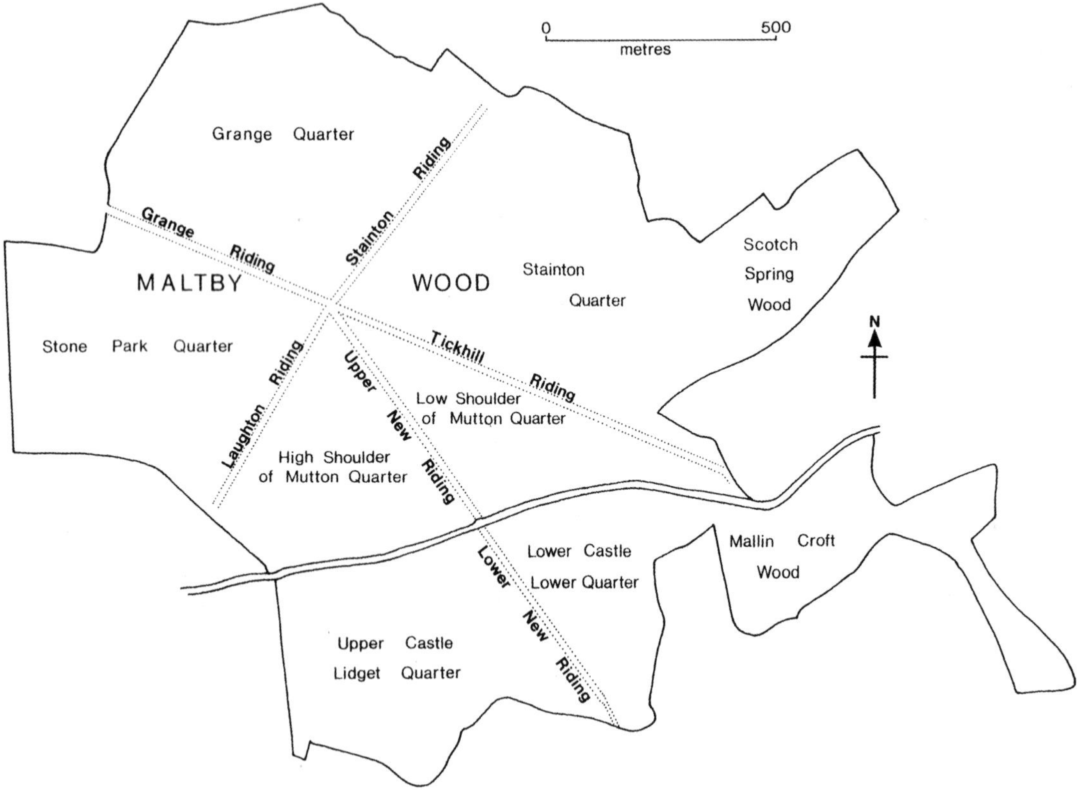

Finally, in former chases, deer parks, wooded commons, coppice woods and in ancient hedges there are living trees indicating, through their form, their past management. These are worthy of consideration as archaeological features. These are **coppice stools, stored coppice, stubs and pollards**. There are ancient coppice stools scattered through many of South Yorkshire's ancient woods. For example in both Canklow Wood in Rotherham and Wincobank Wood in Sheffield there are some old oak coppice stools full of character because of their twisted and gnarled appearance (Figure 5.12). And in Poggs Wood in the Ewden valley there is an ancient

Figure 5.11. Rides in Maltby Wood

Figure 5.12. Ancient coppice stool

multi-stemmed alder coppice stool that could be a descendant of one of those that produced the two cords of 'Owler Wood' (i.e., alder wood) mentioned in the Duke of Norfolk's wood accounts in 1717: *2 Cord of Owler Wood out of poggs ground at 13s p cord £1-06-00* [17]. Stubs are trees cut to about a metre from ground level on woodbanks. Stored coppice, already discussed in Chapter 3 occurs throughout South Yorkshire's former coppice woods, as two- or three-stemmed trees, predominantly of oak, a reminder of the conversion of former coppice woods into high forest. Pollards are very thin on the ground in former wood pastures across the region, notable survivors being the ancient oak at Wortley Hall and two oak pollards on Loxley Common.

What to read about the archaeology of woodlands

ARMSTRONG, L. (1978) *Woodcolliers and Charcoal Burning*, Coach Publishing House Ltd and The Weald and Downland Open Air Museum.

JONES, M (2009) *Sheffield's Woodland Heritage*, 4th edition, Wildtrack Publishing.

MUIR, R. (2005) *Ancient Trees Living Landscapes*, Tempus.

PHILLIPS, H. (1973) *Edlington Wood: An assessment of its recent history, archaeology, geology, natural history and educational and amenity value*, Doncaster Rural District Council, section on archaeology pp. 5–40 by M. Dolby and other experts.

RACKHAM, O. (2006) *Woodlands*, Collins, New Naturalist series, Chapter 8: Archaeology and Land-Forms of Woodland and Wood Pasture.

ROTHERHAM, I.D., JONES, M., SMITH, L. and HANDLEY, C. (2008) (eds) *The Woodland Heritage Manual: A Guide to Investigating Wooded Landscapes*, Wildtrack Publishing, Chapter B.3. (Woodland History and Archaeology); Chapter D.3.1 (Finding and Mapping Archaeological Features; Chapter D.3.2. Detailed Recording of Individual Archaeological Features; and Chapter D.3.3. How to Identify and Survey Ancient and Working Trees).

The annual reviews of the South Yorkshire Archaeology Service, *Archaeology in South Yorkshire*, are a mine of information. For example, the review for 1991–92 has reports on the initial excavations at the rock shelter at Scabba Wood, a study of the field system in Canklow Wood and the excavation at the Iron Age camp in Scholes Coppice; the 1992–93 review has a study of the bell pits in Cawthorne Park Woods; and the 1998–99 review has a report on a second excavation at the rock shelter in Scabba Wood.

Places to visit

Visit prehistoric sites in publicly-owned woodlands. Dead Man's Cave in Anston Stones Wood, Wincobank Hill fort and Scholes Camp in Scholes Coppice are probably the most atmospheric sites. Be careful not to cause any damage at these sites. An illustrated leaflet on Wincobank Hill is available from Sheffield City Council, Parks and Countryside Service, Meersbrook Park Offices, Brook Road, Sheffield S8 9FL. A leaflet on Scholes Coppice has also been produced by Rotherham Metropolitan Borough Council.

Examine bell pits in publicly owned woods and plantations, e.g. Gallery Bottom Wood in Grange Park at Kimberworth, Thorncliffe Wood at Chapeltown and in Newbiggin Plantation (next to Thorncliffe Wood) and Bray Plantation between Scholes and Kimberworth.

Investigate the boundaries of your local wood. Are they in the form of banks? Or stone walls? Or a combination of both? If there is no discernible stockproof boundary look inside the wood in case it has been expanded beyond its old boundaries and beyond the wood in case it has been reduced in size.

Look for charcoal making sites in your local wood and if in the south-west of the region **look for whitecoal kilns**. **A visit to Ecclesall Woods**, with its hundreds of charcoal and whitecoal making sites, is a must for those interested in the archaeology of ancient coppice woods. And of course, there is the monument to the charcoal maker who was burnt to death in the woods and Hector's House, a modern building made entirely from timber and wood.

Investigate the area around the Birley Stone and search for the W.D. markers on the edge of Birley Edge. An illustrated leaflet on the Birley Stone is available from Sheffield City Council, Parks and Countryside Service, Meersbrook Park Offices, Brook Road, Sheffield S8 9FL.

TREES IN PARKS AND GARDENS

FOR A REGION KNOWN throughout the rest of the country mainly for its industrial past in coal mining and iron and steel manufacturing, South Yorkshire is blessed with a number of country house parks and gardens once the property of gentry and aristocratic families that are open to the public. And these parks and gardens are full of fine trees, native and exotic. In the west there is Wortley Hall gardens that surround the former home of the Earls of Wharncliffe and which is now a hotel and conference centre owned by the Trades Union movement. Further east there is Wentworth Castle gardens and park, the former home of the Vernon-Wentworth family, now managed by the Wentworth Castle Trust, and Cannon Hall, the former home of the Spencer and Spencer-Stanhope families with the house (now a museum), the gardens and the park managed by Barnsley Metropolitan Borough Council. At Wentworth Woodhouse, the former residence of the earls Fitzwilliam, although the mansion is in private ownership, the park is open to the public and part of the gardens belong to Wentworth Garden Centre. Further east in Doncaster Metropolitan District are three country house gardens or parks. Campsall Country Park has been developed by Doncaster Metropolitan Borough Council in the grounds of the home (now demolished) of the Frank family; Cusworth Park, containing the former residence of the Battie-Wrightson family, is also run by Doncaster Metropolitan Borough Council with the house as a museum; and Brodsworth Hall gardens, once the property of the Thelluson family, are now a part of the property managed by English Heritage. There are also some notable trees in the municipal parks and gardens distributed across the region, including Sheffield Botanical Gardens with its collection of fine trees.

THE HISTORY OF THE COUNTRY HOUSE PARK

The concept of the park as an aesthetic extension of a country seat and its garden began in the Tudor period and has gone through a number of fashions during the last 500 years. In the Tudor period in the sixteenth century three fundamental changes took place. First, with a stable and strong central government, major landowners in England gradually abandoned their fortified residences – their castles and moated manor houses – and began to build country houses. Secondly, they built these in the middle of existing deer parks or created completely new parks on new sites. Thirdly, they immediately surrounded their new country houses with formal gardens. The fashion for locating a new country house in the centre of an existing deer park is well illustrated in South Yorkshire at Tankersley. The moat of the former moated manor house still survives and still surrounds the nineteenth-century rectory to the north of the church, while in the centre of the former park lie the ruins of the Elizabethan Tankersley Hall. Even more substantial was the Manor Lodge in Sheffield Park built by the 4th Earl of Shrewsbury about 1510 on an eminence with glorious views in every direction. Now largely in ruins except for the Turret House, it was described in his 1637 Survey of the Manor of Sheffield by John Harrison as 'Sheffield Lodge standing on a hill in ye middle of ye Parke'.[1]

The parks surrounding the new country houses that sprang up in the sixteenth and seventeen centuries, were still essentially deer parks, although grazing cattle were a much more common sight than in the medieval period, with both the deer and the cattle being an aesthetic backdrop to the house as much as a source of food. The seventeenth century saw formal design and rigid regularity imposed on existing and new parks. Out went the semi-natural landscape of irregularly-shaped ancient woods, heath and grassland and in came straightness: straight tree-lined avenues and walks and straight canals, with vistas cut through existing woodlands to create views from the house over the park and the estate and in the opposite direction from the park to the house. Nature was put under strict human control.

From 1660 further development of existing parks and the creation of many new ones took place. Existing parks were enlarged, and tree planting became the rage, greatly influenced by the writings of John Evelyn.[2] More trees extending over more and more acres were seen as a great status symbol, symbolising ownership and landed power. The word park came to be a synonym for house, park and estate and whole estates incorporated the name park in their name – local examples being Sandbeck Park and Kiveton Park.

Great swathes were cut through the planted trees, often in the shape of what the French called a *patte d'oie* (goose foot), a semi-circular space from which three, five or seven avenues radiated from it (Figure 6.1). And tree-lined avenues for riding and walking continued to be important – there were, for example, 4,000 planted trees in the avenues at Hampton Court by 1700. Avenues and canals were both features of the French royal park at Versailles created by le Notre and these began to be much imitated in England. In the last two decades of the

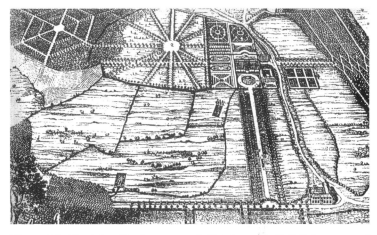

Figure 6.1. *Great tree-lined avenues at Stainborough Hall (later renamed Wentworth Castle) portrayed by Leedert Knyf and engraved by Jan Kip, c 1714*

century Dutch influence became increasingly significant, not only in the growing of tulips but in the introduction of topiary and water features, not only canals, but cascades and fountains.

Then in the eighteenth century came a great revolution in park design. Out went symmetry, orderliness and regularity and in came informality and naturalness. The eighteenth century was the great period of the landscaped park. There were a number of reasons for this great change. It has been said that it reflected political changes following the 'glorious revolution' of 1688 – the replacement of royal despotism by constitutional government – the freeing of the population from tyranny being accompanied, it has been strongly believed, by a desire to free the landscape from the clasp of rigid design. Another important influence that grew as the eighteenth century advanced was the strong impact that foreign travel had on the sons of the country's leading families during their Grand Tour on the continent of Europe. The landscapes they saw in Italy, with their classical ruins, and the landscape paintings they viewed, had a deep impact and there was an increasing desire to sweep away the regularity of the landscapes they were to inherit and to replace them with a more natural landscape. Another reason was supposed to be the great expense incurred in creating and maintaining heavily planted parks, although it must be said that in many cases their more natural successors proved to be just as expensive.

The new landscaped parks were characterised by hundreds of acres of rolling grassland, in some parks substantially re-contoured, by naturally shaped woodland and clumps of trees, and large expanses of water, usually created by widening and deepening the beds of streams to form winding lakes called serpentines (Figure 6.2). These natural-looking but often largely artificial landscapes were dotted with a range of buildings in a variety of architectural styles ranging from necessary edifices such as lodges at the entrances to the park, stable blocks, deersheds and boathouses, to the useful such as temples and other roofed buildings with open sides from which the park could be viewed, and where tea and shelter from inclement weather could be taken during a circuit of the park on horseback or by carriage, to purely monumental obelisks, pyramids and mausoleums.

The rolling grassland sometimes swept right up to the front door of newly-built mansions as they still do in South Yorkshire at Wentworth Woodhouse and Cusworth Hall. In both cases the garden was relegated to a position at the side of or behind the mansion. Where the garden fronted onto the park, existing walls were removed and were replaced by a ha-ha. This was a dry moat with a sloping side facing the park and with a vertical

Figure 6.2. *View across the park at Cusworth Hall from the serpentine lake*

wall on the side nearest the garden. This sunken fence gave un-interrupted views from the house and garden across the landscaped parkland while at the same time ensuring that grazing deer, cattle or sheep did not trample or consume the garden plants. Complete ha-has still survive separating the garden from the park at Wentworth Castle, Wortley Hall and Cannon Hall (Figure 6.3).

Great names are associated with the development of local landscaped parks. Lancelot 'Capability' Brown worked in South Yorkshire, having been in charge of re-designing the park at Sandbeck Park and converting the remains of Roche Abbey into a romantic ruin 'with a poet's eye and a painter's feeling'[3]

Figure 6.3. The ha-ha separating the garden from the park at Cannon Hall

for the 4th Earl of Scarbrough between 1774 and 1777 at a cost of £3,000. In the park at Sandbeck he built a sunken fence (a ha-ha), created lakes, planted trees, laid out walks and a carriageway. Humphry Repton also did some late work on the park at Wentworth Woodhouse. A less-well-known landscape designer who made the biggest impact in South Yorkshire was Richard Woods, at Cannon Hall and Cusworth Hall.

In the nineteenth century the plantings of the eighteenth century matured and the private landscaped parks of the previous century kept their essential outlines and character. The last two centuries have, however, seen great changes of ownership and use of great country houses and their parks, nationally and locally. Some local houses and their parks and gardens like Nostell Priory, in West Yorkshire, have come into

the ownership of the National Trust, others, like Brodsworth, into the ownership of English Heritage, while Cannon Hall and Cusworth have been acquired by local authorities. Wentworth Castle, Wentworth Woodhouse and Wortley Hall are in mixed ownership and/or occupation.

ORNAMENTAL GARDENS SURROUNDING COUNTRY HOUSES

As already noted, the sixteenth century was a period of strong and stable central government which led to the abandonment of castles and fortified houses and the building of country houses (still sometimes surrounded by a moat). The period also saw the wealth of the country increase through the widening of foreign trade and the rise of new leading families and a substantial 'squirearchy'.

Both the leading aristocratic families and the country squires laid out formal ornamental gardens close to their houses, and, for those who could afford it, as discussed above, a park stretched beyond the garden. The ornamental garden was usually square or rectangular and surrounded by a hedge, trellis work or for the most affluent, a wall. This boundary fence was to keep out the wind and grazing animals from the surrounding park or neighbouring farmland.

The layout of the Tudor ornamental garden was formal and symmetrical. A common arrangement was for a central path to lead from the front of the house to a series of parterres which were level areas with ornamental gardens, laid out as knot gardens. These usually square 'knotted beds' consisted of formal geometrical patterns formed by dwarf shrubs, most commonly box, or herbs, for example, thyme, hyssop, rosemary or thrift, which were kept closely clipped. The spaces between the tightly clipped shrubs or herbs were either planted with flowers such as primroses or daffodils or strewn with coloured earth, sand, pebbles, brick dust or broken pieces of terra cotta.

Between the house and the far end of the garden, below the enclosing walls or hedges, covered walks were constructed, of shrub-covered trellis work or clipped yew. The walks contained occasional arbours – sometimes in Tudor documents referred to as 'roosting places' – where members of the family or guests could rest or read or converse. Another important feature of the Tudor garden was the 'mount', an artificially made turfed hill which could be climbed via a winding path and from the top of which the knot gardens could be viewed as could the parkland beyond the ornamental garden boundaries. Often an arbour or a summer house was built on the summit of the mount. As the years passed and the sixteenth century passed into the seventeenth a greater variety of exotic flowers and trees began to be grown in the gardens. For example, the Tradescants, father (d. 1638) and son (d. 1662), introduced from North America the tulip tree (Figure 6.4), the red maple, the lupin, phlox and aster (michaelmas daisy).

Locally many features of a Tudor or Stuart garden survived at Wentworth Woodhouse into the second quarter of the eighteenth century and were portrayed in an engraving of *c.* 1730 (Figure 6.5). At that time the Palladian mansion that faces the park had not been built and the engraving shows the westward facing Baroque mansion with the walled ornamental garden laid out in front of it running to the main entrance in Hague Lane. In front of the house is a large lawn divided into four by a wide path and a central drive leading westwards to the gate on Hague Lane. In the centre of each quarter of the lawn stands a large obelisk which were recent additions to the garden. The 1st Marquis of Rockingham said that these were in place by 1729, although he may later have regretted

their prominent position when Horace Walpole said the view looked liked a bowling alley! On the south side of the lawn were five rows of what appear to be pleached trees, probably fruit trees, and beyond these near the south wall other planted trees and placed among them what is probably a bowling green. On the north side of the lawn are three walled beds. West of the lawn is another area of planted trees (a wilderness?) and beyond this a large area laid out mostly as knot gardens, one in a complicated whorl pattern and another looking like a maze. There are two statues on the walks between the beds. Several of the beds appear to contain shrubs and these may be roses. Lastly, at the southern end of this area of the garden is a mount with winding paths climbing to its summit where there is a small tower.

As already noted, 'naturalness' was the keynote of garden design for most of the eighteenth century. Early in the century Joseph Addison wrote scathingly in *The Spectator* of the formal style of gardening found around every country house: 'We see the mark of the scissors on every plant or bush' he wrote, with every tree 'cut and trimmed into a mathematical figure'. He went on to say that in his opinion an orchard in flower was more delightful than 'all the labyrinths of the most finished parterre'. Topiary gardens that had at last grown into maturity were destroyed and straight avenues and formal groupings of trees were replaced by curving paths and informal 'wildernesses'.

A late eighteenth century landscaping style that embraced both garden and park was the 'Picturesque' style most closely associated with Sir Uvedale Price, a Herefordshire landowner. In his *Essays on the Picturesque* (1796) he criticised the monotony and blandness of William Kent's and Lancelot Brown's designs. Instead he was inspired by the Romantic artists such as Poussin

Figure 6.4. *The tulip tree* (Liriodendron tulipifera)

and Claude and advocated a much more rustic and wild land-scape style. Instead of Brown's smooth serpentine river banks, tonsured lawns and elegant groups of trees, Price favoured broken and crumbling river banks, rutted lanes and irregular groups of trees and shrubs. He put his ideas into practice on his own estate. Humphrey Repton, trained originally as a landscape painter, gradually adopted something akin to the Picturesque approach. Repton criticised Brown's 'mistaken system' of creating sweeping lawns up to the walls of the mansion, and often inserted a balustraded garden terrace between the house and the park.

The nineteenth century saw a great many innovations that transformed existing gardens and resulted in the creation of completely new and exciting gardens. The new ideas, partly

Figure 6.5. *The gardens at Wentworth Woodhouse* c 1730.

fuelled by the introduction from all parts of the globe of new flowering plants, shrubs and trees and hybridisation on a large scale, involved new planting schemes and the creation of specialised gardens. The work of a number of influential Victorian and Edwardian plant collectors (such as Robert Fortune, George Forrest and E H 'Chinese' Wilson), garden designers (such as Gertrude Jekyll) and writers (such as William Robinson and Reginald Farrer) also proved very influential.

Imposed naturalness in the garden, based on the planned disposition of trees and shrubs, which had been such an important feature of eighteenth century gardens continued to be of major significance in the nineteenth century. The 'Picturesque' style gave way to the 'Gardenesque' style, invented by George Loudon, in which the trees and shrubs, both native and exotic, were planted and managed in such places and in such a way that they would reach their peak of perfection of growth. Over time the eighteenth century wilderness became a shrubbery with rhododendrons (Figure 6.6), magnolias and camellias, or a collector's garden or an arboretum with newly introduced trees such as the tulip tree, the gingko or the sequoia or even a single-species area such as a pinetum full of pines or a salicetum full of willows including the weeping willow from China. Much later in the century, in 1870, William Robinson introduced in his book of the same name, the idea of 'the wild garden' by 'naturalizing many beautiful plants of many regions of the earth in fields, woods, copses, (and) outer parts of pleasure grounds'.[4] In the twentieth century this idea has developed particularly into the woodland garden in which native or introduced shrubs, climbers and flowers are allowed to become naturalised in a native woodland environment. This is best seen locally at Hodsock Priory in north Nottinghamshire with native woodland carpeted with snowdrops in February and

Figure 6.6. *Looking towards the shrubbery with its rhododendrons at Wortley Hall*

March, and at Renishaw Hall where the Wilderness is carpeted with bluebells in May, and where a new woodland garden has recently been opened to the public.

'Pastiche' gardens, mimicking gardens of different times and different places and cultures, were also a feature of the nineteenth and early twentieth centuries. The Japanese garden, with its pool, bridge, lanterns and perhaps a tea house and featuring Japanese shrubs such as wisteria and *Acer palmatum*, cropped up in the most unusual places in the late nineteenth and early twentieth centuries inspired by a number of Japanese exhibitions in London and Joseph Conder's *Landscape Gardening in Japan* (1903).[5] Such was the western interpretation of the real Japanese garden, that when shown round one at Friar Park in Oxfordshire, the Japanese ambassador is said to have commented: 'Magnificent. We have nothing like it in Japan'. The nearest complete Japanese garden to South Yorkshire, restored in 2001, is at Tatton Park in Cheshire and the only local garden with Japanese features is at Wentworth Woodhouse.

KITCHEN GARDENS
There is a third element to a country house garden in which notable trees may be found – the kitchen garden. Most country house kitchen gardens were centred upon a rectangular-shaped walled garden ranging in size from one acre in the case of a professional family to twenty or thirty acres if it belonged to one of the leading aristocratic families who had not only their immediate families to feed but also a continuous flow of guests and armies of indoor and outdoor servants and estate workers. It was reckoned that an acre of walled kitchen garden would feed about a dozen people throughout the year.[6] The walled kitchen garden at Cannon Hall is 3 acres in extent, that at Wentworth Woodhouse was 4 acres and the one at Wortley Hall 5 acres.

The walls of a kitchen garden, often as high as 12 feet, were usually of brick, a good storer and transmitter of the sun's heat. The shelter the walls provided resulted in an improved micro-climate within the walls and also immediately to the south of the southern wall or to the east of the eastern wall, where an extra sheltered garden, called a slip garden, was often laid out.

And it is fruit trees, growing against the walls, that are likely to be of great age. When fruits were grown against the walls, depending on which wall they were grown, and whether glass was used, fruiting could be accelerated or delayed. In the north of England acceleration of fruiting and protection against late

frosts was not only aided by draping the wall fruits in canvas and matting or erecting portable glass shelters against the walls but also through the expedient of making the walls themselves into 'hot walls'. Hot walls had internal flues fuelled by furnaces with the hot air escaping through chimneys on the tops of the walls. The north and south walls of the kitchen garden at Wentworth Woodhouse were hot walls and the outlines of nine fire houses that supplied the heat can still be seen on the north side of the north wall.

An enormous amount of time and effort was spent in pruning and supporting the fanned (usually peaches, nectarines, apricots and morello cherries) or espaliered and cordon (pears, apples, plums and cherries) fruit trees (Figure 6.7). Nails were bought in their thousands and close inspection of the walls of a

Figure 6.7. Espaliered pear tree at Cannon Hall

country house kitchen garden will still reveal hundreds of rusty nails protruding from the mortar between the lines of bricks and thousands of nail holes. In the eighteenth century and earlier the fruit trees were attached to the nails with cuttings of cloth called 'shreads' or 'lists' obtained from woollen manufacturers or tailors, but the woollen shreds had been replaced by tarred twine by the nineteenth century.

THE HISTORY OF PUBLIC PARKS

The need for publicly-owned managed green spaces in Britain's towns and cities was gradually identified in the first three decades of the nineteenth century as the country rapidly urbanised and urban centres multiplied in number and spread outwards, leaving the urban population – there was no public transport to speak of – increasingly distant from country lanes and green footpaths and un-industrialised riversides. It was to the urban areas that the early park promoters turned their attention. They stressed the physical and social benefits of parks. The motives of the early park promoters, however, were not entirely selfless and altruistic. It was argued that areas where the working classes could take supervised exercise in their spare time, and preferably in family groups, in a parkland atmosphere, would lead to a healthy workforce, promote stable families and dampen down unrest and militancy at work. They also believed that public parks would be places of social mixing thus easing the tensions between people of different classes.

Official recognition of the need for urban parks dates from 1833 when the Select Committee on Public Walks presented its report to Parliament. In the decade following the publication of the Select Committee report a number of pioneering parks were created. South Yorkshire also saw the creation of two very early parks: Sheffield's Botanical Gardens (open on most days only to subscribing members) were opened in 1837 and in 1841 the Duke of Norfolk donated land for Norfolk Park in Sheffield – but this was for use of the land only and the Corporation did not acquire the site itself until 1909. It was not until the Towns Improvement Clauses Act of 1847 that local authorities could buy or rent land specifically for recreation without a local Act of Parliament and they were still not allowed to maintain through the rates land that had been given to them for park development. The passing of the Ten Hour Act (length of the working day) and the Saturday Half Holiday movement provided further stimuli for the municipal park movement and this was reinforced in 1859 by the Recreation Grounds Act, which encouraged the donation of money and land for park development, and the 1860 Public Improvements Act which gave local authorities the power to acquire and manage parks out of the rates. These acts inspired a further flurry of donations and park creations in the 1860s and 1870s. These included in South Yorkshire Locke Park in Barnsley in 1862, Firth Park and Weston Park in Sheffield, both in 1875, and Rotherham Park (now Boston Castle Park) in 1876. What all these parks had in common was that they were reactive – they were developed to solve perceived problems long after, sometimes decades after, those problems had first arisen. It is now estimated that there are 4,000 Victorian or Edwardian public parks in the United Kingdom together with 30,000 other public green spaces, altogether covering 140,000 hectares (350,000 acres).

At the height of their popularity and place in civic pride – as late as the end of the 1960s in many cases – Britain's municipal parks were not only heavily used, they were also splendidly maintained and superintended. Their lodges were occupied by park keepers, they were surrounded (until the Second World War) by freshly painted cast iron railings and splendidly decorated iron gates, and inside there were immaculate carpet-bedding (and in many cases sculptured bedding) schemes, rock gardens, pruned shrubberies, well-managed specimen trees and bodies of water large and small; the meticulously kept grounds punctuated by a range of un-vandalised and un-graffiti-ed park buildings and other structures including refreshment shelters and pavilions in a variety of architectural styles, band-stands, architectural ruins, bridges, drinking fountains and grottoes.

But things began to go downhill rapidly in the 1970s. The Bains Report of 1972 recommended the amalgamation of local authority Parks Departments with Leisure Services, and with local government re-organisation in 1974 Parks Departments lost their identity and parks managers had to vie for their budgets within the new Leisure Services departments that were often creating high-cost sports centres. Coupled with this, the provision of parks is not a statutory responsibility of local authorities and one way of cutting spending to avert rate-capping by central government was to reduce the costs (for maintenance, new equipment and salaries) of the parks for which they had responsibility.

Perhaps the most significant change was the introduction of Compulsory Competitive Tendering (now replaced by 'Best Value' contracting) brought in under the Local Government Act of 1988 when every maintenance job had to be put out to the lowest tender. The number of park staff was drastically reduced and the local authorities merely became the issuer of contracts to landscape businesses that had no connection with a particular park and its history – 'roving gangs of grass cutters' as they have been described by traditionalists.

By the 1990s the nation's public parks were in deep crisis. The buildings in the parks were shabby or derelict, the grounds were often litter-strewn, dog-fouled, shrubs overgrown, the once magnificent flower beds either gone or only a pale imitation of their former glory, the grassed areas brown or weed-infested. Lodges had been sold, seventy per cent of glasshouses had gone, fifty-six per cent of paddling pools had disappeared, as had many bandstands. Thankfully the mature trees mostly survived (Figure 6.8). The parks were not only under-resourced, strategic greenspace planning was inadequate and there was a lack of local political commitment and leadership. Vandalism and neglect were everywhere in evidence.

Now things are changing for the better. There has been a realisation by local and central government that urban parks still have an important role to play in people's lives in

Figure 6.8. Crocuses and daffodils growing beneath a veteran horse chestnut tree in Clifton Park, Rotherham

the twenty-first century. They are psychological safety valves for people living highly pressured and stressful lives; they encourage healthy exercise; they are important social focal points for communities; they can enhance the image of a town or city and attract 'footloose' industries and other employers; and, finally, it has also being increasingly realised that historic urban parks deserve as much care as historic buildings.

Two significant forces in the changing fortunes of Britain's urban public parks are 'people power' and the National Lottery. Now most historic parks have a 'Friends of ...' group. Such groups badger, cajole and persuade their local authority to act positively and decisively and help to secure funding for park regeneration projects. The Heritage Lottery Fund launched its Urban Parks Initiative in 1998 to fund capital works and revenue costs (mainly fixed term staffing) in parks and in the seven years up to 2004 had invested more than £380m in more than 240 parks across the country.[7]

The native and exotic trees and shrubs that are such a feature of public parks and gardens across the region have two quite different origins. Many, of course, have been planted over the last 150 years by the arboriculturists and other park staff employed by the local authorities who created and managed the parks, but others are the legacy of the previous private owners of the land on which the parks were developed, which was either purchased or donated for public use.

A TREE TOUR OF SOUTH YORKSHIRE'S PARKS AND GARDENS

The parks and gardens attached to former mansions and country houses and Victorian and Edwardian municipal parks contain a variety of ancient, veteran and notable trees.[8] An **ancient tree** is an aged tree, usually with a very wide trunk, a shrinking canopy, often 'stag-headed' and often hollow. Examples of ancient trees are the sessile oak with a trunk of 23 feet (7 m) in circumference at Wortley Hall and the yew at Thryft House (see Chapter 7). A **veteran tree** has some but not all the features of an ancient tree but not necessarily because of its age. It may be a relatively young tree. But a veteran bears the scars of a tough life such as loss of branches, decay in the trunk or roots and fungal fruiting bodies. A **notable tree** is one that stands out in its local environment, because it is an unusual species locally or because it is a local landmark or because of its size (but not its age). Obvious examples of notable trees in South Yorkshire are the magnificent sweet chestnut in front of the house at Cannon Hall and the horse chestnut with seating around it in the village of Wortley. Groups of trees may also be called notable, for example, the Turkey oak avenue in Norfolk Park, Sheffield.

Sheffield Botanical Gardens. Perhaps this is the best place to start, although planting of trees did not begin until 175 years ago. These gardens have the most comprehensive collection of native and non-native trees in South Yorkshire. Moreover each tree carries a small label with its English and botanical name. Here you can become familiar with the form, the bark, the leaves, the blossoms and the seeds of unfamiliar trees before embarking on explorations of other sites where most if not all the trees and shrubs are unlabelled.

If you start your tour via the main entrance on Clarkehouse Road you are immediately bombarded by magnificent specimens or unusual species: within a short space there is a strawberry tree, an Atlas cedar, a copper beech and a fine Corstorphine sycamore. The latter (*Acer pseudoplatanus Corstorphinense*), distinguished by its bright yellow leaves, takes its odd name from the suburb of Edinburgh where the oldest known specimen stood.[9] This Scottish tree is thought to have been planted in 1600 and did not die until 1998 when it was blown down in a storm. It was thought to be a survivor from an avenue that led to Corstorphine Castle. If you then take the path down the slope to the left of the ponds in the rock and water garden, on the left there is a Japanese pagoda tree, a Judas tree, an Austrian pine and a huge beech tree. If you continue down the hill you pass a paper bark maple (*Acer griseum*), an Indian horse chestnut and a 'fastigiate' hornbeam, 'fastigiate' meaning that its branches rise steeply giving the tree a tapering outline.

At this point you need to turn right and walk up the long border beside the southern edge of the gardens. Halfway along you come to what is probably the most important group of trees in the gardens growing around an ancient fossilised tree. This is the Evolution Garden. Growing close to each other are a coastal redwood, a dawn redwood, a giant sequoia or 'Wellingtonia' and a ginkgo or maidenhair tree. Fossils of the coast redwood (*Sequoia sempervirens*) have been found not only in the western United States but also in Britain, although the living tree is only naturally found in the Pacific coast states of America, principally in coastal California, where some specimens are believed to be 2,500 years old. It grows to a great height and the 'tallest tree in the world' in Tall Tree Grove, Redwood Creek, California is almost 368 feet (112 m) tall.[10] It was introduced to Britain as an ornamental tree in the 1840s. Not very far away is a dawn redwood (*Metasequoia glyptostroboides*) with its rough, red, fibrous bark and its bright green needles on short branchlets. The needles turn a russet-brown before falling in the Autumn. Until 1941, when a specimen was recognised in Hupeh province in China, it was believed that this tree was extinct and it was only known from fossils. In 1948 seeds were sent to the Arnold Arboretum in Boston, USA and

from there over the years trees have been planted all over the world.[11] Within a short distance is another sequoia this time the giant sequoia or Wellingtonia (*Sequoiadendron giganteum*) native to Sierra Nevada in California where it was discovered in 1852 (Figure 6.9). It can live for 4,000 years. The tree is popularly known in this country as Wellingtonia, after the Duke of Wellington, on whose estate at Stratfield Saye in Hampshire it was planted in 1857, the year of the duke's death. Nearby is a ginkgo tree (*Ginkgo biloba*), another ancient tree whose fossilised remains have been found dating back 250 million years. It was introduced to Europe from China in the eighteenth century. It is easily recognised from its unusual leaves which are like a fan with a small v-shaped gap in the middle. Lastly, in the Asia Garden, next door to the Evolution Garden, is a specimen of what has been called the most beautiful coniferous tree in the world, Brewer's weeping spruce (*Picea breweriana*) with its weeping branchlets hanging like curtains and festooned with its long cones. This tree, which is native to the mountains of northern California and southern Oregon is named after the botanist W. H. Brewer (1828–1910).

Wortley Hall. The gardens at Wortley Hall contain, in a relatively small area, a wonderful collection of ancient, veteran and notable trees, both native and exotic. At the back of the house just before reaching the parking spaces overlooking the ha-ha there is a very tall Wellingtonia and not far away at the side of the drive there is a Bhutan pine (*Pinus wallichiana*), originating in the Himalayas and introduced into this country in the second decade of the nineteenth century. It is easily recognised from its long banana-like cones. Immediately at the side of the house overlooking the ha-ha into the former Old Park, now farmland, is a veteran horse chestnut tree (*Aesculus hippocastanum*) 15 feet 6 inches (4.7 m) in circumference at breast height (Figure 6.10). The horse chestnut was introduced into this country from its native Greece and Albania in the early seventeenth century. To give some idea of its age, a tree in Northamptonshire known to have been planted in 1762 has a circumference at breast height of 5.37 m. If you walk in a south-easterly direction on the path between the wilderness area and the ha-ha you arrive at a mighty beech tree with a trunk 19 feet 4 inches (5.89 m) in circumference which may be more than 300 years old. Beech, although a native tree, is not native to South Yorkshire but was widely planted in the region's woods and parkland in the nineteenth century. Thirty or 40 metres along the path just before it turns in a south-westerly direction is a veteran sweet chestnut (*Castanea sativa*) with a trunk circumference of 14 feet 9 inches (4.5 m)) and there is an even larger one with a trunk circumference of 18 feet 10 inches. Sweet chestnuts, formerly known as Spanish chestnuts, may have been introduced to this country by the Romans. They grow faster than horse chestnuts and are difficult to age. Many of the sweet chestnuts growing in the famous groves at Croft Castle in Herefordshire, believed to have been planted about 1760 have trunk diameters of more than 2.5m. Further along the path are two veteran sessile oak trees, the one inside the ha-ha having a trunk circumference of 12 feet (3.67 m) and with a great hole in its side. Just beyond these is a large lime tree with a trunk circumference of 13 feet (3.9 m). The walk continues beside the fish pond to the ancient sessile oak with a trunk circumference of 23 feet (7 m). This is almost certainly not a planted tree but a survivor from the period when the gardens were part of the medieval Old Park. It must be at least 600 years old. Further along the path is fringed on both sides by an ancient holly hedge (look closely at the large trunks). On the left beyond the hedge is a small collection of rowans including the

scarlet-berried Sargent rowan (*Sorbus sargentiana*) (Figure 6.11) and the white-berried Hupeh rowan (*S. hupehensis*), both of which originate in Western China. On the path beside the kitchen garden wall just before the hall is reached is an old yew whose canopy rises from a tangle of trunks and then flops on the ground (Figure 6.12). The canopy is more than 180 feet (46 m) in circumference.

Cannon Hall Park and Gardens. This park and its associated gardens also contain a great variety of interesting trees, native and introduced, young and old. For example, a walk can be taken that begins outside the bottom car park. At the bottom of the drive up to the house there are two mature hornbeams on the left-hand side. Although hornbeam is a native tree it is not native to South Yorkshire and north of a line roughly between Cambridge and Bristol it is a planted tree. It is an attractive tree of parkland but was grown in local woods because its timber is very hard (horn = hard) and was used for making cogwheels and butchers' blocks. On the right hand side of the drive just beyond the car park, there is an interesting mixed group of trees including the deodar cedar, Corsican pine and holm oak. The deodar cedar (*Cedrus deodara*) is native to the slopes of the Himalayas and was introduced into this country in 1831. What is unusual about the holm oak (*Quercus ilex*), which is a native of the western Mediterranean that was introduced to this country in about 1500, is that it is evergreen, hence its name holm oak, holm being an old name for holly. The Corsican pine (*Pinus nigra* var. *maritima*) was introduced to this country in 1799. Besides being found in parkland it has long been grown in plantations where its timber was made into pit props. Beside these evergreens there is a small group of 'fastigiate' hornbeams.

To the north of this group of trees there is a magnificent Turkey oak (*Quercus cerris*) with a circumference at breast

Figure 6.9. Giant sequoia in Sheffield Botanical Gardens

Figure 6.10. Horse chestnut at Wortley Hall

height of over 17 feet (5.2 m). The timber of this oak tree, which was introduced from Turkey in the second half of the nineteenth century, proved to be disappointing, being susceptible to warping and distorting and therefore is unsuitable for use out of doors. Despite this it makes a handsome parkland tree. Its most distinguishing feature is its acorn which is produced in a mossy cup. Near the top of the drive on the left there is a tulip tree (*Liriodendron tulipifera*) recognisable from the peculiar-shaped leaves which are long-stalked and have four lobes with a flattened top. The tree is native to North America where it was known as the canoe tree, large canoes being made from its hollowed-out trunk. Beyond the tulip tree just before turning

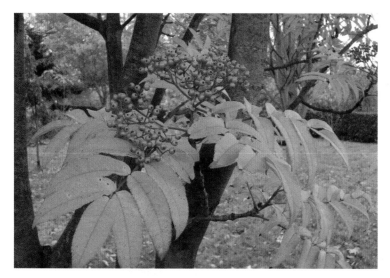

Figure 6.11. The scarlet-berried Sargent rowan (Sorbus sargentiana) *at Wortley Hall*

Figure 6.12. Yew at Wortley Hall

right at the top of the drive is another old oak with a circumference at breast height of over 16 feet (4.9 m).

The main path at the top of the drive turns right along a short avenue of limes. If this avenue is ignored and the visitor takes the path almost straight ahead this leads to a group of hollies and yews that has three interesting trees in it or beside it. Just before reaching the hollies and yews there is a beech tree with a circumference at breast height of 17 feet (5.2 m), in the middle of the hollies and yews there is a giant sequoia and a short distance away towards the mansion there is a dawn redwood.

The tree tourist should then return to the front of the mansion, where at the far end overlooking the park is an enormous sweet chestnut (Figure 6.13). In Spring the twisted bark can be inspected, twisting as one writer put it, like a flamenco dancer's skirt! In Autumn the tree is a glorious sight as its leaves turn to a gorgeous yellow and orange. Just down the slope from the sweet chestnut is another dawn redwood. At this point the visitor should enter the kitchen garden where there are nearly forty varieties of pear some of them reputed to be 200 years old. They are mostly grown against the walls as fans or espaliers. Look out for 'le Lectier' which is full of blossom in mid-April; 'Jargonelle' with its very thick trunk and 'Pitmaston Duchess' which is a most beautiful fan shape.

At the far end of the 'balloon' garden on the right there are two large multi-trunked holm oaks and a cedar of Lebanon

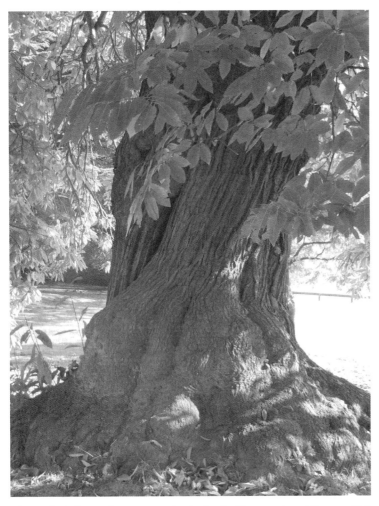

Figure 6.13. Sweet chestnut growing in front of the mansion at Cannon Hall

(*Cedrus libani*) and on the left there is a large Atlas cedar (*Cedrus atlantica*). Similar to the cedar of Lebanon, this cedar is native to North Africa where it grows in the Atlas mountains of Algeria and Morocco. It was introduced to Britain in 1841. From there on the path down to 'Fairyland' there is a very large variegated sycamore. The sycamore (*Acer pseudoplatanus*), which was introduced to Britain from mainland Europe about 400 years ago, has got a bad reputation for spreading relentlessly by seed and taking over native woodlands. But it makes good shelter belts near the coast where it is impervious to salt-laden winds, and in the uplands where it can withstand high winds and even in urban areas it is not affected by pollution. The variegated sycamore makes a fine ornamental tree. From the variegated sycamore, if you turn right and right again you find yourself in a grassed area surrounded mostly by rhododendrons, but if you look carefully you will find two small, but unusual trees, the fruiting medlar (*Mespilus germanica*), originally from the Caucasus, and the Indian bean tree. The latter (*Catalpa bignonioides*) is not from India but the southern United States. The leaves on this tree do not appear before June each year but earlier in the year if you look carefully on the ground beneath the tree you will find the bean- like seed pods which can be up to 16 inches (40 cm) long.

Finally, on retracing your steps to the car park look carefully at the trees beside the serpentine lake where there are some fine specimens of weeping willow.

Wentworth Castle. Like Cannon Hall, the park and gardens at Wentworth Castle, also contain a very varied collection of native and introduced trees. On the walk up to the gardens from the Long Barn Visitor Centre the visitor passes a number of fine lime trees, a London plane, easily recognised from the creamy patches on its trunk, and a weeping ash. The East

Park, dotted with trees including some veteran hawthorns (Figure 6.14), slopes away to the east towards the Serpentine Lake, while to the south is the Great South Avenue in which more than 100 new trees have been planted to replace damaged trees in this double avenue of oaks and limes.

As the visitor crosses the ha-ha over the stone bridge into the gardens there is a fine holm oak and a number of cedars. At this point the Union Jack garden is entered with a number of newly pollarded hollies. Beyond the Union Jack garden as the visitor walks west and north-west towards Stainborough Castle there are rhododendrons on all sides. Inside the perimeter walls of

Figure 6.14. The East Park at Wentworth Castle which is dotted with veteran hawthorns

Stainborough Castle are ten mature Corsican pines. From the Castle a path takes the visitor through the 'Informal' Wilderness to the beginning of Lady Lucy's Walk (Figure 6.15). This is a very fine absolutely straight avenue of tall common lime trees (*Tilia X europaea*) planted about 1920. The Lady Lucy in question was the daughter of Thomas Wentworth who, legend has it, died of a broken heart after falling in love with one of the estate gardeners, and, because of the difference in their social status, was refused permission to marry him by her father. Towards the bottom of the walk a diversion to the right into the Azalea Garden brings the visitor to a gnarled veteran sweet chestnut.

Wentworth Woodhouse. Part of the former gardens to the mansion are now part of Wentworth Garden Centre and can be visited for a small fee. If the visitor walks beside the wall of the kitchen garden the gardens are entered through an arched gateway beyond which there was once a privet maze. This was uprooted in the 1960s but was replanted with yew to mark the Millennium. If the visitor turns right through another gate and walks beside the fallow deer enclosure on the left at the far end there is a large London plane with a circumference at breast height of more than 13 feet (about 4 m).

A side-path and steps lead to a sunken Japanese garden, designed by Countess Maud, wife of the 7th Earl. There was a heavily-publicised and heavily visited Japan-British exhibition at the White City, London in 1910 which contained two large Japanese gardens. Following the exhibition many new gardens were created in the Japanese style. Perhaps Maud Fitzwilliam visited the exhibition and decided to instil a Japanese element in the existing rock and fern garden. A number of features of a Japanese garden survive including the pond against the quarry wall, the remains of Japanese stone lanterns and a number of

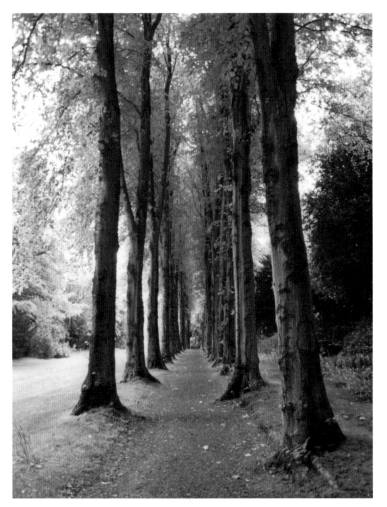

Figure 6.15. Lady Lucy's Walk at Wentworth Castle

Japanese plants including two Japanese maples that glow scarlet in the Autumn.

To the north of the Japanese garden there is a more formal garden, sometimes known as the Italianate garden, with interesting water features. Connecting the two gardens is a small area containing Countess Maud's wisteria-covered tea-house which is overlooked by a Japanese larch. Nearby there are two weeping copper beeches, one of which shelters beneath its weeping canopy, the statue of a large dog. The formal garden contains three large limes and one very large horse chestnut. If the visitor climbs the steps out of the formal garden there are beautiful views from the west down into the Japanese garden. At this upper level there are two large laburnums and running along the outside of the garden wall there is a row of horse chestnuts.

Brodsworth Hall. The drive from the car park up to the house at Brodsworth Hall is lined with interesting trees but these pale into insignificance when the magnificent cedar of Lebanon comes into view on the lawn in front of the house. The circumference of the trunk of this tree at breast height is nearly 23 feet (7 m). Its natural home is in Lebanon and the mountains of southern Turkey. The first written record of a cedar of Lebanon in England was in 1659. The tree was used extensively in his landscaping schemes by 'Capability' Brown in the eighteenth century. In 1891 the Royal Horticultural Society placed it fifth in order of preference as a park tree.[12] Round the southern side of the house and extending at the side of the west lawns and the formal flower garden as far as the classical summer house the garden is edged with a tightly clipped yew hedge in places in the shape of castle battlements in others like giant igloos with statues on plinths in front. In front of the hedge are more tightly clipped evergreen balls –

mainly yew, box, holly and laurel. At the far end of the hedge just in front of the classical temple is a holm oak clipped like a giant globe.

If the visitor takes the path through the middle of the west lawns and through the middle of the formal flower garden, he/she will pass among the shaped beds with their spring or summer bedding, depending on the season, a pair of large deodar cedars and then a pair of monkey-puzzle trees or Chile pines (*Araucaria araucana*) (Figure 6.16). Its popular English name is said to be derived from the fact that a nineteenth century visitor to an early planted tree commented that a monkey would find it puzzling to climb the tree because of its sharp spined leaves and downward pointing branchlets. The French call it *désespoir des singes* (monkeys' despair). It is said that the tree reached England in 1795 after Archibald Menzies, botanist on George Vancouver's ship HMS *Discovery*, saved the seeds that he had been offered as a dessert at a dinner hosted by the governor of Chile and planted them on board HMS *Discovery*. At the far end of the formal flower garden is a long laburnum arch. To the north of the formal flower garden beyond the wild flower meadow is a stand of a dozen Corsican pines.

Between the fernery and the Target House near the quarry face is a dawn redwood, just beyond that a deodar cedar, three ginkgo trees and hanging on the bank beside the Target House is a very large beech tree. Near the top of the Acer Walk that takes the visitor from the Target House along the back of the fernery back to the formal flower garden is a large Wellingtonia with a circumference at breast height of just over 14 feet (4.4 m). Near the old game larder to the north of the hall are a few strawberry trees, *Arbutus unedo* and *A. andrachnoides*, which have lychee-like fruits in October which ripen to a rich

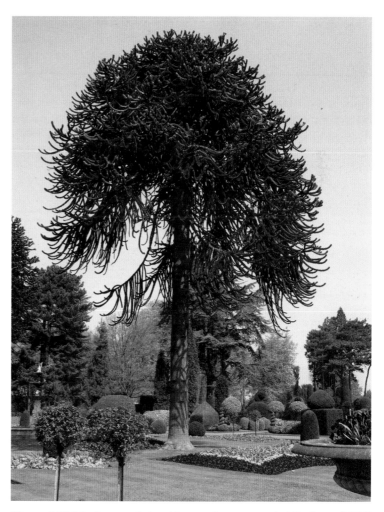

Figure 6.16. *Monkey-puzzle tree (*Araucaria araucana*) at Brodsworth Hall*

strawberry red. The strawberry tree only grows wild in the British Isles in western Ireland. Finally in this part of the garden there are more clipped evergreens in a myriad of shapes. (Figure 6.17).

Cusworth Hall. The park at Cusworth Hall was landscaped in its present form on behalf of the owner, John Battie, with its convex-shaped slope running down to the serpentine lake with its grotto-like boathouse, by Richard Woods in 1761. Since that date many trees have come and gone but there is still a great variety to be inspected. The tour of the park is in the form of an anti-clockwise walk down the slope on the edge of the park to the right of the house, then along the bottom of the park beside

the serpentine lake before turning up the slope again at the far end of the park beside the old kitchen garden wall. After leaving the car park and walking towards the top of the park there is a fine beech tree with a circumference at breast height of 12 feet and 5 inches (3.8 m). As you walk down the slope on the edge of the park on your right you pass a mixed broad-leaved plantation before coming to a magnificent sweet chestnut tree (Figure 6.18). Because of the low growing branches it is impossible to measure accurately the circumference of the trunk at breast height but the size of the tree can be gauged by the fact that a foot or so above ground level the circumference is 20 feet and 4 inches (6.22 m) and the biggest of the low

Figure 6.17. Clipped evergreens at Brodsworth Hall

Figure 6.18. Magnificient sweet chestnut tree at Cusworth Hall

growing branches near the trunk measures more than seven feet (more than 2 m). Nearby there is a holm oak and a Turkey oak and on the island in the serpentine lake there is a weeping willow.

It is at the bottom of the slope at the far end of the park and all the way up the slope that one encounters the widest variety of trees in the park. At the bottom of the slope near the bridge over the lake there is a black Italian poplar, a London plane and a sweet chestnut. On the lower part of the slope there is a veteran sweet chestnut with a circumference at breast height of 18 feet (5.5 m). From there up the slope there is a bewildering variety of trees including two large laburnums, a tulip tree, a number of deodar cedars, a strawberry tree and at the top of the slope two copper beeches and a fastigiate hornbeam.

Public parks. Besides Sheffield Botanical Gardens other public parks across the region have their fair share of interesting trees. For example, **Norfolk Park** in Sheffield boasts two fine avenues of trees, one of lime and the other of Turkey oak, the latter reputed to be the longest avenue of Turkey oak in Europe. The park also boasts an ancient wood, Jervis Lum. There is another fine avenue of limes in **Hillsborough Park**, Sheffield, dating back to the time when the park surrounded Hillsborough Hall built in 1779 and which was in private hands until 1890. **Chapeltown Park**, created in the early twentieth century also has some interesting trees including weeping willows, copper beeches, Norway maples, a hybrid *Catalpa* (*Catalpa ovata*), a ginkgo and a tree of heaven, besides containing part of the former Hesley Wood with mature sessile oak and ash and planted beech. The wood is carpeted in spring and early summer with ancient woodland indicators including wood anemone, bluebell, ramsons, dog's mercury and wood melick. **Hexthorpe Flatts** in Doncaster, which became a park

in 1902 has an area called the Dell, formerly a quarry, which is full of interesting trees including a weeping birch, a weeping willow, a dawn redwood, a tree of heaven, a Tibetan cherry and two ginkgos (Figure 6.19). The park also contains an avenue of London plane trees and another of sycamores. An unusual and richly treed public garden which is worth a visit is **Whinfell Quarry Gardens,** created in 1908. In a recent survey 162 trees in the garden were identified, including two very tall Wellingtonias, one reaching a height of over 91 feet (28 m) and the other 88 feet (27 m). It is said that the seeds from which these trees grew were brought back from North America by the owner of Whinfell House, Samuel Doncaster, a Sheffield industrialist who was a very keen plant collector.

Figure 6.19. Ginkgo (Ginkgo biloba) *at Hexthorpe Flatts*

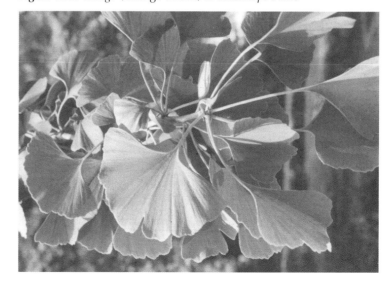

What to read about trees and shrubs in parks and gardens

EDLIN, H. L. (1944) *British Woodland Trees*, Batsford.

EDLIN, H. L. (1958) *The Living Forest: A History of Trees and Timbers*, Thames and Hudson.

JONES, J. and JONES, M. (2005) *Historic Parks and Gardens in and around South Yorkshire*, Wharncliffe Books.

MABEY, R. (1998) *Flora Britannica*, the compact edition, Chatto & Windus.

MILES, A. (1999) *Silva The Tree in Britain*, Ebury Press.

MILES, A. (2006) *The Trees that made Britain*, BBC Books.

MILNER, J. E. (1992) *The Tree Book*, Collins & Brown Ltd.

MITCHELL, A. and MORE, D. (1985) The *Complete Guide to Trees of Britain and Northern Europe*, Dragon's World.

PAKENHAM, T. (1996) *Meetings with Remarkable Trees*, Weidenfeld & Nicolson.

READER'S DIGEST (1981) *Field Guide to the Trees and Shrubs of Britain*.

Places to visit

Tour South Yorkshire's parks and gardens. A good place to start is Sheffield Botanical Gardens because almost all the trees are labelled. Visits at different seasons of the year enable the tree enthusiast to study shape and bark (in Winter), buds and blossom (in Spring), leaf shape and colour (Summer and Autumn) and berries, cones and other fruits (Autumn). A tree identification book that easily slips in the pocket is always useful.

TREES AND SHRUBS IN THE WIDER LANDSCAPE

THIS CHAPTER IS concerned with the trees and shrubs in the wider landscape beyond the ancient woods and country house parks and gardens. It discusses the trees and shrubs that form our linear woodlands – our hedgerows – or were once managed to provide winter feed for livestock or are plantations created to provide an income from the sale of timber or planted by water authorities to protect our water supplies or planted to cover old bell pit workings for ironstone and coal or old colliery tips. It also considers trees that simply stand alone in the landscape – for example in the middle of a field or on a windswept moorland or in a churchyard or mark an old property boundary. Finally, street trees are discussed.

HEDGEROWS AND HEDGEROW TREES

The hedged countryside of England (Figure 7.1) evokes a response from the general public that is equalled only by a bluebell wood in Spring or the sight of large numbers of seabirds nesting on a high sea cliff. But hedgerows are valued not only by the public at large, but by the pastoral farming community, by conservationists and landscape historians. Words and phrases used to describe the hedged countryside range from 'the framework of the countryside', to 'the stitching that holds the countryside together', and 'the patchwork quilt' of the countryside. Many people think that hedges are a peculiar British artefact and that they originated between 150–250 years ago in the great Parliamentary enclosure movement. Both of these assumptions are completely false. Hedges can also be found in a variety of other places, for example in Normandy, in

Figure 7.1. A hedged landscape between Hooton Roberts and Old Denaby

the Austrian Alps, in northern Italy, in the United States from New England to Texas and even in the Andes. In this country some hedges in Devon and Cornwall date from the Bronze Age and in any relatively small area of the English countryside it is likely that there are hedges dating from the Anglo-Saxon period, from the medieval period, from Tudor times, as well as from the Georgian and Victorian periods.

In terms of their physical appearance and associated earthworks, hedges across South Yorkshire come in various forms. Some hedges are composed simply of a stock-proof hedge without hedgerow trees. Others have hedgerow trees at fairly regular intervals. Sometimes the trees show evidence of pollarding in the past. Some hedges stand on low banks; others are on banks against revetted stone walls. In low-lying areas wet drainage ditches often parallel hedges which again may be on a low bank. In terms of management (or lack of it) hedges may show evidence that they were once laid (or 'plashed' as the process was called in the West Riding) by a hedger using a hedging tool, the billhook, and in a tiny minority of cases this may have been done relatively recently (Figure 7.2). Others may have been managed mechanically, either trimmed or shaped or, if managed more severely, they may have been pollarded. Many look overgrown and in need of drastic management and some may have been severely and regularly grazed

Figure 7.2. A hedge being laid near Woodhouse, south-east Sheffield

so that at best they are gappy and at worst have only the appearance of a remnant hedge with very large gaps.

What is often forgotten now is how important hedges were in the past, not just for separating one property from another or being a stock-proof barrier or for providing shade for livestock. The trees in hedgerows provided a valuable renewable resource. For example on the dissolution of Roche Abbey, Henry VIII sold the abbey's properties in Barnby and Bramwith to Richard Turke of London. At the time of the sale it was recorded that growing on the property including in 'the hedges inclosing the landes apperteyning to the same' were 140 oaks and ashes of sixty years and eighty years growth 'moste parte usually cropped and shred'. 'Cropped' in this case most probably means pollarded and 'shred' means the cutting off of the side branches, the harvest being used for various purposes including fodder (called leaf fodder) for livestock. The document goes on to record that sixty of the trees were reserved for housebote, to repair houses in the manor and for stakes for hedgebote 'to repayre and maynteyne the said hedges'.[1] In the nineteenth century hedgerow trees were regularly included in the timber sales on the Duke of Norfolk's estate in Sheffield and Rotherham. For example, at a sale in 1815, along with falls of wood in Greno Wood, Prior Wood and Little Roe Wood, Lot 4 was the 'Hedge Rows in Edward Vickers Farm' consisting of 130 trees with the 'Bark and Tops'.[2]

After centuries of being taken for granted, over the last forty years accelerating hedgerow loss has been brought to the attention of the public in a series of campaigning books such as Marion Shoard's *Theft of the Countryside* (1980)[3] and Graham Harvey's *The Killing of the Countryside* (1997)[4] and campaigns led by organisations such as the Campaign for the Protection of Rural England (CPRE) and the Royal Society for the Protection of Birds (RSPB). It has been the replacement of the working horse by the tractor, the introduction of the combine harvester and the enlargement of fields in those areas where intensive arable farming has become almost a monoculture that have been at the root of the problem. Such areas of intense arable farming include in South Yorkshire large areas in the eastern part of the coalfield zone, more or less the whole of the Magnesian Limestone belt and large parts of the eastern lowlands. By the year 2000 it was estimated that since 1945, fuelled by central government subsidies and The European Community's Common Agricultural Policy (CAP), 150,000 miles (240,000 km)

of hedgerows had been grubbed up in England and Wales. Figure 7.3 shows the hedge boundaries in the Hooton Levitt – Laughton-in-le-Morthen area of Rotherham, in 1830 (map A) and 2000 (map B). The loss of hedgerows in the area is astounding. Even roadside hedges have disappeared over large stretches.

In the coalfield zone it was not only agricultural changes that caused hedgerow loss. Opencast coal mining also played its part. Figure 7.4(A) shows the field boundaries, mostly hedges, in part of Wentworth township in 1854. Figure 7.4(B) shows the same area after opencast coal mining had taken place in the 1940s and 1950s. The area to the south of the stream was

Figure 7.3. The hedged landscape in the Hooton Levitt - Laughton-en-le Morthen area, in map A as surveyed between 1830–1834 and in map B in 2000

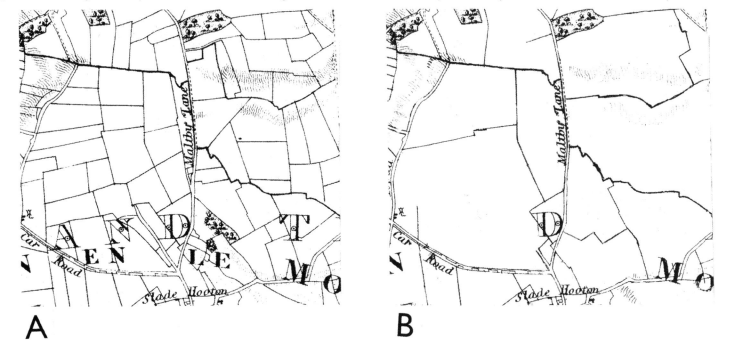

A   B

untouched by opencast mining and retains its mid-nineteenth century field boundaries. Most of the rest of the area lost its old hedges, walls and hedgerow trees and a new field pattern was established, each field separated from its neighbours by concrete post and wire fences (shown by dotted lines). The concrete post and wire fences of the new fields have only recently been replaced by hawthorn hedges.

There are three types of field pattern surrounded by hedges throughout the region. First there are long, fairly narrow, some-times strongly or weakly reverse S-shaped fields that mark the enclosure of bundles of former open-field strips. The reverse S-shape developed because of the need to turn the plough team (usually a team of oxen in the medieval period) at the end of the ploughed strip. Some of these open-field enclosures are likely to date from Tudor times when the open-field system started to break up but others may date from the Georgian or Victorian periods between 1750 and 1830 when the last of the surviving bundles of open-field strips were enclosed.

Figure 7.4. Map A shows field patterns, almost all hedgerows, south of Wentworth village in 1854. Map B shows the same area after opencast mining in the 1940s and 1950s. The new field boundaries (shown by dotted lines) are concrete posts and wire

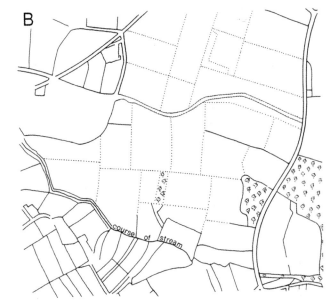

0 ———————————————— 1
kilometre

Then there are the small irregularly shaped fields that reflect 'assarting' activity in the medieval period, that is the painstaking clearance of woodland, scrub and heathland and its enclosure as pasture or cultivated land. This is a particular feature of those parts of the region where the open field system did not become fully developed because the population lived in individual farms or small hamlets as in the Dark Peak and Southern Pennine Fringe zones (where there are more walls than hedges) and in some parts of the eastern lowlands such as the parishes of Fishlake and Sykehouse (see below). Finally there are the large, square or rectangular fields that are typical of the Parliamentary Enclosures that took place between 1750–1830 when through private Acts of Parliament the surviving open fields and common lands were enclosed and shared between landowners in a parish. Figure 7.5 shows the landscape in part of Hoyland Nether township immediately following the enclosure of 1797 in which all three types of field pattern described above, surrounded at that time by a mixture of stone walls and hedges, can be clearly seen. Where a hedge formed part of a parish or township boundary it may be a particularly prominent landscape feature running sinuously across the landscape on a raised bank.

All the landscape clues described above may help us to recognise the origin of the line of a particular hedgerow but do not date the living hedgerow itself. One of the major questions that has tested the minds of a number of leading ecologists, landscape historians and local historians over the last fifty years is 'Is it possible to date a hedge from the shrubs and trees growing in it?' In 1967 Britain's leading local historian, W.G. Hoskins, in his book, *Fieldwork in Local History*, wrote that 'For some years now' he had thought that theoretically hedges of different dates would show significant differences in

their vegetation and that it ought to be possible to arrive at an approximate date for hedges where no documentary date existed from 'a close examination of their constituent vegetation'. He then said that because he had no botanical expertise he had taken his idea no further.[5] He then went on to describe recent pioneering work on hedge dating carried out by Dr Max Hooper of the Nature Conservancy. 'Hooper's hypothesis' or 'Hooper's rule' as it has variously been called came to the

Figure 7.5. Field patterns in part of Hoyland Nether township after Parliamentary enclosure in 1797. At A are long, narrow, reverse-S shaped fields showing the location of enclosed bundles of former open field strips; at B are irregular-shaped fields typical of medieval assarting; at C are regular square or rectangular fields reflecting the recent Parliamentary Enclosure of common land

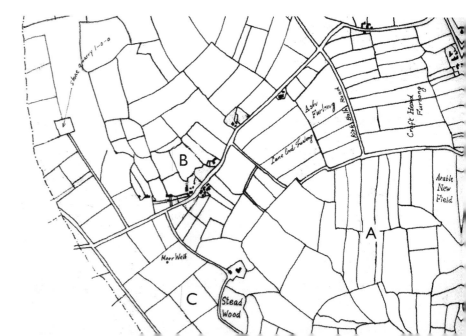

attention of the public at large in its full form in 1974, in the seminal book on the subject, *Hedges*.[6] Simply, Hooper used randomly selected 30 yard stretches of hedge and the equation

$$\text{Age of hedge} = (110 \times \text{number of species}) + 30 \text{ years}$$

Using this equation a random 30 yard stretch of hedge containing eight different species is 910 years old. He then went on to say that the calculation was only an approximate one and could be out as much as 200 years on either side, so that the eight species stretch of hedge would then be calculated to between 710 and 1,110 years old. He did not count under-shrubs such as bramble or climbers like ivy.

He arrived at his equation on the basis that the older a hedge is the more species would have been added to it by natural colonization. And he tested his calculation against more than 200 hedges whose date of origin was known from documentary evidence. He admitted that variations could occur because of differences in climate, soil and regional differences in hedgerow management techniques. He emphasized that the method should be treated with caution and not used as 'an immutable law'. The publication of the equation was met with an enthusiastic response from amateurs and professionals alike and numerous hedge dating studies were undertaken and published. Christopher Taylor, for example, a leading field archaeologist, employed by the Royal Commission on Historical Monuments, used it uncritically in his book, *Fields in the English Landscape* (1975).[7] Just over a decade later Oliver Rackham in his book, *The History of the Countryside* (1986), wrote that he considered the technique to be valuable when used together with other evidence and that it had fallen into unjustified

disrepute because it had sometimes been used uncritically. He considered that it should be used with caution north of Derbyshire, because the number of species is likely to be less for climatic reasons.[8] A much more critical view is taken by another popular landscape historian, Richard Muir. In his recent book, *Be Your Own Landscape Detective* (2007), he directly states that the idea that the age of a hedge can be gauged by counting species is a fallacy. He gives eight reasons for this including the fact that hedges were deliberately planted with more than one species, especially useful fruits; that some hedgerow species are very competitive and will monopolise a stretch of hedge; that some parts of the country, because of better soil and climatic conditions have more potential colonizers than others; and that the more species there are growing in a hedge, the less room there is for new colonists. Instead he places much more emphasis on analysing field shapes and types.[9] The debate continues. For example, in 2011 Cyril Johnson, who wrote an early appraisal of Hooper's technique in 1980, revisited the subject and came to the conclusion that hedge dating from species counts ought still to be part of the landscape historian's toolkit, but only a minor one in conjunction with a range of other evidence.[10]

Three examples will highlight the complexities of hedgerow dating. The first is from a small area between the villages of Thorpe Hesley and Scholes in the Coalfield zone. Figure 7.6 shows the field pattern in 1787 as shown on the first known detailed map of the area. It will be noticed that the hedges between the two lanes once separated narrow fields and each hedge has a faint reverse-S shape. These hedges separated bundles of former open field strips in the one open field of Scholes and a small area of communal meadow commemorated respectively in field names such as Town Field and Old Wife's

Dole. The enclosure of the bundles of open field strips, and their cultivation by individual farmers outside any communal system probably dates from the sixteenth century and if this is so, using Hooper's rule, any random 30-yard stretches of surviving hedgerow within or surrounding the former open field ought to contain between four and six species. In fact only one continuous hedge, down the side of Scholes Lane, remains due to opencast mining on the site. In a sample of twelve random 30-yard lengths of the hedge the number of species varied from three to six, with an average of 4.25. Using Hooper's original

Figure 7.6. *Field patterns in Scholes near Rotherham in 1787. The surveyed hedge lies to the north of Scholes Lane between A and B*

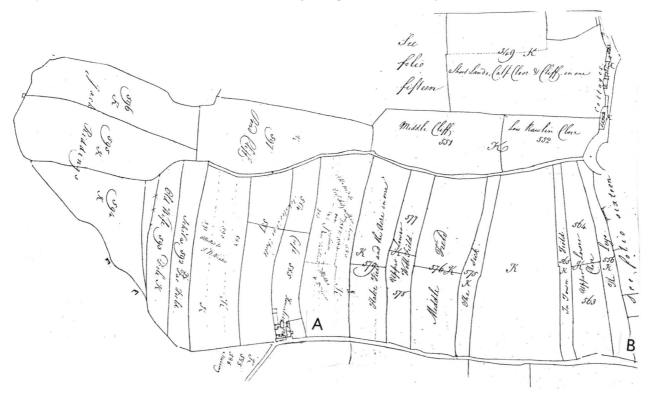

equation this gives an age for the hedge of 497.5 years (i.e. about the year 1500), give or take 200 years, suggesting that it originated sometime between about the year 1300 and the year 1700, which only very roughly coincides with what an analysis of the field shapes suggests, i.e. sometime between 1500 and 1600.

The second example is from a small area in the extreme east of the Coalfield zone (next to the Magnesian Limestone zone) between Hooton Roberts and Ravenfield. There on a walk along the quarter of a mile long Back Lane between the end of Hooton Roberts village and Hooton Cliff Wood as many as thirteen different hedgerow shrubs and trees can be counted including dogwood, native privet and spindle, three species that are rarely found in hedgerows further west (Figure 7.7). On twenty-two randomly selected 30-yard lengths of hedge, evenly divided between the hedges on either side of the lane, the average number of species counted was 5.6, that is, 4.9 on the left-hand side of the lane going up towards Hooton Cliff Wood and 6.27 on the right-hand side. Using Hooper's original equation this would mean that on average the left-hand side of the hedge

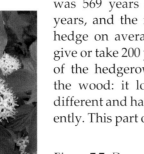

was 569 years old, give or take 200 years, and the right-hand side of the hedge on average was 720 years old give or take 200 years. But the character of the hedgerow changes as it nears the wood: it looks different, it feels different and has been managed differently. This part of the lane also contains

Figure 7.7. Dogwood in flower in Back Lane, Hooton Roberts

hedgerow trees, that are virtually absent in the lower part of the lane. The five 30-yard samples on the left-hand side nearest the wood averaged six giving an age of 690 years give or take 200 years, while that on the right-hand side averaged eight giving an age of 910 give or take 200 years. Does this mean the length of hedgerow on the right-hand side in the top half of the lane originated sometime in the period between the beginning eleventh and the beginning of the fourteenth centuries? In the absence of documentary records this must remain an open question.

The third example comes from the Fishlake area in the far north-eastern corner of the region. The entire area was once the bed of a great post-glacial lake, Lake Humber, and this is reflected in the unrelieved flatness of the area with the highest point being 32 feet (10 m). The area possesses many of the characteristics of what Oliver Rackham has called 'ancient countryside'. This was countryside that was too poor to support villages and a fully-fledged three-field system; instead it is a countryside carved out over thousands of years by individual farmers. It is a landscape of isolated farms and hamlets, small irregularly-shaped fields bounded by species-rich hedges with many hedgerow trees. The settlements are connected by winding lanes and there are many green lanes.[11] Even though there was some open field cultivation in the largest settlements, and though there has been some recent hedgerow removal, the Fishlake area is still a fine example of ancient countryside (Figure 7.8).

The Fishlake area was the subject of the most detailed hedge-row study conducted in South Yorkshire. It was undertaken in 1982 by a team of twenty-five field surveyors under the direction of Mr I. Hinchcliffe of Doncaster MBC's Planning Division and analysed by Colin Howes, Environmental Records Officer at Doncaster Museum.[12] Altogether 647 30-metre lengths of hedgerow were studied. The survey found that 82 per cent of hedges sampled had not received any recent management and only two per cent had been recently laid. Eighty-three per cent of hedges were next to drainage ditches and hedgerow trees were present in 77 per cent of the sampled hedgerows (Figure 7.9). The most common hedgerow trees were oak, ash and willow. Alder, usually associated with damp areas was completely absent. Twenty-five different species of tree and shrub were recorded and seven species of woody and non-woody climbers. Forty per cent of the hedgerows sampled contained only one or two species of trees and shrubs suggesting

Figure 7.8. Field boundaries, all hedgerows, in Fishlake parish in 2000. The parish is bounded in the east and south by the River Don

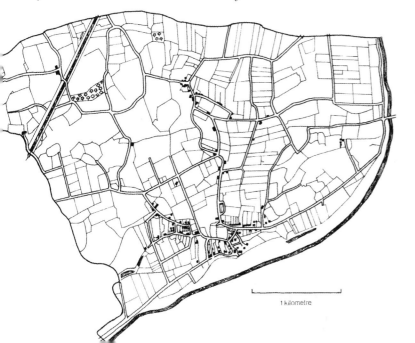

Figure 7.9. Hedge in Fishlake parish with hedgerow trees and blackthorn in flower

they were of nineteenth century origin, probably related to the Parliamentary enclosure award of 1825. Nearly 35 per cent of the hedges sampled had three species suggesting an origin in the eighteenth century, a period of agricultural prosperity and another 16 per cent had four species, suggesting an origin in the early seventeenth century when much drainage ditch digging took place in the aftermath of the heavy flooding in the area following Cornelius Vermuyden's drainage of the Hatfield Levels. Nine per cent of the hedgerow samples had between five and eight shrub or tree species suggesting Tudor or medieval origins. Further study linking specific hedgerows with surviving documentary evidence would be needed to confirm these conclusions.

The overall conclusion that must be reached about species richness and the dates of hedgerows is that species richness alone cannot be used to date hedges. Field shapes and documentary evidence must also be used. Even then conclusions must be provisional. The difficulty with documentary evidence is that in many cases insufficient has survived. Even if relevant documents (including early maps) have survived, those from before about 1750 usually only tell the investigator that a boundary hedge or wall was or was not in existence at the date the document was compiled. Early documents rarely tell us when a boundary was created.

HOLLY HAGS

Holly hags, special woods of holly, have already been mentioned in Chapter 2 in connection with feeding deer in deer parks in winter but they were once also features of the wider farming countryside where they were used as fodder for sheep until at least the eighteenth century. The use of holly for winter fodder was recorded in the Conisbrough manorial rolls in 1318 when five people, including the Abbot of Roche Abbey, were fined for cutting holly, in two cases specifically for feeding to their animals.[13] Another medieval record was in the Sheffield area in 1442 when the Lord of Hallamshire's forester at Bradfield noted in his accounts payment for holly sold for animal fodder in winter.[14] John Harrison in his survey of the Manor of Sheffield in 1637 recorded twenty-seven separate 'Hollin Hagges' that were rented by farm tenants from the Earl of Arundel.[15] The use of holly as fodder in the Sheffield area

was also graphically described by two early diarists. In 1696 Abraham de la Pryme wrote that:

In south-west Yorkshire at and about Bradfield and in Derbyshire they feed all their sheep in winter with holly leaves and bark, which they eat more greedily than any grass. To every farm there is so many holly trees ... care is taken to plant great numbers of them in all farms hereabouts.[16]

Twenty-nine years later, in 1725, a party headed by the Earl of Oxford travelled through Sheffield in a south-easterly direction across an area of common land still called the Birley Hollins. It was noted that they travelled:

through the greatest number of wild stunted holly trees that I ever saw together. They extend themselves on the common for a considerable way. This tract of ground that they grow upon is called the Burley Hollins ... [They have] their branches lopped off every winter for the support of the sheep which browse upon them, and at the same time are sheltered by the stunted part that is left standing.[17]

That holly was considered a valuable crop and had to be protected is illustrated by an entry in the accounts of the Duke of Norfolk's woods in the early eighteenth century. In the winter of 1710 the Duke of Norfolk's woodward noted in his accounts that he had paid Henry Bromhead 'for him and horse going 2 days in ye great snow to see if anyone croped holling'.[18] The impression given is that Bromhead would have had a blunderbuss over his saddle!

The question that naturally arises is: Do any of these holly hags still survive in the landscape? The survival of Bull Wood, a deer park holly hag at Tankersley, has already been referred to in Chapter 2. Writing in 1977 two local researchers, Spray

Figure 7.10. Part of a surviving holly hag on Loxley Common

and Smith, believed that there were at least the remains of five holly haggs in the country to the west of Sheffield. They mention Fox Hagg and Coppice Wood in the Rivelin valley, the holly bushes still surviving at Holly Edge and at Holly Busk near Bolsterstone and a location near the edge of Loxley Common at grid reference SK 308905[19] (Figure 7.10).

PLANTATIONS

Plantations large and small are scattered throughout the South Yorkshire countryside. Most are either of nineteenth or twentieth century origin. Some of the earliest plantations were created on land that had once been covered by mounds of spoil from

shallow bell pits dug to mine ironstone. This is the case of Bray Plantation in Kimberworth which was planted in the 1830s, and on a much larger scale at Tankersley where there are six plantations – Newbiggin Plantation, Potter Holes Plantation, Twelve lands Plantation, Tankersley Plantation, Hood Hill Plantation and Bell Ground. The account books and voucher books of Earl Fitzwilliam's Wentworth estate give considerable detail about the establishment of the plantations at Tankersley.[20] The first mention of planting trees where ironstone mining had taken place occurs in 1815. In that year, on 4 October, the account books record that the estate 'Paid Hanks & Co on account of Trees planted on land in which Ironstone has been got'. Similar entries, sometimes naming a specific plantation occurred in the account books for 1816, 1817, 1820, 1821 and 1822. The voucher books for the same period give details of the purchase of young trees. In 1816, for instance, John Littlewood of Handsworth nurseries near Sheffield supplied '1200 hornbeams, 1000 Scotch Firs, 500 Wych elms, 500 ashes, 1000 hollies and 300 yews' to the estate. That many if not all of these trees were intended for the new plantations is confirmed by a note in the 1817 account book which records a payment to John Littlewood 'for Trees planted in the Ironstone Ground'. By the 1840s the new plantations were listed among the much longer established working woods on the Wentworth estate as 'spring woods' and were providing large quantities of poles and stakes for use in hedge laying and timber for fencing off and repairing the mineral railways and as puncheon wood (pit props) for the coal and ironstone mines on the estate. The last of the plantations, Bell Ground, was created at the end of the 1850s, and is a beech plantation.

Another early nineteenth-century plantation is Sandall Beat Wood just 2 and a half miles (4 km) east of Doncaster town centre, now not only a Local Nature Reserve but also a Site of Special Scientific Interest. It is a favourite public recreational space (Figure 7.11). The site, covering 158 acres (64 ha) was originally an area of heathland, fen and rough pasture. The borough appointed a woodman who supervised the cutting of hundreds of drainage channels in preparation for planting. Planting began in 1810 and continued for a number of years. Thousands of young trees were purchased from the Handsworth nurseries of John Littlewood who supplied oaks, ashes, larches, elms, beeches, sycamores, 'Scotch firs', chestnuts and limes. The present woodland is the result of subsequent

Figure 7.11. Sandall Beat Wood, a nineteenth-century plantation with the character of an ancient wood

replanting, natural regeneration and coppice re-growth. There is an interesting woodland ground flora which includes ancient woodland indicators such as bluebell, wood anemone, dog's mercury, wood sorrel and common cow wheat. Presumably they have spread from small patches of ancient willow carr and alder carr that had survived in the fenny parts of the site when it was planted up. There are also relics of the former heathland vegetation, for example purple moor-grass and a small area of reed swamp. The wood supports a good number of breeding birds including spotted flycatcher and sedge warbler and there are extensive entomological records for the site.

A feature of the western parts of the region in the upper parts of the Rivelin, Loxley, Little Don and Ewden Beck valleys are large reservoirs surrounded wholly or in part by coniferous plantations mostly owned by Yorkshire Water and some by Sheffield City Council (Figure 7.12).

As noted in Chapter 3, the second half of the nineteenth century saw many local coppice woods converted into timber plantations mainly through storing coppice and by extensive planting. This continued into the twentieth century and the Duke of Norfolk's Greno Wood and Hall Wood on the northern outskirts of Sheffield were heavily coniferised and managed by Fountain Forestry. At the time of writing Sheffield and Rotherham Wildlife Trust are trying to raise £1m to buy both woods as conservation and public recreation areas. Wadworth Wood near Doncaster was also heavily planted by the Forestry Commission from the 1920s until the early 1980s. Species planted not only included conifers such as Scots pine, Corsican pine and Japanese larch, but also broadleaves such as beech, birch, Norway maple and particularly large numbers of sycamore.[21] Among other twentieth-century plantations are the privately owned Bawtry Forest and the Forestry Commission's Wharncliffe

Figure 7.12. *Plantations to the west of Bradfield around Agden Reservoir in the foreground and Dale Dike Reservoir in the background*

Woods. The latter were formerly coppiced, but by the 1950s, the constituent woods (nearly ten in number including those with evocative names such as Oughtibridge Hagg, Broomhead Spring and Stead Spring) consisted of open birch, willow and bracken scrub together with areas of mature birch and oak with occasional yew, sweet chestnut and sycamore. Alder persisted beside springs and wet flushes. Since that time almost half of Wharncliffe Woods has been planted with conifers and much of the deciduous woodland has not survived.[22]

There are also nine Forestry Commission-managed community woodlands mainly on former mining sites such as Bentley Community woodland on the site of Bentley Colliery and Thurnscoe Community woodland on the site of Hickleton Main

Colliery. Altogether the development of community woodlands has added 1137 acres (460 ha) of publicly accessible woodland to the South Yorkshire landscape. Another area that has seen much planting over the last thirty years is Rother Valley Country Park. Three hundred hectares on the site were open-cast mined between 1976 and 1981 and it opened as a country park in 1983. 480,000 trees and shrubs have been planted in small blocks as part of the restoration of a mosaic of habitats.

Finally, dotted throughout the region are arable fields recently converted into 'plantations' growing willow for biofuel.

STAND ALONE TREES

Single trees, for example, standing in fields, in moorland cloughs or on windswept stretches of upland, in churchyards and in the centre of a settlement are also important landscape sentinels throughout South Yorkshire. A common sight through-out the region is a lone tree or possible two or three widely spaced trees in the middle of a field (Figure 7.13). Most of these tend to be oaks or ashes. They are usually former hedgerow trees and mark the positions where hedgerows have been removed, mostly in the last fifty years.

In the Dark Peak zone of bleak moorland and gritstone edges there is another lone sentinel, often bent and windblown (Figure 7.14). This is the rowan or mountain ash (*Sorbus aucuparia*) which grows at altitudes of more than 3,000 feet (*c.* 1000 m), higher than any other British tree apart from juniper and some dwarf willows. It is the characteristic tree of the upland farm landscape, growing beside walls along field boundaries or clinging to rock ledges or in sheltered steep-sided moorland cloughs.

Another lone countryside tree is the very scarce black poplar (*Populus nigra*). This is not a woodland tree but a tree of the

Figure 7.13. *A stand alone tree in a field marking the former position of a hedgerow*

riverside in lowland areas. The tree is recognised by its habit of leaning at an angle, by its dark grey rugged bark usually interrupted by large burrs, by its arching branches and its distinctive deltoid-shaped leaves. The native black poplar, not to be confused with the introduced Italian black poplar, is a rare tree in South Yorkshire. A particularly fine black poplar stands on the B6066 near the Shubert Bridge in the Shirtcliff valley between Handsworth and Woodhouse in south-east Sheffield. Stately or notable trees also sometimes stand in the centre of a village or a small town. For example, there is a veteran horse chestnut with a girth of 23 feet (7 m) in the village of Wortley.

Figure 7.14. *A wind-blown moorland rowan on Hallam Moors at about 1,500 feet (457 m)*

Pollard trees, typical in hedges and along dykes in lowland areas, are relatively rare in South Yorkshire, and those that survive are mostly in the eastern lowland areas. For example, a substantial number of pollarded willows survive in the hedgerows in Fishlake parish and white willow pollards line the River Don and the River Went on the eastern and northern boundaries of the parish. There are also some ancient willow pollards in the Rother valley at Woodhouse which have recently been re-pollarded (Figure 7.15).

Trees standing alone or in small groups are also a feature of churchyards. For example Tickhill churchyard is encircled by a ring of stately limes whilst nearer the church there is a weeping ash, a horse chestnut with a girth of 17 feet (5.17 m) and a large sycamore containing a rookery. But the characteristic churchyard tree is the yew. Two of the most famous of

Figure 7.15 Re-pollarded willows in Woodhouse, south-east Sheffield

churchyard yews are at Much Marcle in Herefordshire with a girth of nearly 31 feet (9.4 m) which has been estimated to be over 2,000 years old and at Darley Dale in Derbyshire with a girth of 33 feet (10 m). Unfortunately we have nothing of these sizes or ages in a South Yorkshire churchyard. The most detailed study of churchyard yews in South Yorkshire has been carried out in Doncaster Metropolitan Borough.[23] Yews can be found in twenty-two churchyards throughout the borough ranging from nineteen in Tickhilll churchyard, many of them quite young, to one in Kirk Bramwith, the latter having a girth of more than 10 feet (3.1 m). The church guide claims that it is 600 years old. The biggest group of mature and veteran yews lie in Sprotbrough churchyard where there are six ranging in girth from 3 feet 10 inches (1.16 m) to 9 feet (2.7 m). The belief that ancient yews mark pagan religious sites that were taken over by Christian church builders is still hotly debated, but they may have been planted in churchyards from early Christian times as symbols of immortality. Nor is there any factual evidence that yews were planted to provide the raw materials for longbows. Much of the yew wood for bow making in the Middle Ages was reputedly imported from Spain, the timber of English yews being said to be too brittle and full of knots.[24]

At Thryft House at Bents Green near the southern boundary of Sheffield Metropolitan District stands an ancient yew tree with a girth of more than 15 feet (4.56 m). Much of the north side of the tree appears dead but the south side is flourishing and the branches are full of foliage (Figure 7.16). The tree occupies a right angle in a boundary wall at a habitation site that is of itself of some antiquity, 'Thryft House' ... in the byrlawe of Eklysall' being mentioned in a deed of 1504.[25] H.L. Edlin in his book, *The Living Forest* (1958), suggests that an inch of radius in a yew tree could signify anything from ten to

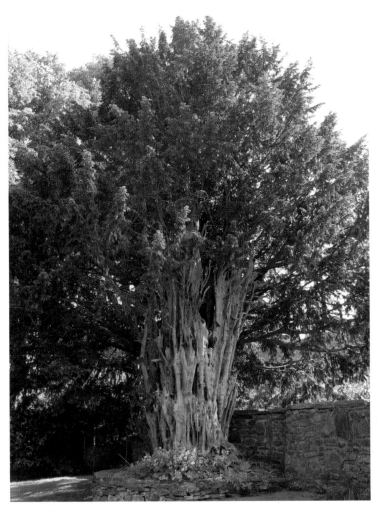

Figure 7.16. The Thryft House yew

seventy years of life.[26] This would give an age of between 286 and 2,002 years for the Thryft House yew! Last year a verifier from the Ancient Tree Hunt organised by the Woodland Trust considered it to be a veteran, which in yew terms is between 1,000 and 2,000 years old. Whatever its age the Thrift House Farm yew tree is probably the oldest living thing in Sheffield and probably in the whole of South Yorkshire. Some people believe that it marks the boundary between the Anglo-Saxon kingdoms of Mercia and Northumbria, which later became the ancient boundary between the counties of Derbyshire and Yorkshire. This old boundary runs along the Limb Brook which is nearly a kilometre away to the south-west therefore this theory seems untenable. However, Thryft House and the yew tree do lie on an ancient boundary. John Gelley's 1725 'Mapp of the Manor of Ecclesall belonging to Mr John Bright' shows that Thryft House Farm stood at that time on the boundary between John Bright's estate and the surrounding lands of the lords of Hallamshire. It is difficult to say how old this boundary is but the Manor of Ecclesall was already in existence in the thirteenth century. What is even more interesting is that we know that some local manorial boundaries were marked by yew trees. In the past it was usual to periodically walk estate, manorial and parish boundaries and record the evidence of old men. These were called perambulations or bounders. Perambulations for the manor of Sheffield have survived for the years 1574, 1575, 1656, 1705, 1719 and 1722. The 1574 perambulation begins *'one ewe* [yew] *tree standing upon my lordes land called Bennett- field is thought to bee a mere* [boundary marker] *between my lord of Ecclesall . . .'.*[27] If the Thryft House yew is a boundary marker, its botanical interest, because of its great age, is greatly enhanced because of its historical significance.

TREES IN URBAN AREAS AND ALONG VILLAGE STREETS

Trees and shrubs grow everywhere in urban areas and large villages. Besides those growing in municipal parks and recreation grounds already discussed in Chapter 6, they have been planted along the sides of streets, on central reservations of major roads, on traffic islands, in school grounds, in cemeteries and even in the car parks of superstores and out-of-town shopping centres. The fashion for planting shrubs and trees that carry berries in autumn and winter has made superstore and out-of-town shopping centre car parks one of the main places at which to spot one of our rarest winter visitors – the waxwing. In Spring a journey by bus or car along urban thoroughfares and village streets is a blaze of colour. In March forsythia provides occasional explosions of bright yellow and on the outskirts the flowering blackthorn in the hedges is quite dazzling. In April it is the flowering cherry and the magnolia that catches the eye, followed in May by the may blossom on the hawthorn. At the eastern end of Wentworth village near the junction of Main Street with Hague Lane is a small plantation of horse chestnuts. The trees themselves, as the leaves unfurl and the 'candle' blossom emerges are very striking, but what attracts the eye and the ear in March and April is the flapping and cawing of the rooks in the upper branches as they repair their nests and settle on their eggs in the rookery.

But the trees that attract most attention in urban areas and in villages across the region are the planted trees, mainly along residential streets (Figure 7.17) but also in streets and roads in commercial and industrial areas. It has been estimated that there are 35,000 street trees in Sheffield including trees on roundabouts and rural verges.[28] In Rotherham the figure is 6,000.[29] The benefits of street trees are manifold. Most obviously

Figure 7.17. Flowering cherry trees bordering Cockshutt Road in Beauchief, Sheffield

they mask or at least reduce the visibility of the harsh straight lines of brick and mortar and add beauty to the most densely populated of areas. They also bring wildlife right into the middle of cities, towns and villages. They are also good for our health. They not only reduce ultra-violet radiation; they reduce air temperatures; reduce atmospheric pollution by removing gaseous pollutants and dust from the atmosphere and dilute polluted air by producing oxygen. And they reduce stress and promote a sense of well-being. A well–treed environment also has economic benefits: it has been shown that they increase property values and can encourage investment to an area from 'footloose' businesses that rely on a skilled but contented labour force.[30]

Street trees are found throughout South Yorkshire in boundless variety. There are sturdy natives such as oak, ash, birch, rowan and whitebeam; introduced species such as sycamore, sweet chestnut, horse chestnut and flowering cherry and rarities such as the tree of heaven and Western balsam poplar. Specialist varieties are also frequently encountered, such as weeping birch, weeping willow, copper beech and fastigiate hornbeam. But the two most common street trees encountered across the region must be the London plane and the common lime. The London plane (*Platanus × acerfolia*) is a hybrid, between the western or American plane and the eastern or oriental plane. The tree was first recorded in this country growing in the Oxford Botanic Gardens in 1670. It has been estimated that more than half the trees in London's streets and squares are London plane, favoured because of its ability to survive in the heavily soot-laden air and to grow well in poor and shallow soils. But it also has its detractors because of the heavy shade that it casts and the habit of its roots of lifting paving stones. The common lime (*Tilia × europaea*) is also believed to be a hybrid between the native small-leaved and large-leaved limes, but most of the stock from which the millions of street trees originate is thought to be originally of continental origin. The main drawback of planting limes is that in summer they become infested with aphids that feed on the leaves and leave behind sticky honeydew that drips constantly on the pavements below.

Limes are favourite trees for planting in avenues which are not confined to country house parks and gardens and public parks. There is an avenue of lime trees along Cemetery Avenue, a short street leading off Ecclesall Road in Sheffield. The name

Cemetery Avenue is the clue. The short street leads to a gatehouse over the River Porter leading to the General Cemetery. Sometimes the distinction between an avenue of trees and simply a double line of trees planted alongside a road or street becomes blurred. This is exemplified by the lime trees that border both sides of Rivelin Valley Road (the A6101) for three miles between Malin Bridge and the junction of the road with the Manchester Road (A57) at Rivelin Post Office. Altogether there are nearly 500 mature lime trees bordering both sides of the road. I like to think of it as an avenue leading to the Peak District National Park.

One of the most unusual avenues of trees is the avenue of holm oaks that winds its way from Moorgate Road up through the grounds of the former Oakwood Hall to the hall, built for James Yates of Yates Haywood, stovegrate manufacturers, but what is now the administrative centre for Rotherham General Hospital.

But it is not just planted trees that have made an impact in urban areas. There are also those that have colonised these areas naturally, often as garden escapes. One of the most colourful of these is the butterfly-bush (*Buddleia davidii*). This shrub, recognised by its honey-scented purple flower spikes, was introduced to this country from China in 1890. Its winged seeds are light and can be blown some distance. It has spread along railway lines and colonised open ground and derelict sites and can even be found sprouting on rooftops and clinging to brick walls. It is particularly widespread in the lower Don valley in Sheffield where it has colonised the side of the railway line and the route of the supertram almost into the centre of Sheffield and it is prolific for a couple of miles alongside Carlisle Street East, Holywell Road and Tyler Street from Burngreave almost as far as the M1 motorway.

One of the most unusual trees growing in an urban area in South Yorkshire is the wild fig tree (*Ficus carica*) which has colonised a stretch of riverside in the east end of Sheffield (Figure 7.18). In a survey carried out in the 1980s fig trees stretched beside the River Don from the middle of Attercliffe to Meadowhall Road beyond the Tinsley viaduct that carries the M1 motorway.[31] In that survey thirty-five mature trees were mapped. At one location they formed a small wood. They were about 26 feet (8 m) high and at least the same across. They were rooted in the base of retaining walls, on a small island and on earth banks. The trees were thought to be about sixty-seventy years old. No young fig trees were found. It is believed the seeds from which the fig trees grew originated in raw sewage deposited in the river during storms when the sewers overflowed. It is also believed that they germinated because of a microclimate that developed because of hot water that was discharged into the river from neighbouring steel works. Since the decline of the steel industry the river temperatures have normalised, the microclimate has disappeared and no young trees have germinated. But the mature trees hung on as they do to this day and constitute the biggest population of wild figs anywhere in Britain. In the 1990s another small colony was found beside the River Sheaf.[32]

Figure 7.18. A fig tree growing beside the River Don at Meadowhall

What to read about trees and shrubs in the wider landscape

HARVEY, G. (1997) *The Killing of the Countryside*, Jonathan Cape.

JONES, M. (2003) A Unique Historic Rural Landscape: The Fishlake-Sykehouse area in *South Yorkshire Yesterday: Glimpses of the Past*, Smith Settle, Chapter 7, pp. 49–55.

MUIR, R. (2007) *Be Your Own Landscape Detective*, Sutton Publishing, Chapter 2.

POLLARD, E., HOOPER, M.D., and MOORE, N.W. (1974) *Hedges*, The New Naturalist series, Collins.

RACKHAM, O. (1986) *The History of the Countryside*, Dent, chapters 9 and 10.

REDMONDS, G. (1990) Hedges and Walls in West Yorkshire, *Old West Riding*, 10, 27–33.

SHOARD, M. (1980) *The Theft of the Countryside*, Temple Smith.

TAYLOR, C. (1975) *Fields in the English Landscape*, Dent.

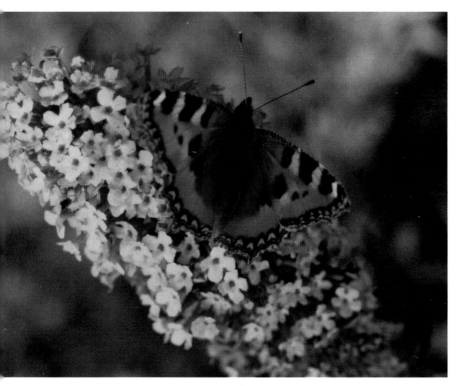

Butterfly bush (Buddleia davidii)

Places to visit

Investigate a local hedgerow. First consult old maps and consider the shapes of the field(s) that it bounds. Draw some conclusions about its possible age. Then do some counting of species in random 30-yard lengths of the hedgerow. Only count woody species – do not count climbers like ivy, bramble or bindweed. Average your counts and apply Hooper's formula. What do <u>you</u> think of the method? Whatever its shortcomings, I like counting species in hedgerows because it makes you look at them carefully and helps hone identification skills.

Visit a local plantation. Compare its character and variety of tree species with a local ancient wood and compare its ground flora with that of a local ancient wood.

A visit to Sandall Beat, an early nineteenth-century plantation on a largely unimproved site of scrub woodland, heath and fen, is interesting because its ground flora contains many ancient woodland indicators that must have spread from the small patches of alder and willow carr on the original site.

Investigate and record the variety of trees, native and introduced, in your **local churchyard**.

When visiting Meadowhall, have a short walk alongside the River Don immediately beside the shopping centre to see **the riverside fig trees**.

LOSS, RESCUE AND RESTORATION

NONE OF THE KNOWN late medieval coppice woods disappeared through the wanton behaviour of wood-men and other exploiters of wood and timber. Woods have disappeared or have been reduced in size over a long period of time as a result of clearance for quarrying and mining operations, through agricultural expansion, industrial develop-ment, the spread of settlement, and road building. For example, a large part of the great pasture wood recorded in 1161 that stretched from the Birley Stone at Grenoside down to the River Don between Wardsend and Oughtibridge was cleared in the medieval period and early modern period for agriculture, leaving only the narrow wooded common on Birley Edge in the west, Wilson Spring halfway down the slope and Beeley Wood beside the River Don. Much later, Hall Carr Wood in Brightside, Sheffield, completely disappeared in the nineteenth century as a result of industrial development as did most of Tinsley Park, this time mostly because of coal mining. Burngreave Wood, also in Sheffield, disappeared as the result of the popu-lation explosion in Sheffield in the second half of the nineteenth century and the need to create a cemetery. A few sessile oaks and a few ancient woodland indicators still survive in the cemetery. Maltby Wood, as described in Chapter 5, was also greatly reduced in size through the development of Maltby Main Colliery during the twentieth century. A great swathe was cut through Smithy Wood near Chapeltown as a result of the construction of the M1 motorway, two swathes were cut through Bowden Housteads Wood in Sheffield through

the construction of the Sheffield Parkway in 1970 and the Mosbrough Parkway in 1990, and another through Wadworth Wood when the M18 was built.

THE DESTRUCTION OF WOODS AT SHIRECLIFFE, SHEFFIELD

One of the best documented cases of woodland destruction occurred in the middle Don valley at Shirecliffe in Sheffield.[1] The area was once covered by a mosaic of ancient woodland comprising Old Park Wood covering 143 acres (58 ha) and the much smaller Scraith Wood, Rawson Spring, Lord's Wood, Oaken Bank and Cooke Wood, making a total of 245 acres (99 ha). The Lord's Wood which covered 27.5 acres (11 ha) was cleared in the eighteenth century for agricultural expansion but the others were managed as coppice-with-standards from at least the beginning of the sixteenth century until almost the end of the nineteenth century (Figure 8.1(A)). But it was in the nineteenth century that things began to change for the worse. First, the western edge of Old Park Wood was severed from the rest of the wood in 1845 by the Manchester, Sheffield and Lincolnshire Railway which involved the construction of the impressive viaduct over Herries Road. By this time the woodlands were also being eaten into on all sides by quarrying and mining activities. Then, in 1857, Wardsend Cemetery came into existence in the north-western corner of Old Park Wood. But the greatest change in the area in the nineteenth century was the creation of a new industrial colony called Parkwood

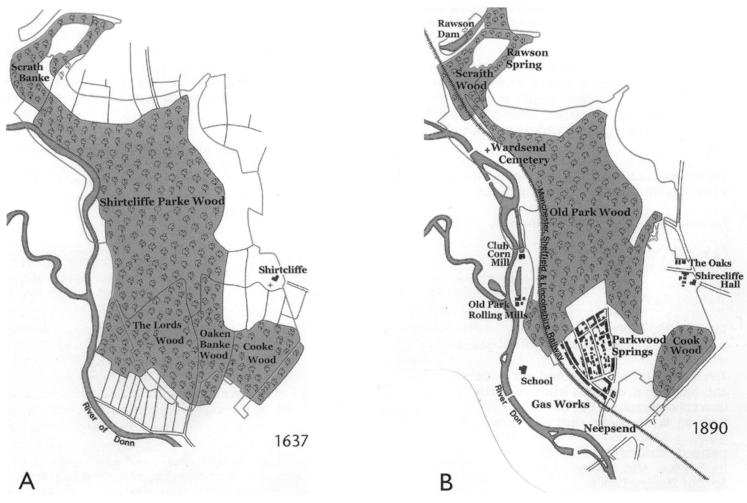

Figure 8.1 *(A) The Shirecliffe area in the seventeenth century; and (B) The Shirecliffe area in the second half of the nineteenth century*

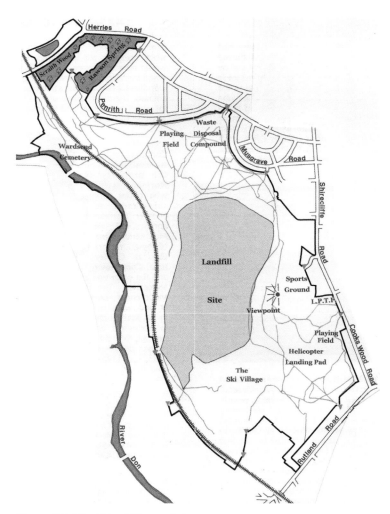

Figure 8.2. The Shirecliffe area today

Springs (Figure 8.1(B)). By 1861 it contained 171 houses and had a population of 792. By the time of the 1901 census the settlement had almost trebled in size to 2,263.

Great swathes of Old Park Wood disappeared in the early twentieth century following an agreement with the Duke of Norfolk's estate to tip ash from the electricity power station at Neepsend in the area formerly covered by woodland. Ordnance Survey maps of 1923–24 and 1935 show extensive areas of tipped ash dispatched to the former woodland by aerial ropeway. Landfill operations began in the 1970s in the abandoned quarry and still continue covering a large part of the central area.

The area once covered by ancient woodland is now mostly a mosaic of acid grassland, meadow and heathland where bare ground has been recently colonised and open woodland dominated by birch and multi-stemmed oak and areas of planted trees, both native and exotic. The only areas of ancient woodland to remain are Rawson Spring and Scraith Wood (Figure 8.2).

SURVIVING, BUT NEGLECTED AND UNMANAGED
Nevertheless, the survival rate of ancient woodland sites, although heavily planted, is surprisingly high considering the rapid population growth and expansion of housing and industry in the nineteenth century. For example in Sheffield the population of the parish was about 20,000 in 1750 and the borough population by 1900 was approaching 400,000. Of the forty-three known coppice woods within the present city boundaries that were in existence in 1600, only two had been lost by 1850, and twenty-nine of the remaining forty-one still stand today.

However, for almost a century, until the late 1980s, ancient broadleaved woods throughout the region, excepting the minority still in private hands (which were often coniferised) were neglected and unmanaged except where dead or dying trees were judged to be a danger to the public. The benign neglect of the publicly owned woods made them much less attractive than in the past (Figure 8.3). They were increasingly even-aged with dense canopies and poorly developed shrub layers. They contained much poorer displays of spring flowers, some breeding birds and butterflies had been reduced in number or were no longer found in woods where they were once common, and local residents were increasingly afraid of walking in the woods because they were dark and gloomy and engendered a fear of personal attack. The more accessible woods were also sometimes heavily vandalised and full of litter. After having survived for hundreds, and in some cases for thousands, of years there was a real danger that our woodland heritage would be squandered. Our ancestors quite deliberately protected the woods by actively managing them; the twentieth century attitude until lately in urban areas seems to have been, at best, to let them take care of themselves, and at worst, to abuse them unmercifully.

Having said that, one ill-judged attempt to introduce active management at Little Matlock Wood, in the Loxley valley, Sheffield, caused much unease, and correspondents to local newspapers criticised what was seen as 'council vandalism',

Figure 8.3. Herringthorpe Wood, Rotherham, showing the impact of close planting including species like beech and sweet chestnut, not native to the site. There is no shrub layer because of the dense canopy and where once there would have been a dense ground flora there is much bare soil

going on to say that once it came to the attention of Sheffield Countryside Management 'the wood was doomed'. It became all too clear that managing public woods in a heavily-populated area in the late twentieth century was as much about public relations as woodmanship and ecological principles.

Three examples illustrate the changing public attitudes, community initiatives and positive action that began to emerge in the 1970s and 1980s: the campaign to save Edlington Wood in Doncaster, renewed management of Bowden Housteads Wood in Sheffield after a century of neglect and the purchase of Broad Ing Plantation at Pilley in Barnsley from the Forestry Commission by Tankersley Parish Council.

THE CAMPAIGN TO SAVE EDLINGTON WOOD IN THE 1970S

Writing in the mid-1970s, Oliver Rackham estimated that at least a third of the country's ancient woodland had been destroyed during the previous thirty years, an estimate that he later revised to a half .[2] By 'destroyed' he meant converted to coniferous plantations as well as being grubbed for agriculture or lost though quarrying, the construction of roads and the expansion of housing and industry. At the beginning of the 1970s, it looked as if Edlington Wood, the largest ancient wood in the Magnesian Limestone zone, then covering more than 350 acres (142 ha) would become part of Rackham's catalogue of recent unprecedented destruction (Figure 8.4).

The site of Edlington Wood was one favoured by our early ancestors, and therefore in archaeological terms it is a site of some importance. It contains an upper Palaeolithic/early Mesolithic rock shelter, the remains of Romano-British field systems and a mysterious linear earthwork, the Double Dyke, that runs across the wood. It is equally important ecologically.

Figure 8.4. *Edlington Wood as shown on the first edition of the One Inch to One Mile Ordnance Survey map published in 1841. Note the intricate system of rides and the two named archaeological features Blow Hall (a burial cairn within a Romano-British field system) and Double Dyke (a linear earthwork)*

The northern part of the site where the limestone outcrops in natural crags there appears to be natural woodland dominated by small-leaved lime, ash and wych elm together with many ancient yews. The rest of the wood has been subject to planting over a long period of time and is a mixture of planted sweet chestnut, sycamore, larch and beech together with naturally regenerated oak, ash, wych elm, lime and birch. The understorey is well developed and contains shrubs typical of limestone such as wild privet, dogwood, spindle, buckthorn and spurge-laurel. There is a diverse ground flora including more than thirty of the ancient woodland indicators listed in Figure 1.14 in Chapter 1. These include unusual species such as tooth-wort (*Lathraea squamaria*), broad-leaved helleborine (*Epipactis helleborine*) and mountain melick (*melica mutans*). The woodland rides support species typical of limestone grassland such as common twayblade (*Listera ovata*), yellow rattle (*Rhinanthus minor*) and ploughman's spikenard (*Inula conza*).

Little is known of its early woodland history,[3] except that recorded woodland in the parish in the Middle Ages was much smaller in area than the present wood. In 1700 the manor of Edlington was purchased by Robert Molesworth, MP who later became first Baron of Philipstown of Swords (in the county of Dublin) and Viscount Molesworth. Under Viscount Molesworth the wood was made into an ornamental woodland through planting and the laying out of a system of rides radiating outwards from the centre. At the centre of the system of rides Molesworth erected a monument in the form of an urn on a square pedestal to a favourite greyhound that was said to have saved his master from being shot by an intruder. Close by the monument was a small woodman/gamekeeper's cottage. After the death of Viscount Moleworth the woodland was converted into a coppice-with-standards and then in 1748, when it covered 350 acres (142 ha) it was bought by the first Marquis of Rockingham of Wentworth Woodhouse and added to his already extensive acreage of coppice-with-standards woods. Eventually, at some unknown date the wood passed from the ownership of the earls Fitzwilliam, the successors to the second Marquis of Rockingham at Wentworth Woodhouse. During the nineteenth century further planting took place. For example, in the Fitzwilliam estate account books it is recorded that in 1824 a

Mr Oldham was paid £99 for planting 'Forest trees' in Ecclesall Woods and Edlington Wood and in Tinsley Park.[4] Other payments were made in 1825, 1830, 1832 and 1842 for planting in Edlington Wood. No doubt further planting took place although the estate account books after the 1840s do not provide details of planting in specific estate woodlands. At some unknown date the wood passed into the ownership of the Earls Nelson of Stafford and the Forestry Commission managed it on their behalf until in the Spring of 1971 it was sold to another private owner, Phillip Lanni, a timber merchant.

Anticipating activity on the site that might result in woodland destruction and affect public access, Doncaster Rural District Council protected the wood by means of a Tree Preservation Order (TPO). In September 1971 the new owner went public with his intentions for the site. These included quarrying and clearance for agriculture and house building. His proposals were met with much local opposition and anger and an action committee was set up to oppose them. There then followed several years of applications from the owner to clear part of the woodland, to introduce quarrying on the site and to fell and to thin.[5] In spite of the TPO the new owner pressed on with his plans. In November 1971 it was learned that planning permission had been given to clear sixty acres in the wood for agriculture that the owner claimed contained no mature trees (and was not covered by the TPO). The action committee arranged meetings with the local MP and the Minister for the Environment (Mr Peter Walker), members of the West Riding Council and the Forestry Commission, but the decision was not changed. Activity by the owner did not stop there. In January 1972 it was learned that felling operations were taking place in those parts of the wood covered by the TPO. Doncaster Rural District Council decided to prosecute and the owner was taken to court and fined. He then applied to open quarries in the wood and to carry out thinning operations. The campaigners were joined in their opposition to the proposed quarrying by the Rural District Council and the Planning Committee strongly recommended refusal. The proposed thinning operations initially received the support of the West Riding County Council but after a year of protest meetings, reports and the support of professional ecologists permission was refused. In November 1973 a group of local and regional specialists in history, archaeology, geology and natural history compiled a 237-page book about the wood, *Edlington Wood*, printed by Doncaster Rural District Council, to further try to convince the owner and the authorities of the importance of the site and the need to protect it.[6]

Problems and protests rumbled on through the 1970s until in 1979 most of the wood (247 acres (100 ha)) was provided with legal protection by being given the status of a Site of Special Scientific Interest (SSSI) by the then Nature Conservancy Council (now Natural England).

RENEWED MANAGEMENT OF BOWDEN HOUSTEADS WOOD AFTER A CENTURY OF NEGLECT

Bowden Housteads is one of the earliest recorded ancient woods in South Yorkshire, being recorded as early as 1332 as a wood pasture.[7] By 1600 it was a coppice-with-standards and was coppiced continuously until almost the end of the nineteenth century. It is typical of ancient woods in that it lies on an ancient parish boundary, and its boundaries, sinuous and zig-zagging, had remained largely intact for at least two hundred years. It was heavily planted in the late nineteenth century. In 1916 the Duke of Norfolk sold the wood to Sheffield Corporation for £6,000 for use as a place of recreation. Since then, not

only was it left virtually unmanaged for more than seventy years, but also a large section of the wood was lost through open-cast coal mining in the 1940s. It was also bisected by the construction of the Sheffield Parkway (A630) in 1970 and the southern part of the wood was further sub-divided by the creation of the Mosborough Parkway in 1990 (Figure 8.5). The wood became increasingly even-aged, with a dense canopy resulting from the closely-planted trees, especially in those areas dominated by beech, causing suppression of ground flora and erosion of bare soils on steep slopes.[8] Because it was gloomy and monotonous it was much less attractive to insects, mammals and birds, and visitors felt less safe walking there. Its ancient boundary walls were also in a state of great disrepair and it was heavily littered in places. A further potential problem was concern that the woodland was becoming drier because the water catchment had been reduced in size and the water table had fallen due to the gradual urbanization of the surrounding area with a potential negative impact on the woodland's ecology.

But it was still a heavily used public open space. In June 1986 a user survey of the wood was conducted among a random selection of adult respondents in 236 households living in those parts of Richmond, Handsworth, Darnall, Manor and Woodthorpe lying adjacent to the wood.[9] In answer to the question 'If you visited a local wood which one it be?' 228 answered 'Bowden Housteads'. Eighty-one per cent of these 228 respondents said they visited the wood on a daily, regular or occasional basis. 115 of these respondents took walks there, seventy-six walked a dog, twenty-nine explored with young members of their family and forty-two used it as a short cut. Eighty-seven of the users said that when they visited the wood they went alone. Among serious problems in the wood

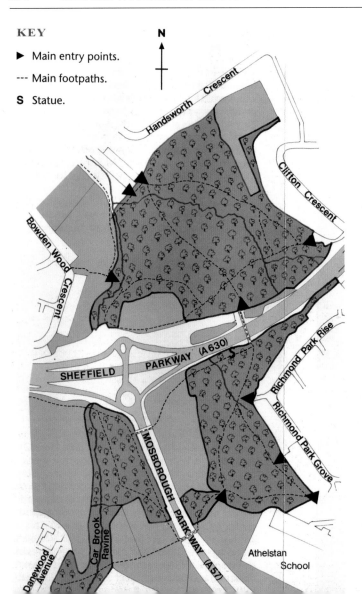

KEY

► Main entry points.

--- Main footpaths.

S Statue.

respondents cited chopping down trees, dumping rubbish, starting fires, using airguns and off-road motorbiking as serious problems. At the end of the questionnaire survey respondents were asked to offer any other comments about the wood. Complimentary comments included 'important for wildlife and relaxation', 'a precious place for children to go and come in contact with nature', 'we need woodlands, need bits of green' and 'somewhere different to walk in – best thing in the area'. But these were balanced by critical comments that emphasized the lack of management such as: 'once meant a lot; now it has deteriorated', 'very dark and gloomy', 'wants cleaning up', 'an unsafe place to walk in or for children to play in', and 'needs supervising by a ranger'.

This then was the situation after nearly three-quarters of a century of public ownership: Bowden Housteads was still heavily used but in great need of sympathetic management.

The City Council's Recreation Department had created a Moorland and Amenity Woodland Advisory Group (MAWAG) in the 1970s made up of council officers and representatives of environmental organisations. In 1985 the group commissioned a study from the author to determine the status and manage-ment history of the major woods in the city, and the ensuing report presented in 1986 made it clear that most of the woods in the City Council's ownership were ancient.[10] The City Council then approved a Woodland Policy, put together by MAWAG, in 1987. Its primary aim was to ensure the protection and perpetuation of the ancient woodlands surviving in the city and to realise their potential in as many ways as possible. The policy sought to maintain the ancient woods in a healthy state, to protect, conserve and encourage their rich flora and fauna,

Figure 8.5. Bowden Housteads Wood

and to preserve their important historical and archaeological value. In all this the public were to be encouraged to play a full part by expressing their views, becoming involved in management, and monitoring effects and consequences. This policy was largely enshrined in the City Council's *Nature Conservation Strategy* document published in 1991.

The Woodland Policy was put into action in Bowden Housteads Wood in the early spring of 1988.[11] This major improvement project in a badly neglected inner city wood, which had remained unmanaged since its purchase from the Duke of Norfolk in 1916, was funded jointly by the City Council and the Countryside Commission. The main operation was thinning, to provide more space for the native trees to develop, and to help diversify the woodland by encouraging the regeneration of the shrub layer and the flowering of the ground flora. The thinning was irregular and several glades were created.

The project involved a major public relations campaign. Before the commencement of operations, public meetings were held and guided walks around the wood were undertaken. 400 letters were posted to local residents about the project, notices were posted up in and around the wood about what was to be done and why, news items appeared in the local press and a broadcast was made on local radio. One important aspect of this campaign was to reassure local residents that felling trees did not mean the destruction of a well-loved wood. The point was made that the sound of a chainsaw should be taken to be a sign of good woodland management practice and not council vandalism (Figure 8.6). The project was a major new departure in woodland management in the city. It was an 'active' rather than a 'care and maintenance' approach, and it

Figure 8.6. Thinning in Bowden Housteads Wood in the Spring of 1988

was sympathetic both to the origins and history of the wood and to the local residents who are its users.

A second management plan for Bowden Housteads, to build on the work undertaken between 1987–1991, was compiled, covering the period from 2000 to 2005 (Sheffield City Council, 2000).[12] In 1999, prior to the plan being put together, a small-scale household questionnaire survey was undertaken (100 persons) and a visitor survey (50 persons). Results of the surveys very much echoed those of the 1986 survey. People said they used the site because of the peace and quiet away from traffic, the wildlife and for exercise. They disliked the continued vandalism, litter, motorbikers and the feeling that it was not an altogether safe place. The improvements most frequently requested were a nature trail, information boards and guided walks, a staff presence and more wildflowers. A small 'Friends of Bowden Housteads' group had been formed in 1996, and this small group of enthusiasts also funnelled local concerns to the woodland managers.

The management plan for 2000–2005 reflected the desire of the city's woodland team to try to solve the problems raised and the requests made by the public. The vegetation management objectives of the plan were to restore natural species composition by continued selective thinning of sycamore, whitebeam and beech and so encouraging natural regeneration. Willow would be encouraged in selected wet areas and the age diversity of the woodland would be further encouraged through the reintroduction of group felling. It was also promised that surveys would be undertaken to monitor ecological change. Additionally access would be improved through upgrading the path system (Trans-Pennine Trail and the National Cycle Route (Sustrans) now pass through the site) and educational and interpretive materials would be produced.

The most recent plan published for the wood covers the period 2009–2013 and aims to build on the work undertaken as part of the plans for 1987–1991 and 2000–2005.[13] The vegetation management will consist of continued small-scale thinning to promote an uneven-aged woodland and a diversity of species, structure and habitats. Operational methods which avoid excessive disturbance will be employed. Native tree and shrub species will be favoured and natural regeneration will be used wherever possible to provide new trees. During thinning operations a proportion of trees will be allowed to develop to over-maturity and natural senescence, and, where not a danger to the public, dead wood, standing and fallen, will be allowed to undergo natural decay processes.

In the early 1990s woodland management was extended to other sites and the winters of 1991–92 and 1992–93 saw management activity in Roe Wood and Woolley Wood. But woodland management is not a one-off operation; it needs to be continuous and long term. It is also costly. What had taken place at Bowden Housteads Wood, Roe Wood and Woolley Wood was just a beginning there. Further management at short intervals over a long period would be necessary in order to achieve and maintain the sought-after uneven structure and the beauty and interest that it brings in its train. Could Sheffield City Council afford to repeat the treatment in the other forty-seven ancient woodlands for which it was responsible? Could it afford not to? That was the challenge.

THE PURCHASE OF BROAD ING PLANTATION FROM THE FORESTRY COMMISSION BY TANKERSLEY PARISH COUNCIL

Although not an ancient wood, the purchase of Broad Ing Plantation at Tankersley by the parish council from the Forestry

Commission underlined the importance of woodlands to local communities and their desire to see them managed for public access and enjoyment. Two hundred years ago the site was partly wooded (called Broad Ing Bushes) and partly farmland, being a meadow and that is what 'ing' means. In the early nineteenth century both the scrub woodland and the meadow became an ironstone mining area, mostly in the form of shallow bell pits and this is the origin of the deep hollows in the wood. After ironstone mining ceased the area was made into a plantation that was felled and replanted on a number of occasions. In 1987, when its purchase was being contemplated by the parish council, Broad Ing Plantation was a small (10 acres (4 ha)) Forestry Commission plantation, managed purely for economic reasons. It had been restocked in 1964 with sycamore (covering just over half of the plantation) and Japanese larch. Under normal Forestry Commission practice it would have been periodically thinned to leave a final crop of larch in 2005 and a final crop of sycamore in about the year 2050. There was no formal access to the plantation and no formal footpaths. Some dumping of rubbish, including glass, had occurred in the southern half of the plantation and there was a large domestic dump again including some glass. Some of the walls around the site were also in disrepair. The plantation was not a particularly attractive site for recreation or education and it was not an important wildlife source but in its favour was its location next to the major settlement, Pilley, within the parish next to the recreation ground. And despite the close planting, native tree and shrub species could still be found both deep within the site and round the edges and a remnant ancient woodland flora including bluebells, wild garlic, greater stitchwort, common cow-wheat, dog's mercury and wood sorrel had also survived.

The Forestry Commission was prepared to sell the plantation to an approved purchaser, in a closed sale. An approved purchaser was one who had the support from the Nature Conservancy Council in the case of a proposed purchase for nature conservancy reasons and from the Countryside Commission in the case of a proposed purchase for scenic, recreational and amenity reasons. In order to gain sponsorship a survey and management plan was commissioned that was delivered in January 1988. [14]

In December 1988 the purchase was completed and the following spring work started on the first five-year management plan. The plan contained a prescription covering the short term, medium-term and long-term objectives. Short-term objectives included thinning 25–30 per cent of the larch and sycamore to encourage a more diverse woodland environment, removing bramble infestation, leaving part of the wood in which planting had been ineffective as a non-intervention area, undertaking some judicial planting of hawthorn, holly and hazel, creating a glade where the ground flora was richest to encourage further spread and flowering, and leaving dead and dying timber and some felled timber to rot and piles of brushwood to provide shelter and nesting sites. Estate work included wall repairs, footpath and ride creation and removal of dumped material. The long-term objective was to arrive at a naturally regenerating native woodland through continued periodic thinning until all of the larch and most of the sycamore had been removed. Other objectives covered educational provision, community involvement and publicity. The main features of the proposed management are shown in Figure 8.7. Work went on at a rapid rate during 1989: walls were repaired, dumped material cleared, thinning and glade creation began, new footpaths and rides were created, an information board

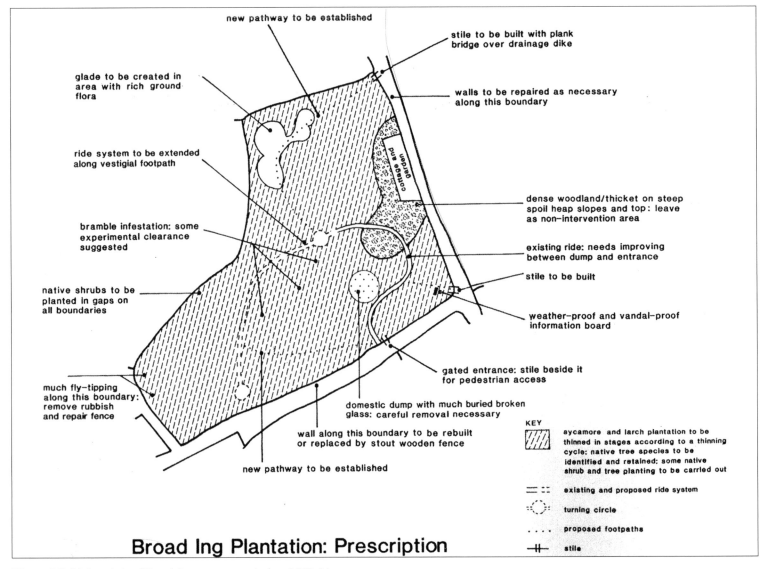

new pathway to be established

stile to be built with plank
bridge over drainage dike

glade to be created in
area with rich ground
flora

walls to be repaired as necessary
along this boundary

ride system to be extended
along vestigial footpath

cottage and
garden

dense woodland/thicket on steep
spoil heap slopes and top: leave
as non-intervention area

bramble infestation: some
experimental clearance
suggested

existing ride: needs improving
between dump and entrance

stile to be built

native shrubs to be
planted in gaps on
all boundaries

weather-proof and vandal-proof
information board

gated entrance: stile beside it
for pedestrian access

much fly-tipping
along this boundary:
remove rubbish
and repair fence

domestic dump with much buried broken
glass: careful removal necessary

KEY

sycamore and larch plantation to be
thinned in stages according to a thinning
cycle: native tree species to be
identified and retained: some native
shrub and tree planting to be carried out

wall along this boundary to be rebuilt
or replaced by stout wooden fence

new pathway to be established

existing and proposed ride system

turning circle

proposed footpaths

stile

Broad Ing Plantation: Prescription

Figure 8.7. Main points of Broad Ing management plan, 1989–94

appeared at the entrance of the wood entitled 'Broad Ing – Our Community Wood' and an illustrated leaflet by the same name was distributed widely. A second detailed management plan covering the period 1999–2003 was compiled which, with support from the Forestry Commission's Woodland Grant Scheme (WGS), enabled the thinning operations, planting and improvement and maintenance of the footpath system to continue. [15]

DEVELOPMENTS DURING THE LAST TWENTY YEARS

Changes of ownership. There have been some interesting developments since the early 1990s. For example, the Woodland Trust has now boosted the number of woods in its ownership in the region to ten: five in Barnsley (Bagger Wood at Hood Green, Birdwell Woods, Miller Hill and Wigfield Wood all at Birdwell, Lower Lee Wood at Thurgoland and Nabs Wood at Silkstone Common); four in Sheffield (Beacon Wood at Loxley, Bitholmes Wood between Deepcar and Wharncliffe Side, Firth Wood and Wantley Dragon Wood both at Oughtibridge); and one in Doncaster (The Shrubbery at Wadworth).

In 1992 Doncaster Council purchased Melton Wood which covers 301 acres (122 ha) and is largely a plantation on an ancient woodland site, from the Forestry Commission. This wood belonged to a succession of local landed families, the Fountaynes, Monktons and Montagus for more than 250 years until 1928 when it was bought by a local builder. It was then sold to the Manvers Main Colliery Company in 1939 from whom it passed to the National Coal Board in 1947. It was acquired on a 999-year lease by the Forestry Commission in 1956 and planting of both broadleaved and coniferous trees took place over the next decade. A long-term programme of management has been introduced to balance the needs of timber production, wildlife and public access and recreation. A feature of the wood is the intricate system of rides which have been in existence for at least 250 years (Figure 8.8).

Perhaps the most important purchase currently under way is the campaign by Sheffield and Rotherham Wildlife Trust to raise £1m to purchase Greno Wood and Hall Wood at Grenoside in Sheffield and to bring them back into a good condition for wildlife and for local people. These woods, covering 481 acres (169 ha), formerly the property of the Duke of Norfolk, and managed for a long period as commercial plantations on ancient woodland sites on his behalf by Fountain Forestry, have been bought by the Esmée Fairburn Foundation to take them off the open market, and a private investor (on behalf of Silvapower Ltd) has bought a much smaller section. The Sheffield and Rotherham Wildlife Trust aims to raise the money to buy the woods from the Esmée Fairburn Foundation within two years for the public benefit. A major bid has been submitted to the Heritage Lottery Fund. Already the Trust is managing the woods and in February 2011 embarked on a major conifer thinning programme covering 133 acres (54 ha) (Figure 8.9). The felled conifers will be sold to provide woodchip for biofuel.

Greno Wood and Hall Wood are both ancient woods and are of the highest heritage value, both being documented as important coppice-with-standards woods for 400 years and being rich in archaeological and ecological features. Greno Wood, as Greno Firth, was first recorded in the thirteenth century. The use of the word 'firth' suggests that at that time it was part of the great hunting ground of the lords of the manor of Hallamshire which also included the extensive Rivelin Chase and Loxley Firth or Chase. On the death of Thomas de Furnival in 1332 it was recorded as wood pasture, in which

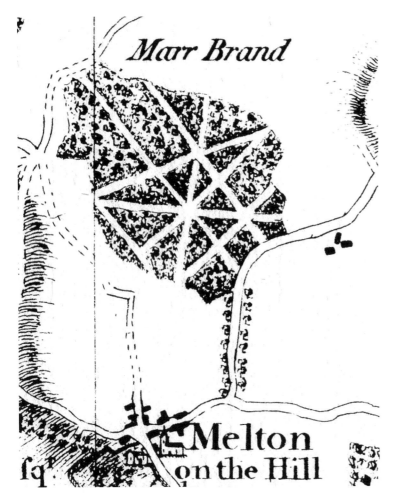

Figure 8.8. Melton Wood as depicted on Jefferys' map of Yorkshire 1775, showing the rides that still survive to the present day

Figure 8.9. Stacking felled conifers in Greno Wood, February 2011

animals would be grazed and timber and wood would be cut. There are a number of records in the fourteenth and fifteenth centuries of individuals being taken to the manorial court for trespassing in or stealing wood from Greno Wood, for example, in 1441 William de Housley was fined fourpence 'for trespass done in the Lord's wood, for breaking down of a hedge next Granowe'.

Both woods are listed in an undated document sent to the 7th Earl of Shrewsbury (he became Earl in 1592 and died in 1616) listing all the coppice woods that provided fuel for 'his Grace's forges'. The underwood in 'Graynowe Spring' was said to be twenty years old and 'redie to coale'. This listing confirms that it was a coppice-with-standards (a 'spring'), that the coppice cycle used was twenty years and that most of the underwood would be made into charcoal. In the same list Hall Wood was said to be in three parts (Upper Hall Wood, Nether Hall Wood and Little Hall Wood) and that the coppice was fourteen years old. Throughout the seventeenth, eighteenth and almost all of the nineteenth century there are many records of the management of both woods in the form of accounts, maps and handbills and contracts for felling, buying and using the wood and timber in the two woods. In Greno Wood is 'Sharps' wood oyl', a small pond where they soaked their willow and hazel rods for basket-making and from which they obtained their water for boiling oak poles for swill-making (see Chapters 4 and 5 for further details). Other archaeological features that survive in and around the two woods are the level areas (the pitsteads) where charcoal stacks were made, woodbanks and walls to keep out grazing animals and the footings of a Romano-British settlement. Greno Wood is one of only three woods in the region with carpets of common cow-wheat (a botanical indicator of ancient woods) which is extinct in most of neighbouring Lincolnshire and East Yorkshire. Common cow-wheat produces a sugary liquid from small glands under its petals on which wood ants feed. Not surprisingly, Greno Wood is the only wood in South Yorkshire with a large colony of wood ants (Figure 8.10).

Re-introduction of small-scale coppicing. On a much smaller scale in the winter of 1993–94 a multi-purpose feasibility study began, in which four experimental areas were re-coppiced – 0.3–0.4 ha areas in four Sheffield woods: Ecclesall Woods, Great Roe Wood, Shirtcliff Wood and Buck Wood. The idea behind the project, which was jointly supported by Sheffield City Council and the South Yorkshire Forest Project, was to find out whether re-coppiced woodland would provide a limited number of woodland craft jobs, create products for which there was a local demand, improve the structural and species diversity of the woodlands and enhance their amenity value.[16] The experiments created much initial interest: on one day in the winter of 1994–95, for example, when the experimental area in Ecclesall Woods was being extended, two guided walks through the woods to explore the history of the site, examine the re-coppicing experiments and to see demonstrations of pole-lathing, charcoal making and hurdle making, attracted more than 300 people. Unfortunately, monitoring of the economic and ecological effects of the re-coppicing experiments, and the reactions of those who use the woods where the experiments took place, has neither comprehensively taken place nor been reported in any meaningful way.

Special interest groups and partnerships. Such groups, some emerging since the beginning of the 1990s, have added new impetus to professional and community involvement in the sustainable management of ancient woodlands across the region. The Gleadless Valley Wildlife Group has been particularly influential in managing and interpreting the important ancient woodlands in the Gleadless Valley in Sheffield. The Friends of Ecclesall Woods, which was formed in 1993 and has a membership varying between 120 and 140, has been a model of community involvement in woodland conservation and management. Members of the group have been involved in practical conservation tasks, particularly the resurfacing of footpaths, but they have also successfully bid for lottery grants to help them in their work. In 2001, for example, they secured an 'Awards for All' grant from the Heritage Lottery Fund which enabled them to fund the undertaking of an archaeological survey of the woods and the creation of an archaeological trail

Figure 8.10. Wood ants' nest in Greno Wood

with an accompanying leaflet.[17] In 2002 they obtained a Local Heritage Initiative grant which has led to the construction of a footpath to the woodcollier's grave, the production of a full-colour leaflet (*A Seasonal Walk around Ecclesall Woods*), and an archaeological survey of the hill-top enclosure and whitecoal pits. More ambitiously they have produced an 85-page book, *Ecclesall Woods, Sheffield: a Flora*, illustrated in colour, again generously supported by the Local Heritage Initiative.[18]

The Working Woodlands Trust, formed in 1997 by a group of local professional woodland workers, has also been a welcome influence in promoting sustainable woodland management in the city's woods. The Trust aims to provide innovative and

enjoyable educational woodland events, provide advice and support for community-based woodland initiatives, promote the use of locally-produced woodland products and provide support for sustainable wood-based businesses. The Working Woodlands Gallery at Ecclesall Woods Sawmill, Sheffield, opened in 2008, is a shop window for Working Woodlands members (Figure 8.11). On the same site a new woodland discovery centre, including an education room and outdoor classroom with display and exhibition space, was opened in the Autumn of 2011.

The South Yorkshire Forest Partnership. A major influence on local attitudes to woodland management in the last two

Figure 8.11. 'Hector's House' in Ecclesall Woods

decades has been the South Yorkshire Forest Project (now Partnership). This project, established in 1991, is a partnership between Barnsley, Rotherham and Sheffield Councils, the Countryside Agency and the Forestry Commission. Its aim is to develop multipurpose forests which will create better environments for people to use, cherish and enjoy. The South Yorkshire Forest area covers most of the Coal Measure country in the three metropolitan districts. Although not just concerned with ancient woodlands, among its objectives are commitments to protect areas of historical, archaeological and ecological interest (i.e. the existing ancient woodlands), to increase opportunities for access and recreation, and to encourage the development of timber-based industries, employment opportunities and woodland products. Following a year of public consultation, the South Yorkshire Forest's first Plan was published in August 1994.[19] This established a policy framework and a strategic approach to woodland management throughout the South Yorkshire Forest area – for private as well as publicly-owned woods – and guided developments into the twenty-first century.

In 1997 the South Yorkshire Forest Team put together a £1½m bid to the Heritage Lottery Fund for a five-year action plan to restore thirty-five Coal Measure woodlands in Sheffield, Rotherham and Barnsley – called *Fuelling a Revolution – The Woods that founded the Steel Country*.[20] In February 1999 it was announced that the bid had been successful and a five-year Heritage Woodlands Project was launched in September 1999 (Figure 8.12). Twenty-two of the thirty-five woodlands within the project were in the ownership of Sheffield City Council, eleven in Rotherham and four in Barnsley. The project also helped Rotherham MBC buy Canklow Wood from the Duke of Norfolk for £135,000, £101,000 of which was provided by the Heritage Lottery Fund. There has been much activity on a

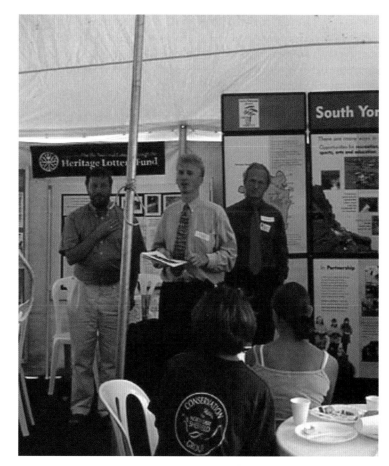

Figure 8.12. *Launch of the* Fuelling a Revolution *project. At the front is Richard Walker, then Director of the South Yorkshire Forest Partnership; and behind him the Right Honorable David Blunkett MP, who officially launched the* Fuelling a Revolution *project*

broad front connected with the project – archaeological surveys, development of management plans, active woodland management programmes, interpretation for local communities, the development of educational materials and activities and the commissioning of public art works.

Active management has taken place in all thirty-five of the *Fuelling a Revolution* woodlands, usually a combination of group felling, thinning and coppicing. The aims of the management have been to maintain or reinstate the semi-natural characteristics of the woodlands by promoting a diverse woodland structure. This, it is hoped, will encourage a rich and diverse ground flora and birdlife and at the same time promote the woodlands as places for safe and accessible recreation and as educational resources. In order to safeguard the ground flora and the archaeology, where the ground is steep or particularly sensitive, working horses rather than wheeled vehicles have been used to remove felled trees (Figure 8.13).

The programmes of interpretation and education developed for schools and for the general public connected with the *Fuelling a Revolution* project have been particularly impressive. For schools, 'school weeks' have been organised in Sheffield, for example, in Wheata Wood (a bodger's camp), Gleadless Valley woods and Bowden Housteads Wood, and woodland play schemes have also been successfully run. In May 2002 a 'big book' for the literacy hour for Sheffield schools pitched at Year 3 pupils – *Sheffield Woodland Detectives* – was launched and has been used in twenty-three of the City's primary schools. For the general public a series of woodland craft courses, run in partnership with The Working Woodlands Trust, have been fully booked. A series of woodland leaflets have appeared: eight were produced for Sheffield woods and seventeen for Rotherham woods. Guided walks and other events such as

***Figure 8.13.** Working horses in Woolley Wood, 2006*

bluebell wood walks were also a feature of the project. There is a *Fuelling a Revolution* website – www.heritagewoodsonline.co.uk – which provides general and site-by-site information for people of all ages about the heritage woodlands and their restoration. An unusual aspect of the project was the commissioning of public works of art to be placed in woods. These range from the construction of a 'dragon bridge' by Jason Thomson over Collier Brook in Birch Wood, Rotherham; a colourful entrance to Rollestone Wood in the Gleadless Valley in Sheffield by artist Karen Gillan in collaboration with local school children; the carving of the face of 'the Wildman of the Woods' into a tree in Hinde Common Wood, Sheffield, by Jason Thomson; and a large sculpture of a steel giant with a hammer in his hand by the same sculptor at the side of the

Sheffield Parkway in Bowden Housteads Wood, reflecting the close connection between South Yorkshire's ancient woods and the development of the steel industry (Figure 8.14).

All the new management plans involve the re-introduction, in some form or other, and at a variety of scales, of thinning, which involves coppicing and felling closely-spaced mature and over-mature timber. If this is to be sustained then old markets for wood and timber will have to be revived and new markets found. There are undoubted opportunities for suppliers of local wood and timber to supply South Yorkshire markets for firewood kindling, rustic poles, log rolls for garden edging, fencing materials, bagged forest bark and mulch material, quality hardwood, biofuel and barbecue charcoal. The market for locally-produced barbecue charcoal in particular is one that is being developed up and down the country. The London Borough of Croydon, for example, in the late 1990s decided to convert the felled wood from its parks and 34 miles of tree-lined streets into charcoal. Sales were expected to be of the value of £50,000 per year. In South Yorkshire, four charcoal-makers (not all are still active), one pole-lathe turner, a basket-maker and a hurdle-maker have set up operations since 1990.

The renewed interest in woodland conservation and management has been marked by an almost universal enthusiasm for the coppicing tradition. There are now, however, some dissenting voices and counsels of caution. Some observers have claimed that too much emphasis has been placed on early successional habitats and on management for the conservation of certain conspicuous and charismatic species such as butterflies and ground flora. Enthusiasts for conservation coppicing have also counselled greater rationality and strategic thinking before embarking on re-coppicing schemes. Clearly, there needs to be careful monitoring of the ecological, economic and recreational impact of the new fashion for 'interventionist' woodland management.

South Yorkshire Biodiversity Research Group. This group, with the Biodiversity and Landscape History Research Institute in conjunction with Sheffield Hallam University, has, since 1994 been conducting research on woodland ecology, history, archaeology and management, organising seminars, conferences and workshops and, through Wildtrack Publishing, publishing conference proceedings and books. Much of their activity has had a local focus. In 2003, for example, a major international conference took place, *Walking and Working in the Footsteps of Ghosts*, which was concerned with the history, ecology, archaeology and management of woodlands with contributors from France, Holland, Spain, Hungary and Sweden as well as from Great Britain. But there were also local contributions and delegates visited local ancient woods. In 2008 a major publication took place in the form of *The Woodland Heritage Manual; a guide to investigating wooded landscapes*. This publication was the culmination of a project called *The Woodland Heritage Champions Project* funded by the Heritage Lottery Fund, the Woodland Trust, the Forestry Commission and English Heritage. The project took the form of workshops for volunteers during which the main elements of the guide would be presented and trialled and feedback would be received from group members. The project was a country-wide project with workshops held in nine different regions of England from Cumbria and North Yorkshire in the north to East Devon and Surrey/East Sussex in the south. The South Yorkshire workshop involved members of three woodland groups: the Gleadless Valley Wildlife Trust, the Friends of Ecclesall Woods and the Steel Valley Project based in Stocksbridge. In 2011 a series of workshops were organised, funded by Heritage Lottery

Figure 8.14. Steel giant in Bowden Housteads Wood

Figure 8.15. *This stretch of unmanaged hedgerow that sits on a low bank at Thorpe Common is the ancient boundary between Rotherham parish and Ecclesfield parish. In the short stretch shown in the photograph there are ten species of tree and shrub: sessile oak, ash, field maple, wild cherry, crab apple, hazel, dog rose, hawthorn, blackthorn and elder. This stretch of hedge also contains two veteran trees, an oak and an ash with multiple trunks partly horizontal and partly vertical that were once part of the hedge when it was laid. Hedges of this type fall within the government's protection legislation*

Awards for All scheme and the South Yorkshire Community Foundation entitled *Discovering Neighbourhood Woodlands.*The workshops introduced local enthusiasts to the ways they could uncover the secrets of the history, archaeology and wildlife of their local woodland. Six short field guides, in leaflet form, were published in connection with the workshops on subjects such as documentary research, identifying an ancient wood-land, woodland archaeology and botanical indicators of ancient woodland.

HEDGEROW PROTECTION REGULATIONS

The government brought in a set of regulations to protect hedgerows in the countryside (not in parks and gardens) in 1997. The regulations were based on a series of historical and archaeological considerations and on the botanical richness of a hedge (Figure 8.15). The CPRE conducted a nation-wide survey of the working of the regulations in 2010 and concluded that although the legislation had improved hedgerow protection to a degree, unfortunately the regulations did not include a land-scape criterion, i.e., the place of a particular hedge within the broader hedged landscape.[21] This means that although an owner would be stopped from removing a hedge that met the protection criteria, neighbouring hedges that did not qualify for protection could be grubbed up. The impact on wildlife, for which the hedgerow network performs a critical corridor function, could be devastating to say nothing of the impact on the landscape character of an area. The regulations were also thought by many local authorities to be too complicated.

CONCLUSION

With all these positive woodland initiatives, the government's hedgerow regulations and the crucial support of the Heritage Lottery Fund, the future of South Yorkshire's trees and wood-lands looks much better now than it did three decades ago. Awareness of the cultural importance of local ancient woods, hedgerows and parkland trees has been raised to a much higher level than hitherto and interest in their critical importance for wildlife as well as their educational and recreational potential has been re-awakened. **But it cannot be emphasised enough that tree and woodland management is not a one-off event; it needs to be continuous and long-term. The work that is currently taking place is very encouraging, but it is just the beginning; the challenge, as everyone knows only too well, is to sustain it in the medium and long term.**

What to read about woodland and hedgerow survival and restoration

CAMPAIGN TO PROTECT RURAL ENGLAND (2010) *England's Hedgerows: don't cut them out - Making the case for better hedgerow protection.* Downloadable from the Internet.
JONES, M. (1995) *Rotherham's Woodland Heritage*, Rotherwood Press.
JONES, M. (1998) The Coal Measure Woodlands of South Yorkshire: Past, Present and Future in M.A. Atherden and R.A. Butlin (eds) *Woodland in the Landscape: Past and Future Perspectives*, PLACE Research Centre, pp. 79–102.
JONES, M. (2009) *Sheffield's Woodland Heritage*, 4th edition, Wildtrack Publishing.
PHILLIPS, H. (ed) (1973) *Edlington Wood*, Doncaster Rural District Council.
ROTHERHAM, I.D., JONES, M., SMITH, L. and HANDLEY, C. (2008) (eds) *The Woodland Heritage Manual: A Guide to Investigating Wooded Landscapes*, Wildtrack Publishing.
SOUTH YORKSHIRE BIODIVERSITY RESEARCH GROUP (2011) Discovering Neighbourhood Woodlands leaflets: *1. Surveying a Woodland; 2. An Introduction to Documentary Research; 3. History, Structure and Form; 4. Pits, Platforms, Banks and Ditches; 5.Botanical Indicators; 6. Worked Trees.*
Downloadable from the Internet (www.ukeconet.co.uk).

Places to visit and things to do

Visit woods throughout the region that have seen active woodland management in recent decades and that have been interpreted through leaflets and interpretation boards. Rotherham Borough Council has published seventeen leaflets on their publicly-owned woods and Sheffield City Council has over the years produced more than a dozen woodland leaflets. Many woods also have interpretation boards.

Find out if your local wood has a **'Friends of'** group. If it does, seriously consider joining it. If it does not, seriously consider forming one.

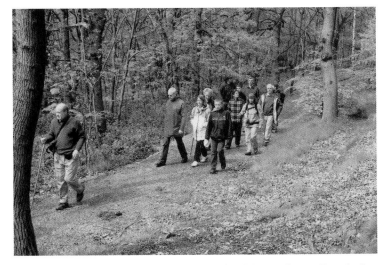

A guided walk through Treeton Wood as part of the Fuelling a Revolution *project*

NOTES AND REFERENCES

Chapter 1

1. Countryside Commission (1998) *Countryside Character, Volume 3, Yorkshire & The Humber.*

2. See, for example, Whitehouse, N.J., Dunnin M.H. and Lindsay, R.A. (1998) Conflicts between palaeoecology, archaeology and nature conservation: the Humberhead Peatlands SSSI in Jones, M. and Rotherham, I.D. (eds) *Landscapes – Perception, Recognition and Management: reconciling the impossible* (proceedings of a Landscape Conservation Forum conference held in Sheffield 2–4 April, 1996) pp. 70–78 and Dunnin, M., Ellis, S. and Weir, D. (1997) The palaeoenvironmental survey of West, Thorne and Hatfield Moors in Van de Noort, R. and Ellis, S. (eds) *Wetland Heritage of the Humberhead Levels: an archaeological survey*, Humber Wetlands Project, pp. 157–189.

3. Limbert, M. (1998) The natural harvest of Thorne Moors, *Thorne and Hatfield Moors Papers*, Volume 5, Thorne and Hatfield Moors Conservation Forum.

4. Innes, J.B. and Simmons, I.G. (1988) Disturbance and diversity: floristic changes associated with pre-elm decline woodland recession in north-east Yorkshire in Jones. M. (ed) *Archaeology and the Flora of the British Isles*, Oxford University Committee for Archaeology, pp. 7–20.

5. Rackham, O. (1988) Wildwood in Jones. M. (ed) *Archaeology and the Flora of the British Isles*, Oxford University Committee for Archaeology, pp. 3–6.

6. Conway, V.M. (1947) Ringinglow Bog, near Sheffield, Part 1, Historical, *Journal of Ecology*, **24**, 149–181.

7. Vera, F.W.M. (2000) *Grazing Ecology and Forest History.* CABI Publishing. Vera's theories are discussed at length in Hodder, K.H., Bullock, J.M., Buckland, P.C. and Kirby, K.J. (2005) *Large herbivores in the wildwood and in modern naturalistic grazing systems*, English Nature, Research Report 648.

8. Radley, J. and Mellars, P. (1963) Hail Mary Hill: Mesolithic Surface Site in the Rother Valley, *Transactions of the Hunter Archaeological Society*, 8, 1958–63, 307–311.

9. Radley, J. and Mellars, P. (1964) A Mesolithic Structure at Deepcar, Yorkshire, England, and the Affinities of its associated Flint Industries, *Proceedings of the Prehistoric Society*, **XXX**, 1–24.

10. Rackham, O. (1980) *Ancient Woodland; its history, vegetation and uses in England*, Arnold, p. 111.

11. Peterken, G. F. (1981) *Woodland Conservation and Management*, Chapman & Hall, p. 12

12. Rackham, O. (1980) p. 61.

13. Eccles, C. (1986) *South Yorkshire Inventory of Ancient Woodland*, Nature Conservancy Council.

14. See, for example, Jones, M. (1986) Ancient Woods in the Sheffield Area: the Documentary evidence, *Sorby Record*, No. 24, 7–18 and Jones, M. (1993) South Yorkshire's Ancient woods: the Historical Evidence in Beswick, P., Rotherham, I.D. and Parsons, J. (eds) (1993) *Ancient Woodlands-Their Archaeology and Ecology: a coincidence of interest*, Landscape Conservation Forum, pp. 26–48.

15. Rodwell, J. and Hey, D, (2010) The King's Wood in Lindrick, *Landscapes*, 11, 1, 47–66.

16. Doncaster Naturalists Society (1993) *A Survey of Wadworth Wood, Doncaster*, p. 21.
17. Shimwell, D. (1973) Natural History: First Survey in Phillips, H. (ed) *Edlington Wood*, Doncaster Rural District Council, pp. 48–56.
18. See, for example, Peterken, G.F. (1993) *Woodland Conservation and Management*, Second edition, Chapman & Hall, pp. 46–62 and Rackham, O. (2006) *Woodlands*, Collins (New Naturalist series), pp. 318–30.
19. For an interesting discussion of botanical indicators of ancient woodland and the influence of past management and plant ecology on indicator species see Spencer, J. (1990) Indications of Antiquity: Some observations on the nature of plants associated with ancient woodland, *British Wildlife*, **2**, 2, 90–102.
20. Jones, M. (1984) Woodland Origins in a South Yorkshire Parish, *The Local Historian*, **16**, 2, 73–82.
21. Species lists for Doncaster woodlands were provided by Bob Smith from Doncaster MBC Botanical Records Office. For a detailed botanical survey of Wadworth Wood see *A Survey of Wadworth Wood, Doncaster* (1993) by Doncaster Naturalists Society.
22. Addy, S.O. (1888) *Glossary of Words used in the neighbourhood of Sheffield*, The English Dialect Society, p. xxii.
23. Huddlestone, J. (1995) *A Geogaphy of Childhood*, Chapeltown & High Green Archive, p. 42.

Chapter 2
1. Hunter, J. (1828–31) *South Yorkshire: the History and Topography of the Deanery of Doncaster*, 2 volumes, J.B. Nicols and Son.
2. Hunter (1828–31) Volume 2, p. 309.
3. Rodgers, A. (1998) Deer Parks in the Maltby Area in Jones, M. (ed) *Aspects of Rotherham: Discovering Local History, Volume 3*, Wharncliffe Publishing, p. 20.
4. Birrell, J. (1992) Deer and Deer Farming in Medieval England, *The Agricultural History Review*, **40**, 112–126.
5. Hunter (1828–31) Volume 1, p. 114.
6. Jones, M. (2007) Deer Parks in South Yorkshire: the Documentary and Landscape Evidence, in Rotherham, I.D. (ed) *The History, Ecology and Archaeology of Medieval Parks and Parkland, Landscape Archaeology and Ecology*, Volume 6, 65–78.
7. Ronksley, J.G. (ed) (1908) *An exact and perfect Survey of the Manor of Sheffield and other lands by John Harrison, 1637*, Robert White & Co.
8. Evelyn, J. (1706 edition) *Silva or a Discourse of Forest Trees*, pp. 229–230.
9. Thomas, A.H. (1924) Some Hallamshire Rolls of the Fifteenth Century, *Transactions of the Hunter Archaeological Society*, 65–79, 142–158, 225–246 and 341–360 and Yorkshire Archaeological Society (1921) *Feet of Fines for the County of York 1218–1231, Record Series*, Volume LXII.
10. Ronksley (1908) p. 228.
11. Wentworth Woodhouse Muniments in Sheffield Archives, WWM D 778–782.
12. Jones, M. (1995) Rents, Remarks and Observations: The First Marquis of Rockingham's Rent Roll Book in Jones, M. (ed) *Aspects of Rotherham, Discovering Local History, Volume 1*, Wharncliffe Publishing, pp. 113–128.
13. Spencer Stanhope Muniments in Sheffield Archives, SSM 60663.

14. Yorkshire Archaeological Society, Record Series (1926), Vol. LXX p. 49.
15. Hall, T.W. (1937) Tankersley Old Hall and Fanshawe Gate in *Incunabula of Sheffield History*, J.W. Northend Ltd, pp. 169–202.
16. Hunter (1828–31) Volume 2, p. 303.
17. Clayton, A.K. (1962) The Break-up of Tankersley Park (1962) *South Yorkshire Times*, 1 February.
18. Fairbank Collection in Sheffield Archives, A288.
19. Jones, M. (1995) Ironstone Mining at Tankersley in the Nineteenth Century for Elsecar and Milton Ironworks in Elliott, B. (ed) *Aspects of Barnsley: Discovering Local History, Volume 3*, Wharncliffe Publishing, pp. 89–115.
20. Wentworth Woodhouse Muniments in Sheffield Archives, WWM SP 16XV.
21. Tomlinson, J. (1882) *The Level of Hatfield Chase and Parts Adjacent*.
22. Ronksley (1908) pp. 55 and 152.
23. Evelyn (1706) p. 229.
24. Ronksley (1908) p. 152.
25. Hall, T.W. (1926) A *Descriptive Catalogue of Sheffield Manorial Records, Volume I*, J.W. Northend, p. 3.
26. Hall, T.W. (1928) *Descriptive Catalogue of Sheffield Manorial Records, Volume II*, p. 12.
27. *Catalogue of the Arundel Castle Manuscripts*, Sheffield City Libraries, p. 201.
28. Hey, D. (1993) Chapter 9, The Dragon of Wantley in *Historic Hallamshire*, Landmark Publishing, pp. 136–153.
29. Hunter, (1828–31) Volume 2, p. 329.
30. McCarthy, A.J. and Rotherham, I.D. (1994) Deer in the Sheffield region including the Eastern Peak District, *The Naturalist*, **119**, 103–110.
31. Curtis, E. (1918) Sheffield in the Fourteenth Century: two Furnival Inquisitions, *Transactions of the Hunter Archaeological Society*, **1**, 31–53.
32. Hall, T.W. (1914) *Descriptive Catalogue of the Jackson Collection*, J.W. Northend, p. 5.
33. Hall, T.W. (1916) *A Descriptive Catalogue of Miscellaneous Charters and Other Documents*, J.W. Northend, pp. 106–107.
34. Hunter (1828–31) Volume 1, p. 154.
35. Hunter (1828–31) Volume 2, p. 407.
36. Hunter, J. (1875) *Hallamshire: the History and Topography of the Parish of Sheffield*, definitive 3rd edition (first published in 1819) edited by A. Gatty, Virtue & Co. p. 56.
37. Curtis, E. (1918) 41.
38. Ronksley (1908) p. 336.
39. Arundel Castle Manuscripts in Sheffield Archives, ACM S283.
40. Bailey, A.E. (2007) *On Common Ground*, privately published.

Chapter 3

1. See, for example, Jones, M. (1998) The rise, decline and extinction of spring wood management in south-west Yorkshire in Watkins, C. (ed) *European Woods and Forests: Studies in Cultural History*, CABI International, pp. 55–72.
2. Hall, T.W. (1914) p. 122 and pp. 325–326.
3. Hall, T.W. (1914) p. 123.
4. Beauchief Muniments in Sheffield Archives, BM994.
5. Miscellaneous Documents in Sheffield Archives, MD 192 folio 72r.
6. Aveling, J.W. (1870) *The History of Roche Abbey*, Robert White, pp. 130–131.
7. Yorkshire Archaeological Society Archive, YAS/DD5/4/46.

8. Lambeth Palace Library, London, A brief estimate of the Yorkshire Woods of Gilbert 7th Earl of Shrewsbury, Shr.P/LPL/Ms 698 folio 1.

9. Scurfield, G. and and Medley, I.E. (1952) An Historical Account of the Vegetation in the Sheffiield District: the Vegetation of the Southall Soke in 1637, *Transactions of the Hunter Archaeological Society*, **7**, 63–77.

10. Wentworth Woodhouse Muniments in Sheffield Archives, MP 46.

11. Arundel Castle Manuscripts in Sheffield Archives, ACM She 169.

12. Hopkinson, G.G. (1963) The Charcoal Iron Industry in the Sheffield Region, 1600–1775, *Transactions of the Hunter Archaeological Society*, 122–151.

13. Goodchild, J. (1996) Lionell Copley: a Seventeenth Century Capitalist in Jones, M. (ed) *Aspects of Rotherham: Discovering Local History, Volume 2*, Wharncliffe Publishing, pp. 28–36.

14. Wentworth Woodhouse Muniments in Sheffield Archives, WWM D778.

15. Duke of Leeds' archive at the Yorkshire Archaeological Society, DD5/35.

16. Wentworth Woodhouse Muniments in Sheffield Archives, WWM A 1273.

17. Wentworth Woodhouse Muniments in Sheffield Archives, WWM A 1273.

18. Arundel Castle Manuscripts in Sheffield Archives, ACM S303.

19. Arundel Castle Manuscripts in Sheffield Archives, ACM S303.

20. Hall, T.W. (1928) p. 3.

21. Hall, T.W. (1930) *A Descriptive Catalogue from the Bosville and the Lindsay Collections*, J. W. Northend, p. 3 and p. 33.

22. Arundel Castle Manuscripts in Sheffield Archives, ACM S283.

23. Arundel Castle Manuscripts in Sheffield Archives, ACM 541.

24. Arundel Castle Manuscripts in Sheffield Archives, ACM S283.

25. Hall, T.W. (1926) p. 48.

26. Arundel Castle Manuscripts in Sheffield Archives, ACM S283.

27. Arundel Castle Manuscripts in Sheffield Archives, ACM S283.

28. Arundel Castle Manuscripts in Sheffield Archives, ACM S283.

29. Arundel Castle Manuscripts in Sheffield Archives, ACM S283.

30. Arundel Castle Manuscripts in Sheffield Archives, ACM S283.

31. Bright Papers (Br A699-745) and Wentworth Woodhouse Muniments (WWM A 257-485) in Sheffield Archives.

32. Wentworth Woodhouse Muniments in Sheffield Archives, WWM D778.

33. Wentworth Woodhouse Muniments in Sheffield Archives, WWM A1273.

34. Collins, E. J. T. (1992) Woodlands and woodland industries in Great Britain during and after the charcoal iron era, *Protoindustries et histoire des forêts, Les Cahiers de l'ISARD*, No. 3, 109–120.

35. Bright Papers (Br A699-745) and Wentworth Woodhouse Muniments, WWM A257-485, MP42,MP44 in Sheffield Archives.

36. Arundel Castle Manuscripts in Sheffield Archives, ACM S308.

Chapter 4

1. Tyers, I. (2002) *Dendrochronological analysis of timbers from the Manorial Barn, Whiston, near Rotherham, Yorkshire*, ARCUS Dendrochronological Laboratory, University of Sheffield.
2. Jones, M (1993) Kirkstead Abbey Grange, Part 1, Speculations on its Origins, *Ivanhoe Review*, No.4 (Spring) 3–12.
3. Ryder, P.F. (n.d.) *Timber Framed Buildings in South Yorkshire*, South Yorkshire County Council.
4. Elliott, B. (2000) Canal Boats made in Barnsley in Elliott, B. (ed) *Aspects of Barnsley: Discovering Local History, Volume 6*, Wharncliffe Books, pp.72–82.
5. Arundel Castle Manuscripts in Sheffield Archives, wood ledgers 1839–1887, ACM S286.
6. Taylor, M. (1995) A Peculiar Aggravation: the Masbrough Boat Accident – 1841, *Ivanhoe Review*, No.8 (Summer), 4–13.
7. For an authoritative account of the early lead industry see Kiernan, D. (1989) *The Derbyshire Lead Industry in the Sixteenth Century*, Derbyshire Record Society.
8. Linnard, W. (1982) *Welsh Woods and Forests: History and Utilization*, National Museum of Wales, p.76.
9. Wentworth Woodhouse Muniments in Sheffield Archives, WWM D365.
10. Ardron, P.A. and Rotherham, I.D. (1999) Types of Charcoal Hearth and the impact of charcoal and whitecoal production on woodland vegetation, *The Peak District Journal of Natural History and Archaeology*, **1**, 35–48.
11. Clarkson, L.A. (1974) The English Bark Trade, 1660–1830, *Agricultural History Review*, **21**, 139.
12. Arundel Castle Manuscripts in Sheffield Archives, wood ledgers 1839–1887, ACM S286.
13. Arundel Castle Manuscripts in Sheffield Archives, ACM S283.
14. Borthwick Institute of Historical Research EW/DD June 1697. Quoted in Elliott, B. (1987/88) Lime, Liquor and Leathermen: Oak-Bark Tanning, the Forgotten Rural Industry of South Yorkshire,1600–1820, *The Hallamshire Historian*, **2**, No. 1, 12–24.
15. Crossley, D. (1989) *Water Power on the Sheffield Rivers*, Sheffield Trades Historical Society/University of Sheffield, Division of Continuing Education, p.9.
16. Elliott, B. (1987/88), Lime, Liquor and Leathermen: Oak-Bark Tanning, the Forgotten Rural Industry of South Yorkshire, 1600–1820, *The Hallamshire Historian*, **2,** No. 1, 14.
17. Wentworth Woodhouse Muniments in Sheffield Archives, WWM A1273
18. Sheffield City Museums (1976) *Bishops' House (Information Sheet 16)*.
19. Borthwick Institute of Historical Research, The inventory is dated 28 April, 1694.
20. Hey, D. (1997) Doncaster People of Ten Generations Ago in Elliott, B. *Aspects of Doncaster: Discovering Local History*, Wharncliffe Publishing, pp.143–147.
21. Arundel Castle Manuscripts in Sheffield Archives, ACM S283.
22. Arundel Castle Manuscripts in Sheffield Archives, ACM S283.
23. Arundel Castle Manuscripts in Sheffield Archives, ACM S283
24. Ronksley (1908) p.167.
25. Arundel Castle Manuscripts in Sheffield Archives, wood ledgers 1839–1887, ACM S286, S289, S290 and S292.
26. Arundel Castle Manuscripts in Sheffield Archives, wood ledgers 1839–1887, ACM S286.

Chapter 5

1. Barnatt, J. and Frith, P. (1983) A Newly Discovered 'Cup and Ring' Carving in Ecclesall Wood, Sheffield, *The Derbyshire Archaeological Journal*, **103**, 41–42.

2. Chadwick, A. (1992) The rock shelter at Scabba Wood in Francis, M.J., Cumberpatch, C., and Whiteley, S.P. (eds) *Archaeology in South Yorkshire 1991–92*, South Yorkshire Archaeology Service, 78–83 and Buckland, P., Chamberlain, A., Collins, P., Dungworth, D., Frederick, C., Merrony, C., Nystrom, P., and Parker Pearson, M. Scabba Wood, Sprotbrough: a prehistoric burial place and an undated enclosure in Saich, D. (ed) *Archaeology in South Yorkshire 1998/1999*, South Yorkshire Archaeology Service, pp. 18–24.

3. Latham, I. D. (1992) The archaeological survey of Canklow Woods, Rotherham in Francis, M. J., Cumberpatch, C.G. and Whiteley, S.P. (eds) *Archaeology in South Yorkshire 1991–1992*, South Yorkshire Archaeology Service, pp. 66–77.

4. Ardron, P.A. and Rotherham, I.D. (2001) *Ecclesall Woods Millennium Archaeology Project Report*, The Centre for Environmental Conservation and Outdoor Leisure, Sheffield Hallam University.

5. Atkinson, S., Latham, I.D and Sydes, R.E. (1992) Investigations at Caesar's Camp, Scholes Coppice in Francis, M.J., Cumberpatch, C.G. and Whiteley, S.P. (eds) *Archaeology in South Yorkshire 1991–1992*, South Yorkshire Archaeology Service, pp. 31–40.

6. Northern Archaeological Associates (2001) *Sheffield Archaeological surveys, Volume II*, for Sheffield City Council, Fuelling a Revolution: the Woods that Founded the Steel Country project.

7. Latham, I.D. (1994) *Results of a Desk Top assessment of the Archaeological Potential of the Wharncliffe Forest*, South Yorkshire Archaeology Field and Research Unit.

8. Cumberpatch, C.G. and Latham, I.D. (1995) A topographic survey of the Roman Ridge at Wath Wood, Rotherham in Cumberpatch, C.G., McNeil, J. and Whiteley, S.P. (eds) *Archaeology in South Yorkshire 1994–1995*, South Yorkshire Archaeology Service, pp. 60–62.

9. Latham, I.D. (1993) An archaeological survey of Cawthorne Park Woods in Cumberpatch, C.G. and Francis, M.J. (eds) *Archaeology in South Yorkshire 1992–1993*, South Yorkshire Archaeology Service, pp. 66–69.

10. Memorandum of Agreement between Charles Bowns for and on behalf of Earl Fitzwilliam of the one part and Henry Longden, Thomas Chambers and George Newton of the other part, 13 December 1793.

11. Northern Archaeological Associates (2001) *Sheffield Archaeological Surveys (Fuelling a Revolution: the woods that founded the steel country), Volume II, Level 2 and 3 Survey Woodlands* for Sheffield City Council, p. 54.

12. Jones, M. (1988) *Inventory Survey of Ancient Woodlands in Rotherham Metropolitan Borough, Progress Report 3 February 1992*, p. 18.

13. Jones, M. (1988) *Inventory Survey of Ancient Woodlands in Rotherham Metropolitan Borough, Progress Report 1 December 1988*, p. 22.

14. Ardron, P.A. and Rotherham, I.D. (1999) Types of charcoal hearth and the impact of charcoal and whitecoal production on woodland vegetation, *The Peak District Journal of Natural History and Archaeology*, **1**, 35–47.

15. Northern Archaeological Associates (2001) *Sheffield Archaeological Surveys (Fuelling a Revolution: the woods that founded*

the steel country), Volume II, Level 2 and 3 Survey Woodlands for Sheffield City Council, p. 61.

16. Jones, M. (1988) *Inventory Survey of Ancient Woodlands in Rotherham Metropolitan Borough, Progress Report 3 February 1992*, p. 13–14.

17. Arundel Castle Manuscripts in Sheffield Archives, ACM S283.

Chapter 6

1. Ronksley, J.G. (ed) (1908) *An exact and perfect Survey of the Manor of Sheffield and other lands by John Harrison, 1637*, Robert White & Co, p. 48.

2. Evelyn, J. (4th edition, 1706) *Sylva or a Discourse of Forest Trees*.

3. Beastall, T.W. (1995) Sandbeck Hall and Park in Jones, M. (ed), *Aspects of Rotherham: Discovering Local History*, Wharncliffe Publishing, p. 97.

4. Robinson, W. (1870) *The Wild Garden*, John Murray.

5. Herries, A. (2001) *Japanese Gardens in Britain*, Shire Publications.

6. Thompson, R. (1901*) The Gardener's Assistant*, new edition edited by W. Watson, Gresham Publishing Company, p. 4.

7. Heritage Lottery Fund, *Parklife*, 2004.

8. Woodland Trust/Ancient Tree Forum (n.d.) *Ancient Tree Guide no 4: What are ancient, veteran and other trees of special interest?*

9. Mitchell, A. and More, D. (1998) *The Complete Guide to Trees of Britain and Northern Europe*, Dragon's World, p. 92.

10. Mitchell and More, p. 138.

11. Milner, J.E. (1992) *The Tree Book*, Collins & Brown, pp. 126–9.

12. Jarvis, P.J. (1979) Plant introductions to England and their role in horticultural and sylvicultural innovation, 1500–

1900 in Fox, H.S.A. and Butlin, R.A. (eds) *Change in the Countryside: Essays on Rural England, 1500–1900*, Institute of British Geographers, pp. 145–164.

Chapter 7

1. Aveling, J.V. (1870) *The History of Roche Abbey*, Robert White, p. 102.

2. Arundel Castle Manuscripts (ACM) in Sheffield Archives, ACM S300.

3. Harvey, G. (1997) *The Killing of the Countryside*, Jonathan Cape.

4. Shoard, M. (1980) *The Theft of the Countryside*, Temple Smith.

5. Hoskins, W.G. (1967) *Fieldwork in Local History*, Faber and Faber, p. 118.

6. Pollard, E., Hooper, M.D. and Moore, N.W. (1974) *Hedges*, The New Naturalist series, Collins.

7. Taylor, C. (1975) *Fields in the English Landscape*, Dent, Chapter 5.

8. Rackham, O. (1986) *The History of the Countryside*, Dent. Chapters 9 and 10.

9. Muir, R. (2007) *Be Your Own Landscape Detective*, Sutton Publishing, Chapter 2.

10. Johnson, C. (Winter 2010/11) Hedge Dating Re-Visited Thirty Years On, *Society for Landscape Studies Newsletter*.

11. Jones, M. (2003) A Unique Historic Rural Landscape: the Fishlake-Sykehouse area in Jones, M. *South Yorkshire Yesterday: Glimpses of the Past*, Smith Settle, pp. 49–55.

12. Howes, C. A. (1986) *Hedgerows and Landscape of the Parish of Fishlake, South Yorkshire*, Doncaster MBC.

13. CCR (Conisbrough Court Rolls) in Doncaster Archives, c/1/8-15 and c/1/8-31.

14. Thomas, A.H. (1924) Some Hallamshire Rolls of the Fifteenth Century, *Transactions of the Hunter Archaeological Society*, 74.

15. Ronksley, J.G. (ed) (1908) *An exact and perfect Survey of the Manor of Sheffield and other lands by John Harrison, 1637*, Robert White & Co, pp. 32–33.

16. Surtees Society (1870) *The diary of Abraham de la Pryme, the Yorkshire antiquary*, Surtees Society, Volume 54.

17. Historical Manuscripts Commission (1901) Lord Edward Harley's (later earl of Oxford) *Journies and tours in the eastern counties 1723–1738*, Portland Mss, Volume 6.

18. Arundel Castle Manuscripts in Sheffield Archives, ACM S283.

19. Spray, M. and Smith, D.J. (1977) The rise and fall of holly in the Sheffield region, *Transactions of the Hunter Archaeological Society*, **10**, 239–51.

20. Jones, M. (1984) Woodland Origins in a South Yorkshire Parish, *The Local Historian*, **16**, 2, 73–82.

21. Bramley D.M. (ed) (1993) *A Survey of Wadworth Wood, Doncaster*, Doncaster Naturalists Society.

22. McCarthy, A.J., Dulieu, K., Rotherham, I.D. and Milego, C. (1993) The Natural History of the Wharncliffe Area, *Sorby Record*, No. 30, 7–19.

23. Howes, C.A. (1999) Historic trees in the Doncaster region: Ancient yew trees in the Doncaster landscape, *Yesterday Today*, **27**, 15–22.

24. Bevan-Jones, R. (2002) *The Ancient Yew*, Windgather Press, p. 153.

25. Hall, T.W. (1914) *Descriptive Catalogue of the Jackson Collection*, J.W. Northend, p. 36.

26. Edlin, H.L. *The Living Forest*, Thames and Hudson, p. 113.

27. Hunter, J. (1819) *Hallamshire, The History and Topography of the Parish of Sheffield in the County of York*, Lackington, Hughes, Harding, Mavor and Jones, pp. 18–19.

28. Personal communication from Nick Hetherington, Head of Streetscene, Sheffield City Council.

29. Personal communication from Ian Kennedy, Trees and Woodlands Team Leader, Rotherham Borough Council.

30. National Urban Forestry Unit/ Trees for Cities/ Countryside Agency (2005) *Trees Matter! Bringing lasting benefits to people in towns*; Sheffield City Council (2001) *Sheffield's Trees and Woodland Strategy*.

31. Gilbert, O.L. and Pearman, M.C. (1996) Wild Figs by the Don, *Sorby Record*, No 25, 31–33.

32. Allen, C., Griffiths, P. and Hobson, C. (1996) National and Local Distribution of the Fig (*Ficus carica*), *Sorby Record*, No. 32, 45–55.

Chapter 8

1. Jones, M and Jones, J. (2007) *The Parkwood Springs Area: Landscape History and Social History*, unpublished report for Sheffield City Council.

2. Rackham, O. (1990) *Trees & Woodland in the British Landscape*, J.M. Dent & Sons Ltd, revised edition, p. 104.

3. Goodchild, J. (1973) 'Recent History' in Phillips, H. (ed) *Edlington Wood*, Doncaster Rural District Council, pp. 1–4.

4. Wentworth Woodhouse Muniments in Sheffield Archives, WWM A339.

5. The rest of this paragraph is based on an account written by J. Kirkland and P.L. Stables entitled 'The Campaign for Preservation' in *Edlington Wood* (1973).

6. See reference 3 for full details.

7. Curtis, E. (1918) Sheffield in the Fourteenth Century: two Furnival Inquisitions, *Transactions of the Hunter Archaeological Society*, **1**, 31–53.

8. Rotherham, I.D. (1996) The sustainable management of urban-fringe woodland for amenity and conservation objectives. *Vegetation Management in Forestry, Amenity and Conservation Areas: Managing for Multiple Objectives, Aspects of Biology*, **44**, The Association of Applied Biologists, 33–38.

9. Jones, M. (1986a) *Bowden Housteads Wood: Household Survey*, Sheffield City Polytechnic.

10. Jones, M. (1986b) *Sheffield's Ancient Woods: some notes on their history and past management with special reference to woods owned by the City Council*, Sheffield City Polytechnic.

11. Sheffield City Council (1987) *Bowden Housteads/ Corker Bottoms 'Greenlink' Management Plan*, Department of Land and Planning.

12. Sheffield City Council (2000) *Bowden Housteads and Spring Wood, Management Plan 2000–2005*, Leisure Services, Parks, Woodlands and Countryside.

13. Sheffield City Council (2009) *Bowden Housteads Wood Draft Management Plan 2009–2013*, Directorate of Place, Parks and Countryside.

14. Jones, M. (1988) *Broad Ing Plantation: survey and management plan*.

15. Tankersley Parish Council (1999) *Broad Ing Plantation Management Plan*.

16. Jones, M. and Talbot, E. (1995) Coppicing in urban woodlands: a progress report on a multi-purpose feasibility study in the City of Sheffield, *The Journal of Practical Ecology and Conservation*, **1**. No 1, 46–52.

17. Ecclesall Woods, Sheffield: Archaeological Trail, illustrated leaflet produced by a partnership between Friends of Ecclesall Woods, Sheffield City Council, Sheffield Hallam University and the South Yorkshire Archaeological Service.

18. Smylie, B. (ed) (n.d.) *Ecclesall Woods, Sheffield: a Flora*, Friends of Ecclesall Woods.

19. South Yorkshire Forest team (1994) South *Yorkshire Forest Plan*.

20. South Yorkshire Forest (1997) *Fuelling a Revolution – the Woods that Founded the Steel Country, application to the Heritage Lottery Fund (No 96-00700)*.

21 Campaign to Protect Rural England (2010) *England's Hedgerows: don't cut them out – Making the case for better hedgerow protection*.

'Charcoal Makers' by John William Buxton Knight (1843–1908)

Index